RELIGION AND CULTURE UNDER MUGHALS

Books by the Same Author

- Indian Muslims Against British Rule (2014)
- Sir Syed Aligarh Muslim University and National Politics (2017)
- Cultural Heritage of Mewat (2020)
- Scientific Development in Islamic Civilization (2023)

About the Author

Dr Aijaz Ahmad was born on 16 August 1969, at Motipur village in the Sant Kabir Nagar district of Uttar Pradesh. After completing his early education in Motipur, Santha and Basti, he joined Aligarh Muslim University in 1985 and completed his BA (Hons), MA and MPhil in history. In 2000, he was awarded the PhD degree from Jamia Millia Islamia, New Delhi, in Modern Indian History. Currently, he is an Associate Professor in History at YMD College Nuh, affiliated with Gurugram University, Gurugram. During his service career, he has published 20 research papers in many national and international journals. In the same period, Dr Ahmad has published twelve books by many reputed publishers. His published books are: 1. *Indian Muslims Against British Rule*; 2. *Sir Syed, Aligarh Muslim University and National Politics*; 3. *Mewati Rebellion of 1857*; 4. *Uprising of 1857*; 5. *History of Mewat*; 6. *Cultural Heritage of Mewat*; 7. *Haryana ka Itihaas*; 8. *Poorv Aupniveshik Bharat Mein Vigyaan Tatha Praudyogiki*; 9. *Triple Talaq*; 10. *Democracy and Discontent in India*; 11. *New Dimensions of Indian Historiography*; 12. *Scientific Development in Islamic Civilization*. *Religion and Culture under Mughals* is the thirteenth book of Dr Ahmad.

RELIGION AND CULTURE UNDER MUGHALS

Aijaz Ahmad

CONCEPT PUBLISHING COMPANY PVT. LTD.
NEW DELHI - 110059

ISBN: 978-93-5594-747-5

First Published 2024

Published and Printed by

Concept Since 1974

Concept Publishing Company Pvt. Ltd.
A/15-16, Commercial Block, Mohan Garden
New Delhi-110059 (India)
T: +91-11-41101460
E: publishing@conceptpub.com, *W*: www.conceptpub.com

Cataloging in Publication--Courtesy: D.K. Agencies (P) Ltd. <docinfo@dkagencies.com>

Ahamada, Ejāja, 1969- **author.**
Religion and culture under Mughals / Aijaz Ahmad.
pages cm
Includes bibliographical references and index.
ISBN 9789355947475

1. Mogul Empire--Religion. 2. Mogul Empire--Social life and customs. 3. Mogul Empire--Kings and rulers. 4. India--History--1526-1765. I. Title.

LCC DS461.A36 2024 | DDC 954.0254 23

To my children
Lubna, Iram, Anam and Sadaf,
who are my greatest creations,
and the reason behind every word in this book.

Preface

The Mughals, a line of emperors descended from Timur and Genghis Khan, not only carved out a vast empire on the Indian subcontinent but also left an enduring legacy of religious diversity and cultural synthesis. The Mughals not only expanded their dominion through military might but also showcased an astute understanding of governance, art and spirituality. Central to the Mughal identity was their patronage of diverse cultural expressions and their embrace of religious pluralism, a rarity in the tumultuous times of their rule. Their reign witnessed the convergence of various faiths, including Islam, Hinduism, Sikhism and others, creating a mosaic of religious pluralism seldom seen in the pages of history.

This book delves into the intricate interplay between religion and culture within the expansive realm of the Mughal dynasty, unravelling the threads that wove together an empire of unparalleled grandeur. It embarks on a journey through the corridors of time, seeking to unravel the rich threads that compose the intricate relationship among the religion, culture and the Mughal rulers. It invites reflection on the enduring legacy of an empire that, despite its imperfections, bequeathed to posterity a cultural and religious tapestry that continues to captivate and inspire.

This book invites readers on a journey through the various religion and culture flourishing under Mughals and their relations, beliefs and policies towards these religions and the people in this great empire. This book also aims to capture the essence of religion and culture under the Great Mughals, providing readers with a nuanced understanding of an era where the spiritual and the temporal coexisted in a delicate balance. This book endeavours to shed light on the the ebb and flow of religious tolerance and the challenges posed by the diversity of religious beliefs within the Mughal realm. It seeks to unravel the stories of religious scholars, the impact of Sufi mysticism and the coexistence of multiple religious traditions that characterized this fascinating period in history.

The Mughal Empire stands as a testament to the fusion of power, culture and religion. Spanning the Indian subcontinent from the early sixteenth to the beginning of the eighteenth century, the Great Mughals left an indelible mark on the tapestry of human civilization. This exploration extends an invitation to delve into the philosophical underpinnings, religious policies and spiritual inclinations of the Mughal emperors. It scrutinizes the Mughal rulers' relationships with various religious communities, including Hindus, Muslims, Sikhs and Christians, shedding light on the nuanced dynamics that characterized their reign. It navigates through the reigns of luminaries like Babur, Akbar, Jahangir, Shah Jahan and Aurangzeb, each leaving an indelible mark on the religious landscape of their time. It examines their engagements with scholars, mystics and religious leaders, painting a vivid picture of the dynamic interplay between temporal power and spiritual pursuits.

This book also proves that the Mughals were not merely conquerors; they were sophisticated patrons of art, architecture, literature and music, fostering an environment where Persian, Central Asian and Indian cultures converged harmoniously. The Mughals' patronage of art, literature and architecture is not only a testament to their refined aesthetic sensibilities but also a reflection of their embrace of diverse cultural and religious expressions. From the towering mosques and mausoleums to the exquisite miniature paintings that adorned their courts, the Mughals left an enduring imprint on the artistic and cultural heritage of South Asia. The Taj Mahal and the grand architectural marvels of Fatehpur Sikri exemplify the Mughals' enduring cultural legacy.

The Mughal Empire, as a crucible of cultural and religious dynamism, continues to be a source of inspiration and contemplation, inviting us to re-examine the intricate intersections of faith and power that defined an era rich in complexity and historical significance. In the vast corridors of history, few epochs rival the splendour and complexity of the Mughal Empire. The pages that follow unravel the threads of faith, spirituality and religious tolerance that defined an empire whose legacy continues to resonate through the ages.

From Babur, the founder of the dynasty, to the zenith of Mughal power under Akbar, Jahangir and Shah Jahan and the eventual decline during the reign of Aurangzeb, this book examines how each ruler navigated the complex interplay between religion and governance. It investigates their policies toward different religious communities, shedding light on the eclectic blend of Persian, Central Asian and indigenous influences that characterized the Mughal approach to spirituality. The Mughals' engagement with Islam, Hinduism, Sikhism and other faiths is a fascinating lens through which we can understand the mosaic of religious coexistence during this period. The Sufi mysticism embraced by many Mughal emperors, alongside their tolerance of diverse religious practices, contributed to a unique atmosphere of syncretism and inclusivity.

In the first chapter it has been dicussed that Babur was a devout Muslim and his conquest against Rana Sanga was often framed as *jihad*, or holy war. However, his approach to governance in India reflected a degree of religious tolerance. While he asserted his dominance and established Islamic practices, he did not impose his faith on the majority Hindu population. Babur was not only a military strategist but also a cultured and learned ruler. He patronized scholars, poets and Sufi mystics, fostering an environment where intellectual and spiritual pursuits thrived. This cultural patronage contributed to the synthesis of Central Asian and Indian traditions.

Babur was well-versed in Persian literature and culture and he brought with him a rich Persianate tradition. His memoir, the *Baburnama*, is not only a personal account but also a literary masterpiece in the Chagatai Turkic language with Persian influences. Babur's love for gardens, an essential element of Persian culture, is evident in the establishment of the famous Gardens of Kabul. This affinity for gardens would later manifest in the Mughal gardens of India. While Babur's architectural contributions in India were limited, his appreciation for aesthetics laid the groundwork for the grand monuments that would follow. Babur's court saw a fusion of Central Asian, Persian and Indian cultural elements, fostering a unique cultural synthesis that would characterize the Mughal Empire. Babur himself was a poet and writer and his literary contributions added to the cultural richness of his court. The *Baburnama*, besides being a historical record, is a testament to his literary prowess. Babur's reign was a pivotal period that set the stage for the cultural and religious amalgamation that would become the hallmark of the Mughal Empire. His nuanced approach to governance and cultural assimilation laid the foundation for the flourishing of art, architecture and intellectual pursuits under subsequent Mughal rulers.

In the second chapter of this book it has been stressed that Akbar played a transformative role in shaping the religious and cultural landscape of India during the late sixteenth century. His reign, from 1556 to 1605, is particularly noteworthy for its policy of religious tolerance and the patronage of arts and culture. He is renowned for his efforts to promote religious harmony and understanding among different faiths. He initiated a series of dialogues and discussions among scholars of various religions, leading to the creation of the *Din-i-Ilahi*, a syncretic faith that sought to incorporate elements from Hinduism, Islam, Zoroastrianism and Christianity. While the *Din-i-Ilahi* did not gain widespread acceptance, Akbar's commitment to religious pluralism left a lasting legacy. He implemented policies of religious tolerance, ensuring that people of all faiths could practice their religions without fear of persecution. He abolished the *jazia* tax on non-Muslims and actively engaged with scholars from different religious backgrounds, fostering an environment of mutual respect. Akbar's court was a vibrant centre of cultural exchange. He married several Rajput princesses, fostering matrimonial alliances that strengthened political ties and contributed to a syncretic blend of Rajput and Mughal cultures. This fusion was evident in art, music and architecture.

Akbar was a great patron of the arts and culture. His court attracted poets, artists, musicians and scholars from different parts of the world. The *Akbarnama*, a historical chronicle commissioned by Akbar, stands as a testament to the era's rich artistic production. His reign witnessed the construction of several architectural marvels, including the Agra Fort, Fatehpur Sikri and the Buland Darwaza. These structures blended Persian, Central Asian and Indian architectural styles, representing the diverse cultural influences present in the Mughal Empire. The Mughal court under Akbar became a centre of literary excellence. Akbar himself was multilingual and promoted the use of Persian as the administrative language. The translation of Hindu texts into Persian, known as the *Akbarnama*, furthered the cultural exchange between the two traditions. His policies of religious tolerance and cultural syncretism laid the groundwork for a uniquely pluralistic society that continued to evolve under subsequent Mughal rulers.

In the third chapter it has been described that Jahangir continued the Mughal tradition of fostering a rich cultural milieu while offering a nuanced approach to religion. Jahangir, like his father Akbar, upheld a policy of religious tolerance. While he personally adhered to Sunni Islam, he did not impose his religious beliefs on his subjects. Jahangir continued the tradition of engaging in interfaith dialogue, maintaining a court where scholars and religious figures from different backgrounds could participate in intellectual exchanges. Jahangir's marriage to Nur Jahan, a Persian princess and a strong, influential woman, strengthened ties between the Mughals and the Rajputs. This matrimonial alliance contributed to a cultural synthesis, blending Persian and Mughal traditions. Jahangir generally maintained the policies of religious tolerance established by his father. He continued to employ and engage with people of diverse religious backgrounds in his court.

Jahangir was a patron of the arts and his reign witnessed the flourishing of Mughal painting. The exquisite art form known as the *Tuzuk-i-Jahangiri*, a memoir written by Jahangir, provides insights into the cultural and political milieu of his time. The period also saw the development of the Mughal miniature painting style, characterized by detailed and vibrant depictions. While Jahangir did not commission as many grand architectural projects as his predecessors, he did contribute to the embellishment of existing structures. The Shalimar Bagh in Kashmir is an example of Jahangir's interest in garden design, a characteristic feature of Mughal architecture. Jahangir was known for his interest in literature and poetry. He patronized poets and writers, contributing to the literary richness of his court. Jahangir, like Akbar, continued the tradition of maintaining a multilingual court where Persian served as the administrative language. This practice contributed to the cultural fusion of Persian and Indian traditions. His rule maintained an environment of religious tolerance and cultural vibrancy, fostering the arts and intellectual pursuits within the Mughal Empire.

The fourth chapter deals with the reign of Shah Jahan who is often remembered for his grand architectural projects and the enduring symbol of love, the Taj Mahal. His reign marked a continuation of the cultural and artistic richness of the Mughal Empire. Shah Jahan, like his predecessors, was a devout Muslim. While Shah Jahan's reign is associated with a certain level of orthodoxy, he generally maintained the policy of religious tolerance established by Akbar. Non-Muslims continued to hold important positions in his administration and he did not actively suppress other religions. Shah Jahan was a patron of Sufi saints and their orders. He supported the construction of Sufi shrines and the promotion of Sufi practices, contributing to the synthesis of mysticism and mainstream Islam within the Mughal Empire.

Shah Jahan is best known for his architectural achievements and his reign is often referred to as the "Golden Age of Mughal Architecture". The construction of the Taj Mahal in memory of his wife Mumtaz Mahal, the Shah Jahan's Mosque at the Jama Masjid in Delhi and the Shah Jahan Mosque in Thatta are iconic examples of Mughal architectural splendour. Shah Jahan's court was a centre of cultural and artistic flourishing. The period saw advancements in Mughal miniature painting, with artists producing intricate and detailed works. The emperor himself was known for his interest in the arts, poetry and calligraphy. Like his predecessors, Shah Jahan maintained a multilingual court where Persian continued to serve as the administrative language. This practice contributed to the fusion of Persian and Indian cultural elements. Shah Jahan's court was renowned for its opulence and luxury. The emperor was a patron of the finest craftsmen and his reign saw the creation of exquisite artefacts and textiles that reflected the pinnacle of Mughal craftsmanship.

The fifth and last chapter is about Aurangzeb whose reign is marked by a departure from the religious tolerance and cultural syncretism of his predecessors. His policies of abolition of many illegal taxes provided much relief to his subject irrespective religious boundaries. Aurangzeb is often characterized by his strict adherence to orthodox Sunni Islam. During his reign, he implemented a series of measures aimed at promoting Islamic orthodoxy, including the enforcement of *Sharia* law, the reimposition of the *jazia* tax on non-Muslims and the prohibition of various cultural practices deemed inconsistent with Islamic teachings. Aurangzeb sought to curtail the influence of Sufi mysticism in the Mughal court and society. He viewed certain Sufi practices as deviations from orthodox Islam and took measures to restrict the activities of Sufi orders.

Aurangzeb was known for his personal austerity, in stark contrast to the opulent lifestyles of his predecessors. He rejected the extravagance of the Mughal court, choosing a more modest way of life. This shift in the ruler's personal choices had an impact on the courtly culture. Unlike his predecessors, Aurangzeb did not commission grand architectural projects. The construction of new monuments and patronage of the arts diminished during his reign. This marked a departure from the tradition of Mughal rulers as prominent builders. The Mughal court under Aurangzeb witnessed a decline in the arts and culture that had flourished during earlier periods. The atmosphere of religious orthodoxy and the emperor's personal frugality contributed to a less vibrant cultural milieu. While Persian continued to be the official language of the court, Aurangzeb did not have the same interest in literature and intellectual pursuits as some of his predecessors. The decline in courtly culture extended to a decrease in literary activities.

During the British period, a detailed study of medieval history started and began to be written in different approaches and thoughts. Some works of those historians are based on research and enquiry and give the exact picture of the past but some works are undoubtedly biased and project the medieval rulers as orthodox Muslim or Islamic rulers. It was all due to the contemporary works of the medieval period in which they were projected as a promoter of Islam. No doubt the medieval rulers were Muslims by religion but they were also aware that the majority of the subjects were Hindus and Islamic rules could not be anyway imposed upon these subjects. But here the question arises that when they were so just to their subjects, why they liked to be written as orthodox which they were not at all in their entire rule. This is the real challenge before the historiographers that the rulers were liked to be posed which they were certainly not. Perhaps the rulers were satisfied with their rule according to the interests of the subjects but they were also eager that their history would be written as protector or promoter of Islam. Perhaps this was a measure to satisfy the Muslim theologians which were a very powerful section in the court.

The Mughals, although very liberal to their subjects, were depicted by Hindutva historians as orthodox and religiously intolerant. The Hindutva authors consider the Mughal period as the Dark Age and even the most liberal Emperor Akbar was shown as a villain and Rana Pratap as the hero of that period. During the British period, some of the Hindu tinge authors began to write the history of medieval India according to their suitability. The Hindutva historians began to change the history written by the Western and Marxist historians by proper enquiry and research. These orthodox historians in order to change the history textbooks declare Maharana Pratap as Great, vilifying Tipu Sultan, rename the Taj Mahal as Tejo Mahalaya, a Shiva Temple etc. This was inevitably a naked form of revisionism, which seeks to reclaim, rename and appropriate all symbols of the medieval past.

As I stand at the culmination of this endeavour, I am filled with gratitude for the multitude of individuals who have contributed to the creation of this work. This exploration into the historical nuances of the Mughal Empire's rich tapestry would not have been possible without the support, encouragement and expertise of numerous individuals. First and foremost, I extend my deepest appreciation to the scholars and historians whose extensive research has paved the way for a more profound understanding of the Mughal era. Their dedication to unravelling the complexities of religious and cultural dynamics under the Mughals has been an invaluable resource. I am indebted to the librarians and archivists who tirelessly curate and preserve the historical documents and manuscripts that have served as the foundation of this work. Their commitment to the preservation of our shared history is commendable. I express my heartfelt thanks to my academic mentors, advisors, friends and family such as Chaudhary Zakir Hussain, Professor M.U. Rabbani, Professor Ziaur Rahman, Sh. S.M. Javed, Professor Waseem Raja, Dr Talha, Dr Saddam, my wife Imrana and my children Lubna, Iram, Anam and Sadaf for their unwavering support and understanding during the countless hours devoted to research and writing.

Aijaz Ahmad

Contents

Chapter 1

Religious Practices Under Babur

Zahiruddin Mohammad Babur (14 February 1483 to 26 December 1530), the founder of the Mughal Empire in Indian subcontinent, was born to Umar Shaikh Mirza and Qutlugh Nigar Khanam in the city of Andijan of Fergana (Khokand) kingdom of Timurid Empire. On the death of Sultan Abu Said Mirza, a great-grandson of Timur and Babur's grandfather, his extensive dominions covering Khurasan and Transoxiana were divided among his sons (1469). Umar Shaikh Mirza got Fergana, Sultan Ahmad Mirza became the ruler of Samarkand, Bukhara and Hissar, Sultan Mahmud Mirza became king of Balkh and Ulugh Beg Mirza became the king of Kabul.

After his father's death on 8 June 1494, Babur inherited his father's precarious throne at the tender age of eleven years and a few months. His life had hitherto been a series of wild adventures, in which, to judge by his own writings, he took a positive pleasure. From the very start, young Babur faced fierce resistance from his nobles and even his uncles, who tried to replace him with his more malleable younger brother. Nonetheless, when only fifteen he managed to seize control of Timur's former capital of Samarkand but soon expelled. Hc also tried afterwards several fruitless attempts to occupy Samarkand.

Finally he established himself, after many vicissitudes, as king of Kabul and it was from Kabul that he set out on his first expedition to India in February 1519.

Babur's Relation with Turks and Mongols

The blood of two great conquerors flowed in Babur's veins. Zahiruddin Mohammad Babur's father Umar Shaikh Mirza, king of Fergana, was the descendant of Amir Timur "the earth-shaker" and Qutlugh Nigar Khanam was the descendant of Genghis Khan "the terrible". Zahiruddin Mohammad was nicknamed "Babur" by his maternal grandfather Yunus Khan, who was descended from Chaghatai Khan, the second son of Genghis Khan, who said that the boy was a little tiger. The term Mughal comes from a mispronunciation of the word Mongol, as the name Mongol was pronounced Mughal in the Fergana Valley. Even Qutlugh Nigar Khanam was called as "Mughal" because she had been given to Omar Shaikh by her father, Yunus Khan, the Mongol Khan of the Stone City (Tashkent).[1]

The Timurid dynasty founded by Timur and Mongol dynasty founded by Genghis Khan were hailed to the same origin or the person known as Tumanay Khan. Genghis was the fifth generation of Tumanay Khan and Timur was the tenth generation from Tumanay Khan. Genghis Khan was descended from Khabul Khan, a son of Tumanay Khan and Babur was descended from Qachuli Khan, another son of Tumanay Khan. Moreover Babur was originally a Mongol but always claimed himself as Timurid because Mongols or Mughals were having a separate identity of being the descendants of Genghiz Khan.

Timur is claimed by both the Turks and the Mongols to be one of them. Timur was technically a Mongol, belonging to the Barlas tribe. But by the time Timur was born, the Barlas clan had become Turkified. If we were to ask Timur, he would probably consider himself a Turk rather than a Mongol. In this way one should prefer calling Timur a Turko-Mongol as he was both and his descendant Babur may be called same as Timur. Even ignoring Timur's claims of relation, the Barlas tribe was connected with the Borjigin clan, the clan of Genghis. The two clans claim a common origin from Bodonchar Munkhag (great grand ancestor of Tumanay Khan) who was alive in the ninth century CE.

Like Mongol and Turk, the Mughals are also called Tartar, Tatar or Tatari. The name Tatar first appeared among nomadic tribes living in north-eastern Mongolia and the area around Lake Baikal. Unlike the Mongols, these peoples spoke a Turkic language. After various groups of these Turkic nomads became part of the armies of the Mongol conqueror Genghis Khan in the early thirteenth century, a fusion of Mongol and Turkic elements took place and the Mongol invaders of Russia and Hungary became known to Europeans as Tatars (or Tartars). As Babur's ancestors were also belonging to the same fusion, some writers write the Indian Mughals as Tatari.

Like the marriage of Umar Shaikh Mirza and Qutlugh Nigar Khanam there was another matrimonial relation between both families. Although, Timur was not a Khan but his ancestors and successors married multiple Mongol queens to increase his legitimacy and get a career boost. Timur's ancestor Qarachar (military commander and advisor of Genghis and Chagatai Khan of Mongol Empire) married the daughter of Chagatai Khan, the second son of Genghis Khan and it is believed that Timur was descending from this marriage. Another blood connection that some of the Timurids claimed was that Timur was a descendant of Genghis via his mother, Tekina Khatun. Even Timur married Saray Mulk Khanam, a descendant of Genghis via Chagatai. Saray Mulk Khanam was the daughter of Qazan Khan ibn Yasaur.Thus Babur has Genghis Khan's blood not just from his mother side, but from his Timurid father's side as well because his paternal ancestors began marrying Genghis Khan's descendants from the time of Timur.

It also must be noted that only the descendant of Genghis Khan could be a Khan or Khanam while Timur's family used the title of Mirza. Khanams were strong powerful figures with a great deal of positive influence on the Mongol order. In the Mughal era in

India, Timur's line was emphasized while Genghis Khan's line was not. *Silsilanamas* started with Timur with no mention of Genghis. Court biographers proclaimed that Timur's achievements were on par with or exceeded Genghis Khan. Mughal emperors called themselves Gurgeniya or Sahib Qiran like Timur and sent money for the upkeep of his mausoleum in Samarkand.

Babur as a Ruler of Fergana and Samarkand

Babur was a military adventurer, a soldier of distinction and a poet and diarist of genius, as well as a statesman. Fergana was a small principality with its capital Andijan but Umar Shaikh Mirza made Akhsikit as his new capital. Babur was governor of Andijan at the time of the death of his father Umar Shaikh Mirza on 8 June 1494. On hearing the sad demise of his father on next day, Babur rushed to Akhsikit, the new capital of Fergana and ascended the throne of Fergana at the age 11 years and few months.[2]

As Babur was the descendant of Amir Timur, he tried to recover Timur's old capital of Samarkand (now in Uzbekistan). At Timurs death, his youngest son Shahrukh Mirza, the ruler of Khurassan, had seized the city and had given it over to be ruled by his son Ulugh Beg Mirza, the famous astronomer; from whom it was taken by his son Abdul Latif Mirza, who, for the sake of the enjoyments of this fleeting world, murdered his own father, an old man so illustrious for his knowledge. After Abdul Latif Mirza's few months' rule Abdullah Mirza mounted the throne and reigned nearly two years. After him the government was seized by Sultan Abu Said Mirza, who conferred it upon his eldest son Sultan Ahmed Mirza. On his death Sultan Mahmud Mirza ascended the throne and after him, Bai-sunghar Mirza (r. 1495-98). Babur occupied Samarkand after a hard struggle of three years against Bai-sunghar Mirza (r. 1495-98) who was also his cousin in relationship. He was able to capture it in November 1497, after a siege of seven months; but he could not hold it for more than 100 days, as he had to leave Samarkand for Fergana to quell a rebellion led by Auzun Hasan and Ahmad

Tambal who acted in the name of his younger brother Jahangir Mirza. Babur failed and now lost both.[3]

He recovered Fergana in June 1498 and won Samarkand for the second time in November 1500, not from a Timurid rival but from Mohammad Shaibani Khan (r. 1500-1510), the chief of the Uzbegs (Babur calls him the foreign robber). Babur then made peace with Jahangir Mirza by ceding parts of Fergana, but the latter ultimately occupied the whole of it. In May 1501, he was badly defeated by Shaibani Khan at Sar-i-pul and forced to surrender Samarkand and give his eldest sister Khanzada Begam in marriage to the enemy. In this way Samarkand, the city of Babur's affections, was thrice taken and lost.[4]

Babur was now once more a throneless wanderer and retired to Tashkent under the shelter of his maternal uncle Sultan Mahmud Khan. With his two uncles, Mahmud Khan and Ahmad Khan, he made several attempts on Fergana. Ahmad Tambal, finding himself no match for such a Timurid-Mongol coalition, invited Shaibani Khan who ultimately inflicted a crushing defeat upon the two Khans (the uncles of Babur) in the battle of Archiyan in June 1503.[5]

Babur lost the battle and compelled to escape with a small band of followers. Sensing Babur's helplessness, most of his officers and warriors alike began to leave his camp. Their families were in Andijan and the deserters saw no hope of retaking that strong city. Babur had managed to lose both ends of his small kingdom; he had been brushed aside almost contemptuously by more powerful schemers. It took him a little while to realize how bad his situation really was. Babur wandered the mountains of Central Asia and took refuge with hill tribes.

Babur's Conquest of Kabul

The battle of Archiyan moulded the future history of Babur and he turned towards a new destination. In October 1504, sensing the futility of ever recovering his patrimony in Central Asia, Babur, his mother and 300 lightly armed men marched southwards across the snowy passes of Afghanistan's Hindu Kush Mountains in search of a base safely distant from the growing Uzbek threat. They set their sights on Kabul, which was previously ruled by Babur's paternal uncle Ulugh Beg II, who died leaving only an infant as heir. The city was then claimed by Muqim Beg, who was considered to be a usurper and was opposed by the local populace. Babur took Kabul from Muqim Beg Arghun usurper almost without any opposition. Arghunids ruler Muqim Beg was forced to retreat towards Kandahar.[6] With this move, Babur gained a new kingdom of Kabul and Ghazni, re-established his fortunes and would remain its ruler until 1526.

Aware that the survival of Timur's legacy rested on his shoulders, in 1508 Babur adopted the exalted Persian title *Padshah* or "supreme king". Moreover, he would have a powerful ally Shah Ismail Safavi (r. 1501-24), the charismatic and seemingly invincible founder of Iran's Safavid dynasty (1501-1736), was just then consolidating his authority across the Iranian plateau. Alarmed by Shaibani Khan's 1507 conquest of Herat, Ismail defeated an Uzbek army in 1510, resulting in the death of Shaibani Khan and the fall of Herat to the Safavids. He also freed Babur's imprisoned relatives, leading to Babur's joyful reunion with his sister Khanzada Begum.

In Kabul Babur didn't lose courage to recover his homeland. After death of Shaibani Khan Babur made his last unsuccessful attempt on Samarkand (1511-1512) induced him to give up a futile quest and to concentrate on expansion elsewhere. After his third loss of Samarkand Babur in 1514, abandoning the possibility of ever regaining Samarkand, he returned to his base in Kabul and again began to look to the north Indian plain, this time not as an object of plunder, but as territory for building a sovereign domain large and stable enough to preserve the threatened Timurid house from extinction. In 1517 Sikandar Lodi had died and was succeeded by his son Ibrahim, who unwisely replaced senior nobles in his service with younger men who were supposedly loyal but were also less experienced. When Babur's expeditions of 1519 and 1520 took him as far as the Punjab's Chenab River, some of those recently dismissed senior Lodi nobles, including the governor of the Punjab and even the sultan's own uncle Alam Khan Lodi, began to see the Mughal commander as a viable alternative to the unpopular Ibrahim. In 1524 they invited him to invade and assume sovereign rule. Again he entered the Punjab, this time with the intent of challenging Sultan Ibrahim Lodi. But on reaching Lahore and Dipalpur, he found that he could not trust the Lodi turncoats nominally under his command and so he returned to Kabul.

Babur's Conquest of India

As of Samarkand and Fergana, Babur had a political claim over India as both the great ancestors of Babur, Genghiz Khan and Timur, had invaded India. The raid of Genghiz Khan had touched only the fringe of the country, but the invasion of Timur caused widespread anarchy in India, as the kingdom of Delhi had already become a shadow of its former self. The Sayyads were hardly the persons to cope with the prevailing anarchy and dislocation and gave way to the Lodis. The kingdom of the Lodis was a loose confederacy of semi-independent governorships held by the *amirs*, the leaders of the Afghan tribes. But Ibrahim, who came to the throne in 1517, was ambitious, tactless, arrogant and impatient; he tried to play the monarch, even to those who detested monarchy. He thus alienated the sympathy of the Afghan nobles who raised the standard of rebellion. The Punjab and Jaunpur openly revolted and the Rajputs also defeated him.

It was in early 1519, at age of 37, Babur first appeared in India. From Kabul he made several incursions into India, which were mere raids until 1525. Babur made a sudden raid on Punjab region (Bajaur) which was part of the dominions of Sultan Ibrahim Lodi and its governor was Daulat Khan Lodi. Babur besieged it and stormed it after a spirited struggle. Babur writes in 1519,

> "As it was always in my heart to possess Hindustan and as these several countries, Bhira, Khush-ab, Chin-ab and Chiniut had once been held by the Turk, I pictured them as my own and was resolved to get them into my hands, whether peacefully or by force."[7]

In 1519, Babur made his way to the Jhelum, meeting with little or no opposition on his march. He crossed the Swat and fording the Indus, made his way almost unopposed to the Jhelum. Most of the local chieftains and the fort of Bhera submitted. Babur regarded the Punjab as his own by hereditary right from Timur, who had conquered it and instructed his troops not to do violence on the people or their flocks and crops. He sent an embassy to the court of Ibrahim Lodi asking for the recognition of his claim to the Punjab, but his envoy Mulla Murshid was detained at Lahore by the governor of the Punjab, Daulat Khan and the letter remained undelivered. Babur marched to Kandhar, took it without any opposition on 6 September 1522 and left his younger son Mirza Kamran in charge.[8]

In India the position of Ibrahim Lodi was growing more and more precarious on account of the revolt of his nobles and relations. The most serious enemies of the Sultan were Alam Khan, his uncle and Daulat Khan Lodi, governor of Punjab, both of whom appealed to Babur for help. Alam Khan went to Kabul and begged Babur to advance to the Punjab and place him on the throne of Delhi. Daulat Khan, apprehending that Sultan Ibrahim would soon deprive him of his position, sent messengers to Babur, offering to acknowledge him as his sovereign and asking his aid against Ibrahim. Babur responded to Daulat Khan's appeal and undertook his sixth invasion of India in 1524. It is also said that Babur was also invited by Rana Sanga the king of Mewar. With this local support Babur was enabled to advance much farther than on previous occasions and ultimately reached Sirhind. But further progress was rendered impossible by the behaviour of Daulat Khan, described by Babur as "rude and stupid". Babur therefore returned to Kabul, where he reorganized and reinforced his army.[9]

Battle of Panipat

On 17 November 1525, Babur, aged forty-two, launched his fifth and final invasion of India, marching from Kabul at the head of an army of 8,000 men, composed of subordinate Timurid princes and their retainers, Pashtun allies from south-eastern Afghanistan and artillery and matchlock contingents advised by Turkish officers from Anatolia. On the way he was joined by Humayun from Badakhshan and Khwaja Kilan from Ghazni. When he crossed the Indus on 16 December the entire army amounted to 12,000 men including non-combatant camp followers.

As Babur advanced towards Sialkot and forced Daulat Khan, who had girded himself with two swords as a challenge against the invader, to capitulate. Daulat Khan's son Ghazi Khan fled but his another son Dilawar Khan joined Babur. Alam Khan Lodi also joined Babur in a forlorn condition. By 12 April 1526, Babur reached Panipat, 65 km north-west of Delhi and secured his defences. Sultan Ibrahim Lodi also advanced from Delhi with a big army to meet the invader and also encamped at Panipat with his huge army.

His centre was strengthened by a line of some 700 movable carts, tied together by ropes of raw hide and between every two carts there were five or six breastworks for the protection of the matchlockmen and artillerymen. The line was not continuous but passages were provided wide enough for 150 horsemen to march out abreast. Babur took his position in the centre. The Mughals also possessed the relatively new technology of matchlock and cannon firepower, which Ibrahim lacked. Most importantly, Babur deployed the same flanking cavalry tactics that Uzbek cavalries had used to defeat him decades earlier in his struggles over Samarkand.

Babur in his Memoir says,

> "... I put my foot in the stirrup of resolution, set my hand on the rein of trust in God and moved forward

against Sultan Ibrahim, son of Sultan Sikandar, son of Buhlul Lodi Afghan, in possession of whose throne at that time were the Delhi capital and the dominions of Hindustan, whose standing-army was called a lakh (1,00,000), whose elephants and whose Begs' elephants were about 1,000".[10]

For eight days from 12 to 19 April the two armies stood face to face. Two advance parties of the Afghans fell upon the Mughul army, the first under Hamid Khan, which came into contact with Babur's right wing, was completely routed by Humayun, the second under Datid Khan and Hatim Khan was similarly routed. Babur says about the number of Ibrahim's army that people estimated the army opposing us at 1,00,000 men; Ibrahim's elephants and those of his *amirs* were said to be about 1,000.[11]

Babur says,

> "...Seven hundred carts were brought in. The order given to Ustad Ali Quli was that these carts should be joined together in Ottoman fashion, but using ropes of raw hide instead of chains and that between every two carts 5 or 6 mantelets should be fixed, behind which the matchlockmen were to stand to fire. Panipat is there with its crowded houses and suburbs. It would be on one side of us; our other sides must be protected by carts and mantelets behind which our foot and matchlockmen would stand."

Babur further says,

> "On our right was the town of Panipat with its suburbs; in front of us were the carts and mantelets we had prepared; on our left and elsewhere were ditch and branch. At distances of an arrow's flights sally-places were left for from 100 to 200 horsemen."[12]

On the 21 April 1526, on Friday the Sultan's army advanced to the attack and the famous first battle of Panipat was started. By midday, the decisive Battle of Panipat had left Sultan Ibrahim's vast army disappeared and he himself lay dead on the field with 15,000 of his men. Babur won the battle by coolness under fire, his use of artillery and effective Turkish wheeling tactics on a divided, dispirited enemy.[13]

Babur himself says,

> "When the incitement to battle had come, the Sun was spear-high; till midday fighting had been in full force; noon passed, the foe was crushed in defeat, our friends rejoicing and gay. By God's mercy and kindness, this difficult affair was made easy for us! In one half-day, that armed mass was laid upon the earth. Five or six thousand men were killed in one place close to Ibrahim. Our estimate of the other dead, lying all over the field, was 15,000 to 16,000, but it came to be known, later in Agra from the statements of Hindustanis, that 40,000 or 50,000 may have died in that battle."[14]

Babur in Delhi and Agra

From the field of Panipat Babur marched to Delhi. On 27 April 1526, the *khutba* was read in his name in the Jami Mosque and the king of Kabul was hailed as the Emperor of Hindusthan. At Delhi Babur remained a few days. While that natural curiosity which was always a marked feature of Babur's character led him to spend much of his time in visiting the tombs, public buildings, gardens etc., of the ancient city, he took effective measures to secure his newly won possession. From Delhi, Babur sent his son Humayun down to Agra, the Lodi capital since 1506, in order to secure the defeated regime's treasury and government palaces. In Delhi, Babur visited the shrines of Nizamuddin Auliya and Khwaja Bakhtiyar Kaki and after three days stay, a governor and a military commandant were appointed for the city. The treasuries were taken over and it was made clear to the citizens of Delhi that a new ruler had come among them.[15]

After securing Delhi Babur passed on to Agra on 4 May 1526, which Prince Humayun had already captured. Agra became Babur's capital in Hindustan and, undoubtedly, a new Samarkand. In Agra fort Raja Vikramadiya of Gwalior's family was staying but Raja himself was slain along with Ibrahim. In Agra Humayun presented Babur a big and precious diamond which he had received from the family of the late Raja Vikramaditya as a mark of gratitude for his chivalrous treatment. This has been identified with the world-famous Koh-i-Nur. Babur, however, affectionately returned it to his son as a gift. The diamond's weight was 8 *misqals* (320 *ratis*) and its cost was equal to two and half days' food of the entire world. Tavernier valued it as £8,80,000. In the fort the other captives were Malik Dad Karani, Milli Surduk and Firoz Khan Mewati. They were all ordered for capital punishment but later freed them with their goods.[16]

Babur's success at Panipat and his occupation on Lodi Empire made him the Emperor of India (Hindustan)[17] and founded Mughal Empire. But his success in Panipat and establishing a new ruling dynasty was not the overall success rather it created many political foes. His small force, burdened by the oppressive weather and located 1,300 km from their base at Kabul, was surrounded by powerful enemies. Down to the Ganga River Valley there were militant Afghan of the East who had set up Bihar Khan as their king and the Rajputs in the south-west under Rana Sangram Singh of Mewar (Udaipur).[18]

While Babur's stay in Agra Sultan Ibrahim's mother Princess Bayda (Buwa) was allowed to stay in Agra court by Babur. Something in the old lady had reminded him of his dead mother, so that he had exalted her to the status of Queen Mother. She attempted to poison Babur on 21 December 1526 by bribing his cook. When he vomited blood just after the meal he realised his poisoning and drank some opium in milk as an antidote. The taster was ordered to be cut to pieces and commanded the cook to be flayed alive. But Babur didn't kill the Ibrahim's mother and her and dispatched her to Kabul. Fearing a hostile reception there, she jumped into a river on the way and drowned. One of her two associates woman was trampled to death by an elephant and the other woman was shot bv a matchlock.[19] From that day Babur made it a rule that food presented to the emperor is first tasted by cook in front of emperor and then only he can have. This policy was followed by all mughal emperors.

Babur's Affair with Hasan Khan Mewati

Even after gaining control over Lodi Empire, Babur was in distress due to his political foes in northern India and also due to the disturbances in his army. Most of the army men were eager to return to their native place but Babur consoled them to stay for the land which they have won after sacrificing their lives. Babur wanted to win over the local chiefs of northern India and assured them the great reward. He also tried to win the confidence of Hasan Khan Mewati who was the chief of Mewat and also the cousin of Ibrahim Lodi.

But Hasan Khan was having conversation with Rana Sanga, the Raja of Mewar, against Babur. Babur says about Hasan Khan,

> "In the fight with Ibrahim, Hasan Khan Mewati's son Nahar Khan had fallen into our hands; we had kept him as a hostage and, ostensibly on his account, his father had been making comings-and-goings with us, constantly asking for him. It now occurred to several people that if Hasan Khan were conciliated by sending him his son, he would thereby be the more favourably disposed and his waiting on me might be the better brought about. Accordingly Nahar Khan was dressed in a robe of honour; promises were made to him for his father and he was given leave to go. That hypocritical mannikin (Hasan Khan) must have waited just till his son had leave from me to go, for on hearing of this and while his son as yet had not joined him, he came out

> of Alur (Alwar) and at once joined Rana Sanga in Toda Bhim (Agra District). It must have been ill-judged to let his son go just then."[20]

Battle of Khanwa

After occupying Delhi and Agra, Babur now turned his attention to the arch-enemy, Rana Sangram Singh (r. 1508-28) of Mewar. This undisputed leader of the Rajput confederacy was an indefatigable fighter, with one arm and one eye lost and eighty scars in his body. He had sent a friendly embassy to Babur at Kabul and offered his help against Ibrahim, but the situation had now changed and Sangram Singh lost no time in declaring war against his rival for the mastery of Hindustan. Babur declared his first *jihad* (holy war) against the "infidels" and sent reinforcement to Bayana which had been besieged by the united forces of Hasan Khan of Mewat and Rana Sangram Singh. On 11 February 1527, Babur himself marched against the enemy and encamped at Sikri where he was joined by the garrison from Bayana. In some skirmishes which followed, the Rajputs inflicted defeat upon his advance guard.

Rana Sangram Singh or Rana Sanga of Mewar was a veteran of many years' military experience. Having ascended the throne of Mewar in 1508, he soon became the principal chief of Rajasthan. Babur says about Rana Sanga:[21]

> "Although Rana Sanga, the pagan, when I was in Kabul, had sent me an ambassador with professions of attachment and had arranged with me, that, if I would march from that quarter into the vicinity of Delhi, he would march from the other side upon Agra; yet, when I defeated Ibrahim and took Delhi and Agra, the pagan, during all my operations, did not make a single movement."

At Khanwa on 17 March 1527, the battle took place. Babur employed the same tactics that he had employed at Panipat. On the two extremities were the flanking columns (Tulghama). Rana Sanga had under his command some 80,000 cavalry, augmented by contingents of surviving Afghans recently defeated by Babur, including Ibrahim Lodi's brother Mahmud, who made common cause in trying to expel the Mughals from India. Though the Rana's host is usually described as a Hindu confederacy, it contained some of the Afghan chiefs whom Babur had failed to conciliate. Another important member was Hasan Khan Mewati of Alwar. The latter, though an adherent of the Afghans, was a Khanzada of Mewat and either a convert or the descendant of a convert to Islam. Badauni describes him as "an infidel who used the Kalima". As the two armies drew near each other, the great disparity in numbers caused despondency in the ranks of Babur's small force.[22]

His men were quaking in anticipation of the struggle with their unknown foes. To encourage his forces Babur made a plan to rouse the religious sentiments in his forces. The flagons and cups of silver and gold, the vessels of feasting, which all brought were broken and renunciation of wine was sworn. That night and next day some 300 begs and persons of the household, soldiers and not soldiers, renounced wine. Babur made the memorable renunciation of his besetting sin, wine and restored the morale of his troops by a stirring oration. Babur called an assembly of all the *amirs* and officers and addressed them:[23]

> "Noblemen and soldiers! Every man that comes into the world is subject to dissolution. When we are passed away and gone, Allah only survives unchangeable. Whoever comes to the feast of life must, before it is over, drink from the cup of death. He who arrives at the inn of mortality must one day inevitably take his departure from that house of sorrow—the world. How much better is it to die with honour than to live with infamy!"

By quoting the couplet from Firdausi's *Shahnama*:

"With fame, even if I die, I am contented;
Let fame be mine, since my body is Death's"

He continued,

> "The Most High Allah has been propitious to us and has now placed us in such a crisis, that if we fall in the field, we die the death of martyrs; if we survive, we rise victorious, the avengers of the cause of Allah. Let us, then, with one accord, swear on Allah's holy word, that none of us will even think of turning his face from this warfare, nor desert from the battle and slaughter that ensues, till his soul is separated from his body."

Babur's words made an instant impression upon his men. All those present, beg and retainer, great and small, took the Holy Book joyfully into their hands and made vow and compact to this purport. Babur used his customary Tulgama tactics—a barrier of wagons for his centre, with gaps for the artillery and for cavalry sallies and wheeling cavalry charges on the wings.

Rana Sanga was having a strong army including the chief of Bhilsa Silhadi with 30,000 horse, Rawal Udai Singh of Bagar (Dongarpur) had 12,000, Medini Rai of Chanderi had 12,000, Hasan Khan of Mewat had 12,000, Rai Chandrabhan Chauhan had 4,000, Bharmal of Idr had 4,000, Narpat Hara had 7,000, Satrvi of Kach (Cutch) had 6,000, Dharmdeo had 4,000, Manikchand Chauhan and Dilpat Rao who had each 4,000, Bir-sing-deo had 4,000, Kanku (or Gangu) and Karm Singh and Dankusi each had 3,000 horse and Mahmud Khan, son of Sikandar Lodi 10,000 horse. Thus, according to the calculations about two lakh one thousand was the total strength of Rana Sanga's army.[24]

On Saturday, 17 March 1527, the battle started about half-past nine in the morning at Khanwa, a small village near Agra. The battle began with a magnificent charge by the Rajput left wing upon the Mughul right. The artillery of Babur stampeded the elephants and the flank charges bewildered the allied force, who, after 10 hours, broke, never to rally under a single leader again. It was a decisive victory for Babur. His small, well-disciplined force cut the huge hordes of the Rajputs to pieces, inflicting very heavy losses upon them. Hasan Khan Mewati was found dead among uncounted heaps of dead bodies. Rana Sanga was wounded and fled from the battlefield and might have died after some years due to poisoning by his own men. After the victory Babur assumed the title of *Ghazi* (victor in a Holy War). In order to reduce Mewat, Babur marched into Hasan Khan Mewati's capital Alwar on 7 April 1527.[25]

Battle of Chanderi

After defeating Rana Sanga at Khanwa, Babur's next target was Medini Rai of Chanderi who was a trusted fellow of Rana Sanga. Medini Rai was a Rajput chief of influence and king-maker in Malwa, who held the great fortress of Chanderi on the north-east of Malwa. Rana Sanga had taken Chanderi from Ibrahim Lodi and had handed over to his friend Medini Rai. The citadel of Chanderi was standing on a hill and below it was the town and outer-fort and below these was the level road. Battle of Khanwa practically destroyed the Rajputs as a fighting force but Medini Rai was still not ready to suurender his fort. Babur encamped before Chanderi on 21 January 1528 and a fruitless negotiation started until a week. Babur firstly offered Midini the Shamsabad area in place of Chanderi but negotiation was failed and the battle of Chanderi started on 28 January 1528. The outworks were occupied without difficulty, but the citadel was not taken without a stout resistance. Finally, Babur's forces defeated and killed the Rajput ruler Medini Rai of Chanderi along with thousands of his men on 29 January 1528. Many of the garrison seeing that all was lost, made an end of themselves.[26]

Babur in Gwalior

Later Babur went to the Gwalior and beautifully describes about the Hindu temples,

> "We rode from the flower-garden to visit the idol-houses of Gualiar. Some are two and some are three storeys high, each storey rather low, in the ancient fashion. On their stone plinths (*izara*) are sculptured images. Some idol-houses, College-fashion, have a portico, large high cupolas and *madarasa* like cells, each topped by a slender stone cupola. In the lower cells are idols carved in the rock."[27]

Babur always praised the Indian architecture of buildings and temples and was never hostile to other religions and places of Hindu worship. During his journey through different parts of the country he had come across several "idol houses" and Hindu pilgrimage centres. He had neither tried to defile or destroy them nor interfered with the religious practices followed there: the Gur-Khattri shrine in Peshawar where Hindus offered their hair as an offering; Kachwa where a Muslim lived among Hindu *yogis* as their disciple and indulged in un-Islamic practices; and Gwalior where a "lofty idol house" stood by a mosque, are examples. The only exception was the destruction of Jaina idols at Urwa Valley near Gwalior, not because they were idols, but because they were "shown naked without covering for their privates".[28]

In the memoirs of Babur which contain very frank opinions on almost everything he had encountered in India, there are hardly any hostile or contemptuous references to other religious faiths. More importantly, his reign is not marked by any acts of bigotry or discriminatory treatment of his subjects on account of their religious faith. On the contrary, his general demeanour underlined his tolerance of other religions.

Defeat of Afghans and Battle of Ghaghra

The Rajputs were thus disposed of, but Babur had still to deal with the Afghan rulers of Awadh, Bihar and Bengal. Babur's next target was defiant Afghans in the east. Babur ordered Chin-timur Sultan to lead his army in pursuit along with other commanders such as Muhammad Ali Jang-jang, Husamud-din Ali (son) of Khalifa,

Muhibbi Ali (son) of Khalifa, Kuki (son) of Baba Qashqa, Dost Mohammad (son) of Baba Qashqa, Baqi Shaghawal of Tashkent. On 2 February 1528, Babur set out on his first eastern campaign against the Afghans under Biban who had routed the Mughal army in Ayodhya and seized Lukhnow. Arriving at Kanauj, Babur crossed the Ganga (Ganges) in the middle of March by constructing a pontoon bridge, defeated the Afghans and hotly pursued them as far as Ayodhya. Biban escaped to Bengal and Bayazid as well as Ma'rif also took to heels.[29]

Babur stayed Ayodhya for a few days and was greatly impressed with the gardens, running water, well designed buildings, trees, particularly mango trees and various birds of coloured plumage. Babur appointed Baqi Tashkenti the governor of Awadh, who also subdued the rebellious local chiefs.[30]

While his stay at Agra, Babur was informed that the Afghans had rallied to Sultan Ibrahim's brother Mahmud Lodi and occupied Bihar and Bengal. Sultan Bayazid, Mahmud Khan, brother of Ibrahim and the newcomer Sher Khan were the main Afghan leader. Their total army was around 100,000 men. Responding to the coalition of Afghans, Babur set out on his second great eastern campaign in January 1529, against a formidable coalition of the Afghan chiefs under Bayazid Farmuli of Awadh (who joined Babur after defeat of Ibrahim in Panipat and Babur restored him Awadh province, but soon Bayazid Farmuli rebelled against Babur).[31]

In three months the Mughal army arrived at Chunar (April 1529), when Mahmud, who was besieging it, took to flight. Sher Khan abandoned Benares, several Afghan leaders surrendered to Babur and Mahmud Lodi, finding himself deserted, sought refuge with the Bengal army which was massed on the frontier. Babur moved eastward and encamped on the junction of Ganga and Ghaghra River just opposite to the Afghan army. On 6 May 1529, was fought the battle of Ghaghra and after a fierce struggle the enemy, attacked in front, rear and flank, broke and fled. Artillery was again decisive, helped by the skilful handling of boats. Ma'raf and several other Afghan chiefs joined him, while Biban, Bayazid and Mahmud Lodi retired. Jalal Khan, the late boy-king of Bihar, acknowledged Babur as overlord and a treaty of peace was concluded with Nusrat Shah, by which Babur's sovereignty in Bihar was recognized.[32]

The three battles Panipat, Khanwa and Ghaghra made Babur master of northern India. This was the last exploit of Babur's stormy career. Babur's dominion was now secure from Kandahar to the borders of Bengal, with a southern limit marked by the Rajput desert and the forts of Ranthambhor, Gwalior and Chanderi.

Building of Babri Mosque and Related Controversy

During Babur's regime Baqi Tashkenti built a mosque in Ayodhya[33] in 1528. It is said that Babur had ordered to built this mosque while his stay in Ayodhya to settle the affairs of Bayazid Farmuli. In its proof there were two inscriptions, one inside the mosque and another outside the mosque. The inscription inside the mosque was as:[34]

1. *Ba farmuda-i-shah babur ki adilash*
   Banayast ta kakh-i-gardoon mulaqi,
2. *Banakard ain muhbit-i-qudsiyan*
   Amir-i-saadat nishaan mir baqi,
3. *Buvad khair baqi chu saal-i-banaish*
   Ayaan shud ki guftam-buvad khai baqi. (935H)

The translation of the inside inscription is as,

> "By the command of the Emperor Babur whose justice is an edifice reaching up to the very height of the heavens, The good-hearted Mir Baqi built this alighting-place of angles; *buvad khair baqi*! (may this goodness last forever!) The year of building it was made clear likewise when I said, *buvad khair baqi*—935."

The inscription gives the date of the complete construction of the building in the last line, e.g. *buvad khair baqi* (B=2, v=6, d=4

—total=12; Kh=600, ai=10, r=400—total= 810; B=2, a=1, q=100, i=10—total=113: Grand Total= 935).

The inscription outside the mosque was as follows:[35]

1. *Banani-i-anki dana hast akbar*
   Ki khdliq-i-jumla alam la makaani,
2. *Durud mustafa bad az satayish*
   Ki sarwar-i-anibiyd do jahani
3. *Fasana dar jahan babur qalandar*
   Ki shud dar daur giti kamrani.

In the first couplet the poet praises Allah, in the second Mohammad (PBUH) and in the third Babur. The explanation of the above inscription is as,

> "In the name of one who is the wisest of all, who is the creator of the universe, but Himself has no abode; in thanks giving to the Prophet of all prophets in the two worlds; in celebration of the glory of Babur qalandar (the recluse) who has achieved great success in the world."

After the battle of Panipat Babur had visited the Awadh region and he himself says, "I halted some days in this station, for the purpose of settling the affairs of Oudh and the neighbouring country and for making the necessary arrangements" could not be presumed that Babur stayed there to demolish the temples. There is also some doubt whether he had actually gone to Ayodhya. The details of his activities during his stay in this region are not available in the *Baburnama*, as the pages covering this period are missing. Therefore, in the absence of any other contemporary accounts describing his activities during this period, the verses inscribed on the walls of the mosque form the only contemporary evidence indicating the circumstances in which the mosque was constructed. While the religious fervour of Mir Baqi is clear from these verses, particularly from the reference to the Prophet, it is important to underline the fact that there is no mention that the mosque was erected by demolishing a place of idol worship. No such reference is available in contemporary Persian chronicles also.

During the late medieval and early modern periods, there was no controversy over Ayodhya mosque. Most of the historians opine that the cult of Rama seems to have become popular only from the twelfth century. Yet even in the fifteenth and sixteenth centuries Ramanandis had not settled in Ayodhya on a significant scale. It became a centre of the Rama cult, as controlled by the Ramanandi order (*akhara*), only from the eighteenth century. Most of the Rama temples came into being only after that. It was only in the nineteenth century that British officials and writers began to give wide circulation and lend authority to the story that on Babur's orders a temple had been destroyed and a mosque built on the site. This fitted in with the British understanding of India.

Huen Tsang who was in India in the seventh century CE describes a place called Ayodhya which was then a major centre of Buddhism with many monasteries and *stupas*. He refers to about 300 monks of both the Mahayana and Hinayana Buddhism, who studied in Ayodhya. Huen Tsang also does not mention any place of Rama worship, even though he has recorded the existence of "ten Deva temples" (Vaishnava temples) in Ayodhya in the seventh century CE.[36]

Persian chronicles of also do not refer to the destruction of a temple at Ayodhya, the texts by Hindus are also silent about it. The most significant silence is that of Goswami Tulsidas, a great devotee of Rama and author of the *Ramacharitmanas*. Judging from his description of Ayodhya, an intimate knowledge of the area cannot be doubted. Yet he does not mention the existence of a temple at the Ramajanmasthan and its destruction by Muslims. Since he was greatly concerned with the rise of the *malecchas* he could not have overlooked it.

Sarvapalli Gopal writes that there is no conclusive proof that the mosque built at the time of Babur was on a temple site or that a temple had been destroyed to build it. It is true that the mosque incorporates pillars which have non-Islamic motifs; but the explanation for this may well lie in the employment of Hindu craftsmen in the building of mosques or the incorporating of material from any derelict building in the vicinity which could have had a non-religious function or even have been associated with non-Hindu sects. In fact, the style of these pillars is thought by some to be more Jaina than Hindu and it is possible that parts of the mosque may have been picked up from Jaina buildings. Ayodhya had been a Buddhist and then a Jaina centre before followers of the Rama cult started settling there in large numbers in the eighteenth century and building temples under the patronage of the Muslim Nawabs of Awadh.[37]

Babur had a habit of writing a diary of daily events which was known as *Tuzuk-i-Babri* or *Memoire of Babur*. In his *Memoire*, he mentions all the events related to him including social political and religious affairs. Even he mentions flora-fauna, fruits, birds, geography, society and politics, war, peace and even the history of India. However, in his *Memoire*, Babur did not mention any such event of destruction of temple and construction of a mosque on that place. Not even any contemporary work proves or shows doubt of his temple destruction in Ayodhya. Notwithstanding, his message to Humayun was rather a slap on the face of the Hindutva authors who day-night trying to prove him a tyrant and religious intolerant.

Babur never thought of draining the Indian wealth, or ruining the religion, culture and society of India, or dismantling the Indian religious places. He had actually no land to return or to drain the wealth. Right from the defeat of Ibrahim Lodi, Babur tried to settle his *amirs* in Agra and even called their relatives to come and settle in Agra, the final abode of his dream. He was a true politician and better knew how to rule such a country whose inhabitants were fond of their religion and culture. He was quite sure that India is his last destination and Indians are their subjects and it was his duty to take care of his subjects. He never tried to interfere with their religion and guided his *amirs* and his sons to respect the sentiments of the Indian people if they continue to rule India for a longer time.

It is notable that until the age of Akbar and also during his age, Lord Rama had no place in the temples and minds of the people. During the whole medieval period, Lord Krishna and Lord Shiva (in the form of *linga* worship) were the dominant gods occupying the religious places of Mathura, Vrindavan and Varanasi. Akbar himself promoted the Krishna cult through Raja Man Singh at Vrindavan and Shaivism through Raja Todarmal at Varanasi.

During the medieval times, no contemporary text proves Ayodhya a Hindu religious place of worship. During the age of Akbar, on the instructions of Raja Todarmal, a Vaishnavist poet Tulsidas (*c.*1532/1543-1623), wrote a text titled *Ramcharitamanas*, based on the Valmiki's *Ramayana* at Varanasi. Tulsidas was close to several movers and shakers at the Mughal court including Raja Man Singh. As the *Ramacharitmanas* of Tulsidas was in vernacular language Hindi, it became much popular in the Hindi-speaking belt of north India. By the efforts of Raja Man Singh and Todarmal, *Ramacharitmanas* began to be read and played as Rama Play (Ram Lila) throughout north India.[38] The rendering of the *Ramayana* in the local dialect in the form of *Ramacharitmanas* helped in projecting Rama as the most popular *avatara* of Vishnu and a deity in north India. As such sects associated with the *bhakti* of Rama emerged and Ayodhya naturally became the main centre of their activity.

During the age of Akbar Rama gained an importance through his officials' efforts. It was in his age his chronicler Abul Fazl writes the description of Ayodhya in his famous work *Ain-i-Akbari*. He refers to Ayodhya as "one of the holiest places of antiquity" and "the residence of Ramachandra, who in the Treta Age combined in his person both the spiritual supremacy and the kingly office". Abul Fazl does not mention the existence of a temple dedicated to a person with spiritual and temporal power and its replacement by a mosque. Nor does he record any religious strife in the area. In the succeeding centuries Rama emerged as God and his temple began to be built in the north as well as in the rest of India in the modern period.

P. Carnegy writes that in 1720 CE when Nawab Saadat Khan was appointed the Mughal Viceroy in Awadh, Hindu activity in the city gained ground. It seems he intended to differentiate the attitudes of the Shia and the Sunni Muslim governors towards their Hindu subjects. He probably wanted to justify the establishment of the Ramanandi *akharas* (sects) after that time. When the second Nawab Safdarjang shifted the seat of government from Ayodhya to Faizabad, Raja Naval Rai, a minister at the court of the Nawab, encouraged the construction of Hindu temples in Ayodhya. Raja Naval Rai was a Hindu Kayastha and was said to have been a staunch devotee of Shri Rama. Local traditions relate that Raja Naval Rai supported and extended Vaishnava activity in Ayodhya. It is said that because of his efforts several temples and settlements of *sadhus* and people learned in the Shastras came up. Carnegy provides us a list of 209 such institutions and temples in Ayodhya in 1870.[39]

To cite the restrained language of Judith Brown, the British tended to break up the Indian population in terms of community and analysed Indian society as a plural one of different peoples who needed special outlets in political life! These "imagined religious communities", in Romila Thapar's phrase, were also seen as basically hostile to each other; and the assumption that in Ayodhya a temple had been destroyed and replaced by a mosque was of a piece with this hypothesis. That Muslim rulers in India often acted on non-religious grounds and, like all rulers everywhere, were primarily interested in the maintenance of their political power, was ignored.[40]

Montgomery Martin, who was assigned the task of compiling historical and topographical data on eastern India by the English East India Company, observed that Ayodhya was a Hindu city and the adjacent Faizabad was a Mohammadan city. He published his report in 1838. Martin provides us information regarding several cities and districts adjoining Gorakhpur, but he does not distinguish the other cities by the nomenclature "Hindu" and "Mohammadan". He describes the cities of Prayag (Allahabad), Kashi (Varanasi), Haridwar (Hardwar), Dadri or Dardara Kshatra and the district of Benares, but does not call them Hindu cities. The other British historians like Hans T. Bakker, H.E. Neville, Koenraad Elst also advocated that Babur built the mosque after demolishing the Hindu temple which was the birthplace of Rama.

It was the British government who in order to follow the divide and rule theory made Ayodhya and Babri Mosque site disputed. In 1819, John Leyden translated the memoirs of Babur and he wrote that Babur had encamped near Ayodhya on 28 March 1528. In 1826, Erskine remarked that he had found a document that confirmed that Babur had remained in Ayodhya for a fortnight and was involved in building activities. Montgomery Martin was the first British observer who related the myth of Vikramaditya but he was convinced that the story was myth and no more. In 1838, Montgomery Martin wrote that the people of Ayodhya maintained that a mosque had been raised by Babur. He wrote that in the construction of the mosque, carved black stone-pillars had been used and as they were un-Islamic they confirm the destruction of temples by Muslim zealots. However, Martin felt that the Babri Masjid had not been built from the debris of the temple said to have been erected by Vikrama of Ujjain. In 1866, H.M. Elliot asserted that Babur came to Ayodhya and destroyed the famous temple. He added that the mosque was constructed about the time of his expedition to Bihar. Montgomery Martin writes in 1860 that the people of Ayodhya imagine that, after the death of Vrihadbala, their city was deserted and continued so until the time of Vikrama of Ujjain, who came in search of the holy city, erected a fort called Ramgarh, cut down the forest by which the ruins were covered and erected 360 temples on the places sanctified by the actions of Rama, of his wife Sita, of his brother Lakshmana and of his general Mahavira (Hanuman). However, Benet expressed surprise at the erection of 360 temples and observed in 1877 that at that time there were only forty-two such temples in Ayodhya.[41]

It was on the basis of these writings that the idea gained popularity. It is quite evident that no temple-mosque controversy was known in Ayodhya till the nineteenth century. Local stories were put into circulation and claims were raised over the places of worship in Ayodhya. The British played a significant role in strengthening the claim by providing the local stories with a historical basis. They stamped on the belief that Babur had destroyed the Ramjanmabhumi Temple and erected a mosque in its place. The Hindutva historians from nineteenth century to the current period, more especially Hans T. Bakker, H.E. Neville, Koenraad Elst, etc., confirmed the Ramjanmabhumi Temple idea and make Babur responsible for destroying a temple and building a mosque over there in Ayodhya.[42] British historians rationalized that British rule was a boon for the Hindus because it liberated them from the intolerant rule of the Muslims. He made the point indirectly that the British Empire was better than the earlier Mughal Empire.

The first official publication dealing with the history of the region was *A Historical Sketch of Tahsil Fyzabad; Zilla Fyzabad* by P. Carnegy in 1870. He asserted, on the basis of "locally affirmed" information, that three temples in Ayodhya were destroyed and mosques were constructed at their sites by the Mughals. Carnegy's account was reproduced almost verbatim by H.E. Neville in the *Gazetteer of Faizabad* published in 1905. Neither Carnegy nor Neville had anything but local affirmation. However, their opinion seems to have become an accepted fact. In the *District Gazetteer of Fyzabad*, H.E. Neville says without giving any proof and reference, "In 1528, Babur came to Ajodhya (Aud) and halted a week. He destroyed the ancient temple" (marking the birthplace of Rama of Treta Yuga) "and on its site built a mosque, still known as Babur's Mosque."[43]

The reports of Neville also published in *Barabanki District Gazetteer* that

> "numerous disputes have sprung up from time to time between the Hindu priests and the Mussalmans of Ayodhya with regard to the ground on which formerly stood the Janmasthan temple, which was destroyed by Babur and replaced by a mosque".[44] Several British

> officials had published their observation on the city of Ayodhya in the nineteenth century. The majority of such works started appearing after the annexation of the Kingdom of Awadh in February 1856. After successful suppression of the Revolt of 1857, the British openly fanned the episode to appease their Hindu helpers during the crisis.

Many British writers on Ayodhya believe that long before the penetration of the Islamic forces in Ayodhya the place was covered by a thick jungle. At that time Ayodhya, at best, was known as a famous hunting ground. They are therefore surprised at the emergence of Ayodhya as an important centre of Hindu pilgrimage. Benet writes, "It may, however, be remarked here that Hindu revival at Ayodhya is one of the most remarkable things in modem India".[45]

Some British scholars even deny the Hindu claim of Janmabhumi on the site of mosque but they advocate that most of temples at Ayodhya were built by Man Singh and Todarmal during Akbar's reign and Raja Naval Rai, a minister of Nawab of Awadh. Alexander Cunningham, Archaeological Surveyor to the Government of India, was convinced that some important Buddhist traces were hidden under the great mounds in Ayodhya. H.C. Irwin, lamenting the dearth of evidence, wrote: It is asomewhat humiliating confession, but it is probably a true one, that of the history of Oudh, from the time of Syed Salar's expedition to the appointment of Saadat Khan as Subahdar of the province in 1720 CE, a period of nearly 700 years, we have next to no real information. Written Hindu records there are almost none. Local Hindu traditions there are in abundance, but it seems almost impossible to connect them with any degree of certainty with such facts as are to be gathered from the Mohammadan historians.[46]

However it is a matter of great concern that after 500 years some Hindutva organizations and political parties demolished a marvellous symbol of architecture and Muslim religious place Babri Mosque on 6 December 1992. Very surprisingly the Indian government and supreme judiciary by quoting the reference of

Hans T. Bakker, H.E. Neville, Koenraad Elst, passed the decision in favour of the majority community and approved to build a huge Rama Temple on that place. Ironically it happened in the presence of a secular and democratic constitution protecting the rights and religion of the Indian Muslims.

These temple theories were proved false propaganda after the destruction of mosque and findings of the excavation under the same structure in 1992. The remains which were unearthed during temple construction in 1921 were belonged to the Buddhism of which Ayodhya was an important religious centre right from the time of Buddha himself.[47] The mound was a place of Buddhist structure dismantled by any influential Hindu Raja, most probably Pushyamitra Shunga. The recent excavations prove the city of Ayodhya was a Buddhist religious place during the time of Ashoka and Kanishka.

Babur as a Muslim

Babur's memoirs reveal him a warrior, conquerer, humble man, nature lover and a man of secular character. He always enjoyed a genuine joy of life and love of nature which are not usually associated with a ruthless conqueror. Judged by the standards of his age, he was not cruel. Again and again he pardoned and showed clemency in strong contrast with the practice of his time and race.

Babur himself was a true Muslim and had great impact of his father on religious belief. He was very lenient even towards his enemies. After his victories, Babur, unlike the generals of the past, did not allow the local population to be looted by his soldiers and their traditions and customs were trampled under foot. By these actions, Babur shows how noble and religious a person he is. He even courted Lodi's mother, Princess Bayda. Living in this hot country, he pays great attention to the construction, cultural and educational sphere. In a short period of time, Babur sponsored efforts to stabilize the political environment in India, unify the Indian lands, improve the cities, regulate trade and create gardens. The beautification of India, the construction of architectural monuments, gardens, libraries, caravanserais, which are still famous in it, spread on a large scale, especially during the period of his sons and descendants.[48]

Babur was a true Muslim and his unwavering faith in Islam was received from his father Umar Shaikh Mirza. Babur writes about his father that he was a true believer (Hanafi sect) and pure in the faith, not neglecting the five times prayers and, his life through, making up his Omissions. He read the Quran very frequently and was a disciple of, a Suifi Shaikh of Nakshbandi order, Khwaja Ubaidullah Ahrari, who honoured him by visits and even called him son. At Babur's birth Shaikh Ahrari visited the palace and assisted at his naming. Babur's father had been one of his many disciples and Babur himself, while still a young man in Central Asia, once dreamt that Shaikh Ahrari appeared before him and allowed him to seize Samarkand, which he actually did soon after that dream. Ahrari died in 1491 when Babur was about seven years old but his influence was life-long. From his capital in Agra, Babur maintained close ties with Naqshbandi *shaikhs* in Central Asia, even though Chishti *shaikhs* were then dominant in Delhi.[49]

The teacher and spiritual guide of Babur was Khwaja Maulana-i-Qazi Abdullah. This family had come to be the Religious Guides (Muqtadda) and pontiff (Shaikhul Islam) and Judge (*qazi*) in the Fergana country. He was a disciple of his Highness Khwaja Ubaidullah (Ahrari) and from him had his upbringing. He was a wonderful man; it was not in him to be afraid; in no other man was seen such courage as his. This quality is a further witness to his sanctity. When the enemy, after taking possession of Andijan, heard of Babur's arrival, they (Tambal) martyred Khwaja Maulana-i-Qazi Abdullah by hanging him, with dishonour, in the Gate of the Andijan citadel. Undoubtedly, he was a saint (*wali*); what better witnesses to his sanctity than the fact that within a short time, no sign or trace remained of those active for his death?[50]

He was always prayed to Allah in every of his problems and even serious illness. He used to considerevery trouble as his fault and the reason of Allah's displeasure. He writes,

> "A few days later in Bigram when I had fever and discharge, followed by cough and I began to spit blood each time I coughed, I knew whence my reproof came; I knew what act of mine had brought this affliction on me."

He quotes the verse of Quran that Whoever shall violate his oath, will violate it to the hurt of his own soul; but whoever shall perform that which he hath covenanted with Allah, to that man surely will He give great reward. Babur frequently prayed,

> "O Lord! we have dealt unjustly with our own souls; if Thou forgive us not and be not merciful unto us, we shall surely be of those that perish."[51]

Babur was an outstanding warrior, military strategist and as a ruler in India a lenient to his subject. As a man Babur was a firm believer in Islam fully believed the Quranic messages and applied to the people of India that "Your religion for you and mine for me". He gave full religious freedom to the people all religions of India particularly Hindus. A mosque was built in Ayodhya in his time over a raised mound. However, there was not a Hindu, Buddha or Jaina temple on that site as claimed by some Hindus. Babur had made clear instructions that no worshipping place or building should be dismantled. Babur himself patronized Hindu temples and individuals and in Ayodhya itself he gave a revenue-free grant of a large piece of land to a Hindu ascetic.[52]

In India Babur was mostly engaged in extending his empire and didn't find enough time in strengthening his empire and establishing his policies. He followed the rules and laws which were followed during Lodis. Undoubtedly his religious policy was the same as Lodis and definitely it was lenient to other religions of India. Babur inherited his religious policy from the Lodis. It is well known that Lodis didn't promoted discriminatory policies against Hindus. During Lodi rule the Hindus were employed on almost lower posts and even some very important higher posts. However *jazia* and pilgrim tax were continued. Babur followed the same as of Lodis'. Some of the Lodi officials continued to serve when Babur came into power. He projected no great changes in the government of the country except the design of a royal road from Agra to Kabul. But the Hindus, he met with, occupied no humble position. Babur tried to strengthen the position of Muslims by exempting from paying stamp duties thus confining the tax to Hindus alone.

Babur was secular in nature and lenient to his subjects but not kind to his enemies. After the conquest of India, Babur fully realised that to rule India, a land of Hindu majority, rulers must adopt the policy of tolerance and respect towards all religions. He left his testament to Humayun, a remarkable historical document which proves Babur's sagacity and wisdom as a ruler. The testament provided the guidance to all the Mughal rulers on how to rule India. Later on, the Mughal emperors followed it earnestly. They Indianised themselves by adopting Indian customs and traditions and were loved by both Hindus and Muslims alike.

While sending his testament to Humayun, Babur made him realise the importance of being the ruler of India where followers of different religions lived. He advised him to fulfil this responsibility with great care and sensitivity. Humayun followed his father's advice and remain lenient to his Hindu subjects. He made a grant of 300 acres of land in Mirzapur district in the Uttar Pradesh for the maintenance of Jangamvadi Math of Banaras. Babur's recommendation for Humayun focus on the following matters:[53]

(a) Respect all religions without any prejudice and never hurt anyone's sentiments related to his/her religion, tradition and culture.

(b) In order to respect Hindus, never slaughter a cow as it is considered a sacred animal by Hindus. This practice will create goodwill among people.

(c) Never demolish any worship house belonging to any religion. Follow a policy of justice and tolerance. Treat your people with kindness and without discrimination.

(d) Nobody should be forced to convert to Islam. Preaching should be by peaceful means.
(e) Avoid Shia and Sunni conflicts. It would make Islam weak and vulnerable.
(f) Understand the different qualities that your people belonging to different religions possess and give importance to all communities.

The above statement of Babur showed that he was an ideal ruler for each and every community of India. Babur didn't have interfered the ongoing religious practices in India. As one could see saint-poet Chaitanya movement was on the peak at his time in Bengal and Orissa. Chaitanya (1485-1533) had influenced and converted many Muslims into Hindu fold but on this ground, he was not even questioned and rather honoured in the society. He even converted the Muslim governor of Orissa. He also converted a group of Pathans, men from the rugged north-western region of the subcontinent, settled in the east, who were not Hindus in the first instance, even as Hinduism is not a proselytizing religion. They earned the sobriquet of Pathan Vaisnavas.[54]

In 1530, Humayun the favourite son of Babur became severely sick due to malarial fever while staying in his country estate Sambhal. His physicians declared that the case was hopeless. Theologians suggested him for the charity of most valued thing, Kohinoor diamond. However, Babur, a firm believer in Allah's miracle, declared to sacrifice his own life for his beloved son and he prayed for that. After that Humayun began to recover and Babur fell ill and died. He was buried at Kabul in one of his beloved gardens.[55]

Babur declared war against Rana Sanga and Medini Rao as *jihad* only to boost the morale of his military as until that time his forces were exhausted and wanted to return to their original homeland. If some historian claims him as fanatic and intolerant to the Hindus definitely they don't find word to define his war against Ibrahim Lodi which was more bloody and disastrous.

While branding Babur as a Muslim fanatic, the Hindutva historians also must project the fact that Babur occupied Delhi and

Agra by killing more than 40,000 Muslims. Unfortunately they don't highlight the fact of killing such a large number of Muslims. However, he could not be branded as intolerant to Muslims because in warfare there is no religion of faith but only religion of killing the enemy by hook and crook. In military science it is the universal rule to kill the enemy and adopt various tricks to win the war either on the pretext of religion and race or promoting nationalism.

Babur as a Scholar

Babur owes his literary fame chiefly to his charming memoirs, but in the eyes of his contemporaries, he had many other claims to scholastic distinction. His cousin, Mirza Haidar Doughlat, points out that he was second only to Amir Ali Shir in the art of Turkish composition. He has written a *diwan* (collection of odes) in the purest and most lucid Turkish. He invented a style of verse called *mubaiyan* and was the author of a most useful treatise on jurisprudence which has been adopted generally. He also wrote a tract on Turki prosody, superior in elegance to any other and put into verse the *Risalah-i-Walidiah* of His Holiness. He was also skilled in music and other arts. He invented the Babari mode of handwriting, transcribed the Holy Quran and presented a copy to the Sheriff of Mecca.[56]

The contemporary records bear ample testimony to his princely patronage of learning. In spite of his incessant military and political activities, he bestowed the most careful attention on the education of his sons. The eldest, Humayun, grew up a fine physicist, mathematician, astronomer and geographer.

Death of Babur

The Ghaghra victory brought Babur's campaigns to a close and in the next year (1530) he died. He was a comparatively young man, being only in his forty-seventh year; but the hard life he had led had certainly enfeebled his constitution and the climate of India proved fatal. The story of his death is well known. It is said that after his last attempt to conquer Samarkand Humayun retired to his *jagir* at

Sambhal, but after six months fell seriously ill and was brought to Agra. The skill of the best physicians failed to cure Humayun. One of Babur's high officers, saint Mir Abu Baga distinguished for his piety, said to Babur that Almighty Allah might vouchsafe to spare Humayun's life in return for the sacrifice of Babur's most precious possession and suggested that the great diamond (Kohinoor diamond) captured at Agra be the offering. Babur said, "No, my own life is the most precious of my possessions and I devote it to this end". He three times walked about the dying prince and retired to pray. Returning he exclaimed, "I have borne it away".[57]

Shortly after, Humayun recovered and Babur, whose health had already been failing, was taken ill and this illness continued for two or three months. Babur nominated Humayun as his successor and a few days later, passed away on 30 December 1530, at Agra at the age of 47. In a short time Death, the sunderer of societies, the gamerer of graveyards, the plunderer of palaces, bore him away to the mercy of Allah, the compassionating, the compassionate and his son reigned in his stead. His body buried, as he directed, at Kabul, in a favourite garden near the city. Close to his unpretentious grave a mosque was erected many years later by his descendant, Shah Jahan.

Notes

1. Annette Susannah Beveridge (1922). *The Memoirs of Babur* (tr. *Baburnama* of Zahiruddin Muhammad Babur Padshah Ghazi), vol. I, London, p. 19. (Qutlugh Nigar Khanam was the second daughter of Yunus Khan, a descendant of Chaghatai Khan, the second son of Genghis Khan and Aisan Daulat Begum, the daughter of his chief Ali Sher Beg. Babur was a direct descendant or 6th generation of Amir Timur (Timur, Miran Shah, Mohammad Mirza, Abu Said, Umar Shaikh, Babur). Babur was tenth generation of Genghis Khan through his mother (Genghis Khan, Chaghatai Khan, Muatukan, Yesuntawa Khan, Dawa Khan, Aisan-bugha Khan, Tughluq-timur Khan, Khizr Khwaja Khan, Muhammad Khan, Sher Ali Aughlon, Wais Khan, Yunus Khan, Qutlugh Nigar Khanum, Babur.)
2. Babur writes that meantime a strange event occurred. The fort of Akhsi was situated above a deep ravine and along this ravine stand the palace buildings and from it, on Monday, Ramzan 4 (8 June), 'Umar

Shaikh Mirza flew, with his pigeons and their house and became a falcon. (*The Memoirs of Babur,* vol. I, *op. cit.*, pp. 13 & 29.)

3. Edward S. Holden (1895), *The Mogul Emperors of Hindustan*, New York, pp. 59-60; Majumdar, R.C. (1974), *The Mughul Empire: History and Culture of the Indian People*, vol. VII, Bombay, p. 24. Babur writes, "Just at that time I had a wonderful dream: His Highness Khwaja Ubaidullah (Ahrari) seemed to come; I seemed to go out to give him honourable meeting; he came in and seated himself; people seemed to lay a table-cloth before him, apparently without sufficient care and, on account of this, something seemed to come into his Highness Khwaja's mind. Mulla Baba (Pashaghart) made me a sign; I signed back, "Not through me! the table-layer is in fault!" The Khwaja understood and accepted the excuse. When he rose, I escorted him out. In the hall of that house he took hold of either my right or left arm and lifted me up till one of my feet was off the ground, saying, in Turki, 'Shaikh Maslahat has given (Samarkand)'. I really took Samarkand a few days later." (*The Memoirs of Babur,* vol. I, *op. cit.*, p. 132.)
4. Majumdar, vol. VII, *op. cit.*, pp. 24-25.
5. *Ibid.*
6. *The Memoirs of Babur,* vol. I, *op. cit.*, pp. 198-99.
7. S.M. Edwardes & H.L.O. Garrett (1930), *Mughal Rule in India*, London, p. 3.
8. *Ibid.*, p. 5.
9. *Ibid.*, pp. 5-6; *The Memoirs of Babur,* vol. II, *op. cit.*, pp. 454-59; see also Williams, Rushbrook (1918), *An Empire Builder of the 16th Century*, London, p. 140; John Leyden and William Erskine (1826), *Memoirs of Zaheeruddin Mohammad Babur* (tr. of *Tuzuk-i-Babari* of Zahiruddin Mohammad Babur), London, pp. 335 & 361; and Ishwari Prashad (1939), *A Short History of Muslim Rule in India: From the Conquest of Islam to the Death of Aurangzeb*, Allahabad, pp. 216-18.
10. *The Memoirs of Babur,* vol. II, *op. cit.*, p. 463.
11. *Ibid.*, p. 470; Edwardes & Garrett, *op. cit.*, p. 6.
12. *The Memoirs of Babur,* vol. II, *op. cit.*, pp. 468-69.
13. Babur says, "Our right was Humayun, Khwaja Kalan, Sultan Mohammad Duldai, Hindu Beg, Treasurer Wali and Pir-qulil Sistani; our left was Mohammad Mirza, Mahdi Khwaja, Adil Sultan, Shah Mir Husain, Junaid Barlas, Qutluq-qadam, Jan Beg, Pay-master Mohammad and Shah Husain (of) Yaragi Mughul Ghanchi. The right hand of the centre was Chin-timur Sultan, Sulaiman Mirza, Mohammadi Kukuldash, Shah Mansur Barlas, Yunas-i-ali, Darwish-i-mohammad Sarban and Abdullah the librarian. The left of the

centre was Khalifa, Khwaja Mir-i-miran, Secretary Ahmadi, Tardi Beg (brother) of Quj Beg, Khalifa's Muhibb-i-ali and Mirza Beg Tarkhan. The advance was Khusrau Kukuldash and Muh Ali Jang-jang. Abdul Aziz the Master of the Horse was posted as the reserve. For the turning-party (Tulghuma) at the point of the right wing, we fixed on Red Wali and Malik Qasim (brother) of Baba Qashqa, with their Mughals; for the turning-party at the point of the left wing, we arrayed Qara-quzi, Abu'l-mohammad the lanceplayer, Shaikh Jamal Barin's Shaikh Ali, Mahndi and Tingri-birdi Bashaghi Mughal; these two parties, directly the enemy got near, were to turn his rear, one from the right, the other from the left." (*The Memoirs of Babur,* vol. II, *op. cit.*, pp. 472-73.)

14. *The Memoirs of Babur,* vol. II, *op. cit.*, pp. 474-75. Ibrahim Lodi had with him a force of 1,00,000 men and 1,000 elephants while Babur's army was 24,000 strong. The Afghan army came straight on at a rapid march and Babur sent out his flanking columns to wheel round the Afghans and deliver a violent attack on their rear, while his right and left wings charged straight on. Babur sent timely reinforcement to the left wing under Mehdi Khwaja which was hard pressed, as well as to the right wing which felt the brunt of the Afghan attack. From the centre Ustad Ali Quli Khan with his artillery and Mustafa with his match locks began their action. Ibrahim's centre gave way and the Afghans, beset on all sides by arrows and fire and crowded into a narrow space with no room to use their arms, could neither advance nor retreat. The battle ended at noon when the Afghans were completely routed and took to flight, leaving some 20,000 dead, including Sultan Ibrahim Lodi. (Majumdar, *op. cit.*, p. 33.)
15. *The Memoirs of Babur,* vol. II, *op. cit.*, pp. 475-78.
16. *Ibid.*, Edwardes & Garrett, *op. cit.*, p. 8.
17. Babur describes about India as, "Hindustan is a country of few charms. Its people have no good looks; of social intercourse, paying and receiving visits there is none; of genius and capacity none; of manners none; in handicraft and work there is no form or symmetry, method or quality; there are no good horses, no good dogs, no grapes, muskmelons or first-rate fruits, no ice or cold water, no good bread or cooked food in the bazars, no Hot-baths, no Colleges, no candles, torches or candlesticks.... Peasants and people of low standing go about naked. They tie on a thing called *lunguta,* a decency-clout which hangs two spans below the navel. From the tie of this pendant decency clout, another clout is passed between the thighs and made

fast behind. Women also tie on a cloth (*lung*), one-half of which goes round the waist, the other is thrown over the head. ...Pleasant things of Hindustan are that it is a large country and has masses of gold and silver. Its air in the Rains is very fine. Sometimes it rains 10, 15 or 20 times a day; torrents pour down all at once and rivers flow where no water had been. While it rains and through the Rains, the air is remarkably fine, not to be surpassed for healthiness and charm." (*The Memoirs of Babur,* vol. II, *op. cit.*, pp. 518-19.)

18. Babur says, "On our first coming to Agra, there was remarkable dislike and hostility between its people and mine, the peasantry and soldiers running away in fear of our men. Delhi and Agra excepted, not a fortified town but strengthened its defences and neither was in obedience nor submitted. Qasim Sambhali was in Sambhal; Nizam Khan was in Blana; in Mewat was Hasan Khan Mewati himself, impious mannikin! who was the sole leader of the trouble and mischief. Mohammad Zaitun was in Dulpur; Tatar Khan Sarang-khani was in Gualiar; Husain Khan Nuhani was in Rapri; Qutb Khan was in Etawa; Alam Khan (Kalpi) was in Kalpi. Qanauj and the other side of Ganges was all held by Afghans in independent hostility, such as Nasir Khan Nuhani, Ma'ruf Farmuli and a crowd of other *amirs*. These had been in rebellion for three or four years before Ibrahim's death and when I defeated him, were holding Qanauj and the whole country beyond it. At the present time they were lying two or three marches on our side of Qanauj and had made Bahar Khan the son of Darya Khan Luhani their *padshah*, under the style Sultan Muhammad. Marghub the slave was in Mahawin (Mathura); he remained there, thus close, for some time but came no nearer". (*The Memoirs of Babur,* vol. II, *op. cit.*, p. 523.)
19. Holden, *op. cit.*, p. 89.
20. *The Memoirs of Babur,* vol. II, *op. cit.*, p. 545. (Babur writes, "His trusted man, Karm-chand by name, who had come from him to me in Agra when his son (Nahar i.e. Tiger) was with me there, came now from that son's presence in Alur and asked for peace. Abdu'r-rahim Shaghawal went with him to Alur, conveying letters of royal favour and returned bringing Nahar Khan who was restored to favour and received *parganas* worth several laks for his support". Babur further says that in the way, at Sunkar, Hasan Khan Mewatis son Nahar Khan escaped from Abdur Rahim Shaghawal's charge. (*The Memoirs of Babur,* vol. II, *op. cit.*, pp. 578 & 581.)

21. Williams, Rushbrook (1918), *An Empire Builder of the 16th Century*, London, p. 140; *Memoirs of Zaheeruddin Mohammad Babur, op. cit.*, pp. 335 & 361.
22. Edwardes & Garrett, *op. cit.*, p. 9.
23. *Memoirs of Zaheeruddin Mohammad Babur, op. cit.*, p. 357.
24. *The Memoirs of Babur,* vol. II, *op. cit.*, pp. 562 & 573.
25. *The Memoirs of Babur,* vol. II, *op. cit.*, p. 575. Babur writes:
    "For Islam's sake, I wandered in the wilds,
    Prepared for war with pagans and Hindus,
    Resolved myself to meet the martyr's death,
    Thanks be to Allah! A *Ghazi* I became."
26. *The Memoirs of Babur,* vol. II, *op. cit.*, pp. 595-96. Babur says, "By Allah's grace this renowned fort was captured in 2 or 3 hours, without drum and standard, with no hard fighting done. A pillar of pagan-heads was ordered set up on a hill north-west of Chandiri. A chronogram of this victory having been found in the words *Fath-i-daru'l-harb* (Conquest of a hostile seat), I thus composed them:
    Was for a while the station Chanderi
    Pagan-full, the seat of hostile force;
    By fighting, I vanquished its fort,
    The date was *Fath-i-daru'l-harb.*"
27. *The Memoirs of Babur,* vol. II, *op. cit.*, p. 613.
28. Sarvapalli Gopal (Penguin, 1992). *Anatomy of a Confrontation: The Babri Masjid-Ram Janmabhumi Issue*, New Delhi, p. 28. Babur says, "Three sides of Urwa are solid rock, not the red rock of Biana but one paler in colour. On these sides people have cut out idol-statues, large and small, one large statue on the south side being perhaps 20 *qari* (yards) high. These idols are shewn quite naked without covering for the privities. Along the sides of the two Urwa lakes 20 or 30 wells have been dug, with water from which useful vegetables (*Sabzi Karliklar*), flowers and trees are grown. Urwa is not a bad place; it is shut in (T. tur); the idols are its defect; I, for my part, ordered them destroyed." (*The Memoirs of Babur,* vol. II, *op. cit.*, pp. 611-12.)
29. *The Memoirs of Babur,* vol. II, *op. cit.*, p. 601; Majumdar, *op. cit.*, p. 36.
30. Harold Lamb (1961). *Babur, the Tiger; First of the Great Moguls*, New York, pp. 311-15.
31. *Ibid.*
32. Edwardes & Garrett, *op. cit.*, p. 11.
33. In ancient times the country round about Ayodhya was known as Kosala and both find mention in ancient literature. The first three

Vedas, however, do not mention either Kosala or its capital, Ayodhya; it is only in the *Atharvaveda* that the city has been described as having been built by the gods and being as prosperous as paradise itself. According to the Jaina tradition, twenty-three out of the twenty-four *tirthankaras* were of this line, of whom live were born in Ayodhya itself including Adinatha (or Rishabhadeva) who was the first. The earliest and best known kings of Kosala were the Ikshvakus (Ikshvaku, the eldest son of Vaivasvata and Manu, obtained from his father the kingdom of Ayodhya and became its first ruler) who made celebrated the Kosala country of which Ayodhya was the chief city. It was in Ramachandra, the eldest son of Dasharatha, that the glory of the Kosala royal dynasty reached its culmination. He is credited with the establishment of an ideally lawful state, the proverbial Rama-rajya. Kosala emerges into great prominence in this period, its princes carrying Aryan civilization as far as Ceylon. The story of this epoch has been immortalised by Valmiki and immensely popularised by the great mass of subsequent literature on Rama. At the time of emerging Magadha as an empire, the ruler Kosala Prasenjit was an intimate ally of Magadha ruler Ajatashatru, the son and successor of King Bimbisara. To this period Gautama Buddha and the *tirthankara* Mahavira were said to have enjoyed the patronage of Prasenjit in whose reign Kosala became an important centre of their proselytising activities. About the beginning of the last quarter of the fourth century BCE, the Mauryas superseded the Nandas. In *circa* 184 BCE, Pushyamitra, the Brahmana general of the last Maurya king, assassinated his master and captured the throne thus founding five Shunga dynasty which lasted till 75 BCE. There is no doubt that Ayodhya was included in the dominions of the Shungas and was probably a viceroyalty. It seems that from the time Prasenjit Ayodhya was the important centre of Buddhism as well as Jainism. At least Budhism fully flourished at Ayodhya until the conquest of fanatic Brahmana ruler Pushyamitra of Shunga dynasty and he might have destroyed the Buddhist and Jaina religious establishment and the prosecution was continued until Gupta rulers who promoted Hinduism against Buddhism. It is clear from the record of the Chinese pilgrim Fa-hien, who travelled in India for more than ten years (*c*.400-411 CE) during the reign of Chandragupta II. He passed through Awadh and visited the city of Sha-chi (Saket) where he found that the Buddhists and the Brahmanas were not on good terms. Here he saw a *stupa* where the four Buddhas had walked and sat and also the tree that had sprouted from the toothbrush stick thrown away by the Buddha. The famous Chinese pilgrim Hiuen Tsang

(630-644 CE) passed through Awadh reached the O-yu-to (Ayodhya) country. According to Hiuen Tsang, there were about 100 Buddhist monasteries, more than 3,000 Mahayani and Hinayani monks and only ten *deva* (non-Buddhist God) temples, the non-Buddhists being but few in number. As regards Pi-sho-ka (Saket), the pilgrim says that this city had twenty monasteries in which 3,000 monks lived, who were all adherents of the Sammatitya school. There were about 50 *deva* temples and the non-Buddhists were numerous. During the early medieval time, the first Muslim invasion of Awadh or Ayodhya is ascribed to the legendary hero Syed Salar Masud Ghazi, popularly known as Ghazi Mian. He is said to have occupied Awadh some time before 1030 CE. All along the old Lucknow road there are numerous tombs which the local Muslims say are those of the followers of Syed Salar. Muizuddin Mohammad bin Sam (Shihabuddin Ghori) is said to have conquered Awadh after taking Kanauj and it is supposed that either he himself or one of his lieutenants occupied Ayodhya. (*Uttar Pradesh District Gazetteers Faizabad*, Allahabad, 1960, pp. 27-41.)

34. *The Memoirs of Babur*, vol. II, *op. cit.*, pp. lxxvii-lxxviii; *Uttar Pradesh District Gazetteers Faizabad*, *op. cit.*, pp. 46-47.
35. *The Memoirs of Babur*, vol. II, *op. cit.*, pp. lxxviii-lxxix.
36. Sarvapalli Gopal, *op. cit.*, p. 25.
37. *Ibid.*, pp. 11 & 38.
38. Wendy Doniger (2009), *The Hindus: An Alternative History*, New Delhi, p. 552.
39. Sarvapalli Gopal, *op. cit.*, pp. 39-40.
40. *Ibid.*, p. 12.
41. Sarvapalli Gopal, *op. cit.*, pp. 46-47 & 54. Apart from British historians, the British government in order to suppress the Muslim revolutionaries of 1857 targeted almost all Muslim population and appeased the Hindus because they helped the British in hour of crisis during the Revolt. In Ayodhya too, after the suppression of the Revolt of 1857, Hindu activity in Ayodhya was allowed to grow. It is reported that during the Revolt, British life and property in Ayodhya and Faizabad were endangered and some landlords offered help to the British and "a similar offer was made by the *mahants* of the Hanumangarhi". It is therefore certain that after the successful suppression of the Revolt, all those who had helped the British were to be suitably rewarded. All land in Ayodhya was *nazul* (government land) and therefore it was easy for the government to distribute land as reward for services rendered during the Revolt. The Bairagis received

land in Ayodhya and its adjoining areas. Land belonging to Muslim institutions was confiscated. The former royal gardens Hayat Baksh and Farhat Baksh passed into Hindu hands. The former was assigned to Pandit Uma Datta by the British government and the latter was partly owned by the Raja of Jaipur and partly by the Digambara sect.

42. Hans Bakker has told that Babur was responsible for destroying the Rama Temple and building a mosque over there. However, based on a detailed survey of the literary, epigraphic and archaeological sources, Hans Bakker has come to the conclusion that "the cult in which Rama was worshipped as the supreme form and main manifestation of Vishnu did not rise into prominence before the eleventh and twelfth centuries CE". His study also indicates that there were very few temples dedicated to Rama in the twelfth century and these were in places other than Ayodhya. (Sarvapalli Gopal, *op. cit.*, p. 26.)

43. *District Gazetteer of Fyzabad*, Lucknow, 1905, p. 173. Van der Veer, on the other hand, draws upon local belief. He not only affirms the view, but also refers to the miracles which followed the destruction of the temple, "Mir Baqi destroyed the temple, but his efforts to build a mosque failed because each night everything that had been built during the day fell down again. This continued until Mir Baqi grew desperate and proposed to give up. Then the Faqir Khwaja dreamt that the mosque should not be built right over the *garbha* (sanctum) of the temple, but somewhat behind it. Thus the mosque was built in such a way that the *garbha* of the temple remained open to the Hindus for centuries in the form of a pit into which they could throw flowers". (Sarvapalli Gopal, *op. cit.*, p. 30.)

44. *Barabanki District Gazetteer*, Lucknow, 1902, (Annexure 21), pp. 168-69. It is said that much before Babri Mosque controversy, there was another episode of Hindu-Muslim conflict. A group of orthodox Sunni Muslims, under the leadership of Shah Gulam Hussain, claimed that the temple of Hanumangarhi had supplanted a mosque which existed there earlier. Shah and his followers pretended that a *masjid* formerly existed in the immediate vicinity of Hanumangarhi and that the *bairagi fakirs* have either destroyed it, or by defacing and building upon it have converted it into a part and portion of their own buildings, whilst the *bairagis* strenuously deny the existence of any such *masjid* either now or in preceding years. In July 1855, Gulam Hussain led a party of his followers, numbering about 500, to oust the Hindus from the temple. The *bairagis*, the occupants of the temple, had the support of about 8,000 people, among whom were some large

landholders and their retainers from the neighbouring countryside. In the ensuing conflict a large number of Muslims were "soon laid prostrate, the remainder returned and gained the Babri Masjid where they were soon surrounded and cut to pieces". At the gate of Babri Mosque seventy-five Musalmans were buried, the spot being known as the Ganj Shahidan or the martyrs' resting place. The defeat of Gulam Hussain and his followers at the hands of the Hindu *bairagis* created considerable consternation among the Muslims of Awadh, both Sunni and Shia. Nawab Wajid Ali Shah appointed a committee of inquiry, consisting of a Muslim, a Hindu and a representative of the British, in order to defuse the situation. After very detailed investigations the committee came to the conclusion that there was no *masjid* at the Hanumangarhi. The Muslims resented this decision and Maulvi Ameer Ali Amethavi started organizing a movement to reclaim the *masjid*. The Nawab toyed with the idea of constructing a mosque adjacent to the temple to assuage the feelings of the Muslims, but this was strongly opposed by the Hindus. General Outram stepped in and insisted on the maintenance of law and order. The Maulvi, however, continued his threatening attitude towards the temple and eventually, trusting to the secret support of the Nawab, advanced to its attack; but was met by Nawab's troops commanded by English officers, with the result that he was himself killed and his followers dispersed. The *mahant* of Hanumangarhi was quick to realize the implication of the proceedings initiated by Gulam Hussain and Ameer Ali. The proposal of the Nawab to build a mosque adjoining the temple was quite alarming to him. He apprehended that the decision of the government need not necessarily go in favour of the Hindus if the agitation were to be renewed in future. A counter-claim on the areas controlled by the Muslims could be an effective move to foil the designs of orthodox Muslims to gain possession of the temple. The demand for the Janmasthan thus originated as a defensive ploy. Soon after the Revolt of 1857 the *mahant* took over a part of the Babri Masjid compound and constructed a *chabutara*. This attempt of the *mahant* was opposed by the local Muslims. On 30 November 1858 Maulvi Mohammad Asghar, *khatib* and *muazzin* of Babri Masjid, submitted a petition to the magistrate complaining that the *bairagis* had built a *chabutara* close to the mosque and that they had written "Rama, Rama" on the walls of the mosque. Similar complaints were made in 1860, 1877, 1883 and 1884. In 1885, the *mahant* filed a suit to gain legal title to the land and for permission to construct a temple on the *chabutara*. His suit and appeals were dismissed. The details of this event are available in British records and in Urdu and Persian accounts which also make it clear that the dispute was over the Hanumangarhi temple and not about the Babri Masjid. (Innes, McLeod, *Lucknow & Oude in the Mutiny: A Narrative and a Study*, London, 1895, pp. 58-59; Innes, McLeod, *The Sepoy Revolt: A Critical Narrative*, London, 1897, pp. 32-33; Martin, R. Montgomery, *The Indian Empire*, vol. II, London, 1858, p. 77; and Sarvapalli Gopal, *op. cit.*, pp. 30-33.)

45. Sarvapalli Gopal, *op. cit.*, p. 54.
46. Mohammad Faiz Baksh's *Tarikh Farah Baksh* relates that after the signing of the Treaty of Allahabad in 1765 the influence of the Mughals in Ayodhya started declining. The Mewati soldiers who represented the Mughals were withdrawn. The absence of the Mewatis provided freedom of movement to the spear-wielding *sannyasins*. The *sannyasins* were well known for disturbing the peace of Ayodhya and after 1765 the law and order situation in Ayodhya deteriorated. Raghunath Prasad wrote that in the eighteenth century in Ayodhya, the *bairagis* and the *sannyasins* were involved in a fight for domination in the area. (Sarvapalli Gopal, *op. cit.*, pp. 40 & 54.)
47. The fanatic Hindus began to build a grand Rama Temple over that site of Babri Mosque from 11 May 2020. On levelling the ground they unearthed a lot of Buddhist remains, which created a new cry over the site. It is presumed that in ancient times it was a Buddhist worship place named as Saket, only 45 miles away from the Lord Buddha's birthplace Bhulia. It is also said that Lord Buddha had spent six or seven years in Saket and Emperor Ashoka and Kanishka had developed Saket as a religious place and built a lot of Buddhist monasteries. During the age of Guptas, when Hinduism was again revived, these monasteries were might have been dismantled by the local Hindu rulers. The Shungas, the Guptas and regional Hindu rulers of later period were responsible for mass level conversion and even the destruction of the Buddhist places which were the greatest danger in the absence of the Islam. During the time of Babur, his generals might have built a mosque on a site surrounded by the mounds in which the Buddhist remains were buried because a mosque is a must for the Muslim establishment. Ayodhya was an important place and Huen Tsang had also visited the city as a Buddhist centre. Much later during the sixteenth century, the generals of Babur build a mosque on that ground which was known as Babri Mosque.

48. Kholikov Rozik Ikhtiyorovich "Zahiruddin Muhammad Babur the Great Commander", published in *International Journal of Trend in Scientific Research and Development* (*IJTSRD*), ISSN: 2456-6470, vol. 6, Issue 6, October 2022, p. 1396. URL: www.ijtsrd.com/papers/ijtsrd52079.pdf
49. *The Memoirs of Babur*, vol. II, *op. cit.*, pp. xxix & 15. At the Battle of Panipat, Delhi's leading Chishti *shaikh* of the day, 'Abd al-Quddus Gangohi, had prayed for the success of his Lodi patrons. But when the latter were defeated, the Mughal victors captured the *shaikh* and forced him to walk the 65 km back to Delhi. Babur's attitude to living Chishtis who had opposed him obviously differed from his respect for the shrines of revered Chishti saints. (Muzaffar Alam, "The Mughals, the Sufi Shaikhs and the Formation of the Akbari Dispensation", *Modern Asian Studies*, 43, No. 1 (2009), pp. 137-51.)
50. *Ibid*, pp. 89-90.
51. *The Memoirs of Babur*, vol. II, *op. cit.*, pp. 449-50.
52. Sarvapalli Gopal, *op. cit.*, p. 25.
53. Sri Ram Sharma (1972). *The Religious Policy of the Mughal Emperors*, Bombay, pp. 24-27; see also *Dawn* (Eng. Daily), 25 December 2010. ("Oh my son! The realm of Hindustan is full of diverse creeds. Praise be to God, the Righteous, the Glorious, the Highest, that He hath granted unto thee the Empire of it. It is but proper that you, with a heart cleansed of all religious bigotry, should dispense justice according to the tenets of each community. And in particular refrain from the sacrifice of the cow, for that way lies the conquest of the hearts of the people of Hindustan; and the subjects of the realm will, through royal favour, be devoted to thee. And the temples and abodes of worship of every community under Imperial sway, you should not damage. Dispense justice so that the sovereign may be happy with the subjects and likewise the subjects with their sovereign. The progress of Islam is better by the sword of kindness, not by the sword of oppression. Ignore the disputations of Shias and Sunnis; for therein is the weakness of Islam. And bring together the subjects with different beliefs in the manner of the Four Elements, so that the body politic may be immune from the various ailments. And remember the deeds of Hazrat Taimur Sahib Qiran (Lord of the conjunction) so that you may become mature in matters of Government. And on us is but the duty to advise."
54. Sarkar, J.N. (1988). *Chaitanya's Life and Teachings*, New Delhi, pp. 149-50 and 169-70.

55. Havell, E. B. (1904). *A Handbook to Agra, The Taj, Sikandara, Fatehpur Sikri and the Neighbourhood,* Calcutta, pp. 12-13. (The diamond Kohinoor was gifted to Humayun when he was sent to Agra by Babur immediately after the battle of Panipat. The Raja of Gwalior, slain at Panipat, had left his family and the heads of his clan at Agra. In gratitude to Humayun, who treated them magnanimously and protected them from plunder, they presented to him a *peshkash* (token of homage) consisting of a quantity of jewels and precious stones. Among these was one famous diamond which had been acquired by Sultan Alauddin. A judge of diamonds valued it at about half the daily expense of the whole world.)
56. Beni Prasad (1940). *History of Jahangir*, Allahabad, p. 14.
57. Majumdar, *op. cit.*, p. 38; Holden, *op. cit.*, p. 92; *A Handbook to Agra, op. cit.*, pp. 12-13.

Chapter 2

Religious Freedom Under Akbar

Jalaluddin Mohammad Akbar (1556-1605) was born on 15 October 1542 to Nasiruddin Mohammad Humayun and Hameeda Bano Begum at Amarkot, a Rajput principality in Sindh. Amarkot was a Rajput principality under Rana Virsal alias Rana Prasad. It was apparent, moreover, that Akbar was blessed with a gift for memory and remarkable intelligence, even though his tutors were unable to teach him to read or write, as he was apparently dyslexic. Fortuitously, the young heir was placed under the regency of Bairam Khan, whose competent generalship had facilitated Humayun's restoration of Mughal rule.

During the last days of Humayun, he had divided his realm between Mirza Hakim in Kabul and Akbar in Hindustan. It was only after his younger brother had died (1585), the whole Afghanistan was included in his empire. On his father's death, Akbar was at Kalanaur in the Gurdaspur district, where he was carrying on operations against Sikandar Sur, who had taken refuge in the Fort of Mankot. Bairam Khan at once took steps to proclaim Akbar Emperor of India and had him formally enthroned in a garden at Kalanaur on the 14 February 1556, a brick throne being improvised for the occasion. He had previously been proclaimed at Delhi on the 11 February.[1]

During the last days of Humayun, there were three Afghan chiefs; first the King Adil Shah Sur who was forced to retire to Chunar in Bengal; second was Sikandar Sur was the only serious rival in the Punjab and was still awaiting a suitable opportunity to regain the throne; and third was Ibrahim Sur another claimant of the throne. From Chunar King Adil Shah Sur raised Hem Chandra (Hemu), originally a shopkeeper of Rewari, to the position of first minister and chief commander and sent him to oppose Humayun and recover Delhi. On his way Hemu defeated Ibrahim Sur and set towards Delhi and at the time of Humayun's death he was in the field at the head of a vast Afghan army, to contest the throne of Hindustan with Akbar.

Nominally acting on behalf of Adil Shah, Hemu really aspired to carving out a Hindu kingdom on the ruins of Muslim power. The accession of young Akbar offered him the opportunity for striking at Delhi. With a huge body of cavalry and elephants, he marched from Gwalior to Agra whose governor Iskandar Khan, the Uzbeg, failed to defend it against the superior force of the invader and fled to Delhi. Hemu took Agra and then advanced on Delhi. Hemu defeated the Mughal forces and much valuable booty fell into the hands of the victor. Tardi Beg Khan, the governor of Delhi, fled from the battlefield to Sirhind. The capture of both Delhi and Agra placed Hemu in a very strong position. Hemu at the height of his power took the title of Raja Vikramaditya and made his Afghan soldiers call him Hemu Shah.

Second Battle of Panipat

In late 1556 Hemchandra (Hemu), a Hindu general who had formerly served the dislodged Afghan regime, seized Delhi and set himself up as the city's "liberator" and new sovereign with the title of Vikramaditya. When the report of the fall of Delhi reached Akbar at Jullundur, the majority of his nobles advised an immediate retreat to Kabul as their numbers were no more than 25,000 while Hemu could boast of an army of more than 50,000 Afghans and Rajputs and 1,900 elephants. The terrible famine was also raging in the country at the time and they were in the midst of a hostile population, who sympathized more or less with the enemy. But Bairam Khan refused to entertain the idea of retreat and declared that the throne of Hindustan was not one to be abandoned without a struggle.[2]

Leaving Khizr Khwaja Khan at Jullundur to subdue Sikandar Sur, Akbar and Bairam marched towards Delhi. At Sirhind, they were joined by the fugitive governors, Iskandar Khan, Tardi Beg Khan and Ali Quli Khan, who had been forced to leave Sambhal. Here Bairam Khan took the drastic step of executing Tardi Beg Khan for his failure at Delhi while Akbar was away on hunting. From Sirhind, Akbar and Bairam advanced towards Delhi to meet the enemy Hemu who was now master of Delhi and Agra. Hemu or Maharaja Vikramaditya also marched against them with full confidence of victory.

The two armies met on the historic battlefield of Panipat on 5 November 1556. Initially Hemu succeeded in throwing into confusion the right and left wings of his foe and sought to secure a decisive victory by charging the Mughal centre with all his elephants. He was on the point of gaining victory when an arrow struck him in the eye and pierced his brain and he fell unconscious in the saddle. This turned the tide of the battle. Hemu's army lost its morale and dispersed. Two thousand were killed during retreat and all of Himu's elephants fell into the hands of the Mughals who obtained a complete and decisive victory. Hemu himself was brought before Akbar and Bairam Khan by Shah Quli Khan Mehram. On Bairam Khan's advice Emperor Akbar drew his sword and dispatched the defeated general on the spot. Hemu's head was sent to Kabul, while his body was hung at one of the gates of Delhi.[3] The second battle of Panipat sealed the fate of the Afghans and the story of the Mughal Empire now begins.

Capture of Delhi and Agra

After the victory at Panipat Bairam Khan appointed his servant Pir Muhammad Sherwani to suppress Haji Khan, an officer of Sher Shah, who was acting independently in Alwar and to capture the family and property of Hemu which were there. Haji Khan fled before the arrival of the Mughal army and Hemu's wife also escaped, but Pir Muhammad captured his vast wealth and his octogenarian father whom he put to death.

Akbar along with his huge army entered Delhi in triumph on 6 November 1556 and Agra was also recovered. Akbar halted at Delhi for about a month and then returned to the Punjab to complete the operations against Sikandar Sur. The Mughals marched from Sirhind to Lahore and forced Sikandar to take refuge once more in the fortress of Mankot and after a protracted siege Sikandar surrendered in May 1557. Sikandar was treated generously and received *jagirs* in Bihar, where he died two years later. Of the remaining two Sur claimants, Ibrahim Khan withdrew from the contest and Adil was killed in 1557, while making a vain attempt upon Bengal. In December Akbar left for Delhi and on the way at Jullundur, Bairam Khan, then aged more than fifty, married his nineteen year old cousin Salima Begam.[4]

Bairam Khan's Regency (1556-60)

Bairam Khan (18 January 1501-31 January 1561) was born in Badakhshan in Central Asia. He was originally called Bairam "Beg". Later, he was honored as "Kha" or Khan. His father Seyfali Beg Baharlu and grandfather, Janali Beg Baharlu, had been part of Babur's service. Pirali Beg Baharlu, Bairam Khan's great-grandfather was the brother of Babur's wife Pasha Begum. At the age of 16, Bairam entered Babur's service. He played an active role in the early Mughal conquests of India. He later contributed greatly to the establishment of the Mughal Empire under Humayun. He was consigned with the position of *muhardar* (keeper of the seals). He also took part in military campaigns in Benares, Bengal and

Gujarat. Bairam Khan accompanied Humayun during his exile in Persia and helped conquer Kandahar before serving as its governor for nine years. He played a leading role in Humayun's reconquest of Hindustan, as a commander in 1556. Humayun honoured him as Khan-i-Khanan (king of kings). Later, he became commander-in-chief of the Mughal army, powerful statesman and regent at the court of Akbar.

After enthroning Akbar as Emperor of India at Kalanaur on 14 February 1556, Bairam Khan beame Regent (prime minister and guardian) of the Empire as Akbar was only 12 years of age at that time. From this time until he was eighteen, he remained under the tutelage of a great noble, Bairam Khan, his prime minister and guardian. Bairam Khan made arrangements for the education of Akbar but Akbar instead of devoting himself to books, he spent his time in hunting, in elephant-fights and other such pursuits, leaving the actual work of the administration to Bairam Khan. In December Akbar left for Delhi and on the way at Jullundur, Bairam Khan, then aged more than 50, married his 19 year old cousin Salima Sultan Begam, a niece of Humayun, a mark of the sovereign's regard for his distinguished services. Akbar established his court at Agra, the Lodi capital. The Regent Bairam Khan carried on the work most successfully and the strong fortress of Gwalior and the rich province of Jaunpur were annexed to the Empire, though an attempt upon Ranthambhor failed.[5]

Bairam Khan's right-hand man Pir Muhammad Khan had gradually raised to the very high position. He was also appointed tutor to the prince and won royal favour and confidence, so much so that he became almost as powerful as Bairam Khan himself. Bairam would brook no rival and availed of the earliest opportunity for dismissing the upstart. One day he even insulted his patron by refusing admission when he made a courtesy visit to his house during his illness. Pir Muhammad Khan was at first sent in confinement to Bayana and then allowed to go on pilgrimage to Mecca by way of Gujarat. Though Bairam Khan was amply justified in discharging this ungrateful servant, Akbar was displeased.[6]

After Pir Muhammads' dismissal Bairam Khan appointed Shaikh Gadai, a Shiah of no eminence to the important position of *Sadr-us-Sudur*. This appointment raised a storm of indignation among the orthodox Muslims who, to quote Badauni, "flew into a rage at the advancement, honour and unseasonable exaltation of Shaikh Gadai". The unbecoming treatment which Bairam Khan, under Shaikh Gadai's influence, meted to Shaikh Mohammad Ghaus when he visited Agra in April 1559, highly displeased Akbar who revered the Shaikh (Mohammad Ghaus) and afterwards became his disciple.[7]

As early as May 1557, Bairam Khan suspected that Akbar had begun to dislike him; he misinterpreted the accidental running of two royal elephants near his tent as an attempt on his life and held Atga Khan responsible for the displeasure with which he was occasionally treated by his young sovereign. The execution of Tardi Beg Khan and Musahib Beg, the dismissal of Pir Mohammad Khan, the cold treatment of Shaikh Mohammad Ghaus and the two elephant incidents (1559-60) when Bairam put to death two drivers of the royal elephants, on the first occasion, because a drunken royal elephant had wounded one of Bairam's elephants and, on the second, another royal elephant had rushed towards the boat of the minister on the Yamuna where he had been airing, all these added to the displeasure and vexation of the growing ward and made him all the more conscious of his real position. These were the circumstances that led to Bairam Khan's downfall.[8]

In spite of their differences in minor details the root cause of the regent's fall was the desire of the prince to be the king in fact as in name. As Akbar advanced in years to manhood he found that he was a mere puppet in the hands of his guardian who did not consult him in the gravest matters of public importance and did not allow him the least power in financial affairs, so much so that his personal expenses were sanctioned by Bairam with stringency. Akbar wanted to set himself free and this could be done only by the dismissal of his all-powerful guardian, for Bairam would not have tolerated subordination to one whose obedience he had so long enjoyed. This desire of the young emperor to drop the pilot was further strengthened by a series of incidents which highly displeased him and completely alienated him from his valued guardian.

The Emperor Akbar, on entering his eighteenth year, began to feel the bonds of dependence and resented the galling tutelage in which he was kept by Bairam Khan. The leaders of the opposition against the regent, however, formed a small faction whose personnel was drawn from the members of the *harem* and their relations or more properly Akbar's foster-relations known as Atga-Khan: Maham Anaga, the chief nurse of the emperor who had risked her life when the prince was thrown open to the gun shots of Mirza Kamran at Kabul, her son Adham Khan, her relations Shihab-ud-din Ahmad Khan, governor of Delhi and Mirza Sharaf-ud-din Husain and Jiji Anaga who had suckled the prince, her husband Shams-ud-din Atga Khan with his brothers and sons as well as Hamida Begam, the queen-mother.[9]

They began to poison the mind of the Emperor by insinuating that Bairam Khan had become virtual master of the kingdom and was actually thinking of setting Akbar aside and of placing a son of Kamran upon the throne. The dismissal of so powerful a man like Bairam Khan by the young emperor was not an easy task. A secret plot was made by Akbar and the opposition party. On 19 March 1560, Akbar and the collaborators left Agra on the pretext of hunting. As his mother was lying sick at Delhi, Akbar made this his motive to proceed to that city. At Delhi the enemies of Bairam did their utmost to hasten his dismissal. Shihab-ud-din Ahmad Khan made arrangements for the defence of the city and officers from all directions were called to join the emperor. Atga Khan was the earliest to arrive and others followed. From Delhi the Emperor sent Bairam Khan a message to this effect:[10]

> "As I was fully assured of your honesty and fidelity, I left all important affairs of State in your charge and thought only of my own pleasures. I have now determined to take the reins of government into my own hands and it is desirable that you should now make the pilgrimage

> to Mecca, upon which you have been so long intent. A suitable *jagir* out of the *parganas* of Hindustan shall be assigned for your maintenance, the revenues of which shall be transmitted to you by your agents."

On receiving Akbar's message from Delhi, Bairam Khan was surprised and immediately sent envoys to the Emperor and unsuccessfully begging his pardon and assuring him of loyal service in future. Early in April 1560, he left Agra announcing that he was going on pilgrimage to Mecca. But Bairam Khan realized that he was being followed by Mughal army under Pir Mohammad and Munim Khan. Under these circumstances Bairam Khan revolted against Empire. Meanwhile Akbar in person had marched to Sirhind. Here Munim Khan joined him from Kabul. After his defeat Bairam Khan offered to surrender on condition that he would be assured of safe conduct to the Emperor.

In October 1560, at Hajipur (in Hoshiarpur district) Bairam Khan presented himself before Akbar who received him kindly and offered him the alternatives of service as his personal companion or as a *jagirdar* of Kalpi and Chanderi and pilgrimage. Declining to serve where he had ruled, the great minister chose the second and left for Gujarat where at Patan he was assassinated on 31 January 1561, by some Afghans led by one Mubarak Khan whose father had been killed at the battle of Machiwara in which Bairam was in command. Bairam Khan's widow, Salima Sultan Begum, was married to the Emperor and his infant son Mirza Abdur Rahim grew up in royal favour and gradually raised high in position till he became the Khan-i-Khanan in 1584.[11]

Petticoat Influence (1560-62)

In the absence of Bairam Khan the *harem* party under Maham Ananga had the most influence on government and Emperor Akbar. The historians quote that the next three years Akbar remained under a "petticoat government of the worst kind". The *harem* party and Maham Anaga in particular secured important positions as the natural reward of the great services they had recently rendered. Her one idea was to advance her son, Adham Khan, a man of very bad character, to high office. She further showed her incapacity by bringing into office Pir Mohammad Sherwani, a cruel and brutal man. Under his new advisers, the Mughal kingdom was still a comparatively small state and it was now decided to commence an aggressive policy of expansion.

The first victim was Baz Bahadur, the ruler of Malwa. The Mughal army led by Adham Khan and Pir Mohammad Khan invaded Malwa and marched unopposed to Sarangpur where at last the musician-king Baz Bahadur was easily defeated by the superior army of Akbar and put to flight on 29 March 1561. All his treasures, elephants and his *harem* fell into the hands of the victors but his beloved, the famous Rupmati, the romantic theme of artists and poets, took poison. Baz Bahadur remained a fugitive at various courts until November 1570, when he surrendered to Akbar at Nagaur and joined his service.[12]

The period of the control of Maham Anaga and her worthless son was now drawing to a close. In November 1561, Atga Khan was appointed *vakil* or the prime minister. This appointment displeased Maham Anaga and Munim Khan who had been holding the position since the discharge of Bairam Khan. The *harem* party was now broken into two groups: the Maham Anaga group and the party of Atga Khan. The appointment of Atga Khan as *vakil* had provoked the displeasure of the Maham Anaga group and the malcontents found in the unscrupulous Adham Khan. On 16 May 1562, the hot-headed youth, accompanied by a few ruffians, burst in upon Shams-ud-din as he sat in the hall of audience and murdered him. Adham Khan then attempted to enter the royal apartments where Akbar was sleeping at the time. But the Emperor, warned by his servants of what had occurred, armed himself and, entering the hall suddenly, struck Adham Khan to the ground. In the punishment Adham was twice thrown from the terrace by royal order and put to death.

Akbar himself broke this news to Maham Anaga who made the simple but dignified reply that he did well and forty days later followed her son to the grave.[13] From now the days of Akbar's dependence were over. Henceforth the Emperor was to take supreme control of affairs.

In 1560 Akbar overthrew his all-powerful guardian who had maintained his throne; in 1562 he overthrew the Maham Anaga group who had assisted him to drop his pilot but abused the power he had bestowed on them. After getting rid of ladies intervention and assistance in 1562 Akbar was his own master consulting whomsoever he liked and successfully ruled the country until his death in 1605. In 1564 Akbar revealed the same strength of character as of Adham Khan's punishment when he did not hesitate to order death sentence on his maternal uncle Khwaja Muazzam for having murdered his wife. The Rajput alliance and Akbar's prohibition in 1562 of the practice of enslaving prisoners of war were expressions of that marked individuality of the young emperor.

Policy of Sulh-i-Kul

After getting rid of his powerful guardians and ladies intervention and assistance in 1562, he successfully ruled the country until his death in 1605. As a ruler, Akbar was in all circumstances most tolerant and liberal to his subjects. Abdul Latif, a man of liberal attitude was the tutor of Emperor Akbar. Abdul Latif was so liberal in his views that among Sunnis he acquired the reputation of being a Shia and among Shias that of being a Sunni. India was vast country and as a ruler of each and every religion and community, Akbar justified his duty by adopting his policy of Sulh-i-Kul (universal toleration). His Rajput policy, religious policy, promotion of different religions and religious leaders, matrimonial alliances, Ibadat Khana, Din-i-Ilahi, etc., all were part of his policy of Sulh-i-Kul.

The fundamental of Akbar's policy, Sulh-i-Kul, was obnoxious to Sunni orthodoxy and Jesuit Catholicism. The Fathers were anxious to prove that Akbar was about to embrace Christianity by describing him as an enemy and persecutor of Islam. Most of the charges made by Badauni do not stand the test of scientific criticism. From the Muslim chronicles as well as Jesuit accounts we find that throughout the reign of Akbar and even after the promulgation of the Din-i-Ilahi, Muslims could pray, observe fasts and festivals, give the name of Ahmad and Mohammad to their children and go on pilgrimage to Mecca. In fact, Akbar, with his principle of universal toleration, was far in advance of his age. In his age he stood alone, not only in Islam, but in the whole world; Catholic and Protestant Christendom might both have gone and sat at his feet. No wonder that the Din-i-Ilahi could obtain hardly twenty-five converts of note and died with its author. The "ethical rationalism" of Akbar, which was to have united all, pleased none; it was many centuries too soon. It appealed neither to the Hindus nor to the Muslims.

Akbar established matrimonial alliances between the two communities of Hindus and Muslims and maintained communal harmony in the country. Akbar's marriages with Hindu princesses further contributed to the liberalizing process. He provided religious freedom and even freedom of converting Muslims to the Hindu fold. He appointed Hindus on the higher posts of revenue, military and administration.

Akbar improved upon the matrimonial practice by allowing his Hindu spouses to perform their religious rites in the palace. This had its effect upon his religious attitude to his people. Akbar, thus, came to be surrounded by Hindu influences at home which must have worn away the natural repugnance of a Muslim for Hindu practices. Akbar's marriages with Hindu princesses and his relations with the Hindu *rajas* provided the means for bringing Hindu teachers of all shades of opinion to the religious discussions in the official presence. These meetings were thrown open to the adherents of other religions as well. Akbar's relations with the State of Bikaner procured for him the services of Karm Chand who had once served as a minister at the court of Bikaner. He was a Jaina and through him were introduced to the court such eminent Jaina scholars as Man Singh and Jai Chand Suri.

All these things played an important part in shaping Akbar's religious policy. But it was his mind that gave definite shape to the policy of tolerance to the several religions in his kingdom. Many of these factors, if they tended to create a liberal atmosphere were themselves in their turn created by Akbar's natural liberalism and political far-sightedness. Akbar's religious policy was due to political rather than religious reasons. It was the realization of the fact that the Truth is an inhabitant of every place and undoubtedly in every religion. Although there was no religious tussle or controversy among the Hindus and Muslims yet he wanted to bridge the each and every gap in the society.

Rajput Policy

The Rajputs had been the chief bulwark of Hinduism in the past and chief opponent of Delhi Sultans, Afghans and Mughals. Akbar not only tried to win over for the imperial cause but also tried to make them as permanent ally to control the empire for longer time. Akbar's Rajput policy began as a response to the internal politics of one of the Rajput lineages, the Kachhwaha clan, based in the state of Amber in northern Rajasthan. In 1534 the clan's head, Puran Mal, died with no adult heir and was succeeded by his younger brother, Bhar Mal. Puran Mal, however, did have a son who by the early 1560s had come of age and challenged Bhar Mal's right to rule Amber. Feeling this pressure from within his own clan, Bhar Mal approached Akbar for material support, offering in exchange his daughter in marriage in 1562. It happened in the middle of January 1562, Akbar made a pilgrimage to the tomb of the famous saint of Ajmer, Khwaja Muin-ud-din Chishti. On the way Raja Bhar Mal of Amber paid homage to the emperor and offered him the hand of his daughter. Akbar agreed and during his return journey the marriage was celebrated at Sambhar. This pilgrimage to Ajmer, which henceforward Akbar made annually until 1579, is a landmark not only in Akbar's but also in Indo-Muslim history.

In 1562, the Kachhwaha chieftain entered Mughal service, with Akbar assuring him of support in maintaining his position in the Kachwaha political order, while his family entered the royal household. Besides his daughter, Man Singh, the nephew and adopted son of Raja Bhagwan Das, the heir of Raja Bhar Mal was taken into the royal service. Akbar's marriage with the Rajput princess offered a suitable opportunity and he decided to make the most of it. Mariam-uz-Zamani or Harka Bai (but no chronicler mentions the Rajput name of the daughter of Bhar Mal of Amber), the princess of Amber, afterwards became the mother of Emperor Jahangir in 1569.[14] For several generations thereafter, the ruling clan continued to give its daughters to the Mughal court, thereby making the chiefs of these clans the uncles, cousins or even fathers-in-law of Mughal emperors. The intimate connection between the two courts had far-reaching results. Not only did Kachhwaha rulers quickly rise in rank and stature in the Mughal court, but their position within their own clan was greatly enhanced by Akbar's confirmation of their political leadership. Akbar's support also enhanced the position of the Kachhwahas as a whole and hence Amber state, in the hierarchy of Rajasthan's other Rajput lineages.

Neighbouring Rajput clans soon realized the political wisdom of attaching themselves to the expanding Mughal state, a visibly rising star in north Indian politics. Around 1564, the Rathor *raja* of Merta, in western Rajasthan, submitted to Akbar and gave him his daughter in marriage. Mughal support now gave this lineage, a junior branch of the Rathors of Jodhpur, a political edge over local rivals. The same pattern continued across Rajasthan. In 1569 the Hada Rajputs surrendered the stronghold of Ranthambhor in order to gain Mughal backing for leverage against their own kinsmen in south-eastern Rajasthan. About the same time, the Baghela Rajputs of Bhatta surrendered the fort of Kalinjar to Akbar. The next year the Rathors of Bikaner submitted to Mughal power, as did the Bhatis of Jaisalmar. In 1583, Udai Singh of the Rathor clan of Jodhpur was recognized as the ruler of Marwar, in western Rajasthan, initiating that powerful house's collaboration with Mughals. Driving these arrangements, though, was not just the incentive of courtly patronage. The clans of Rajasthan well understood that refusal to engage with the Mughals would bring the stick of military confrontation.

Alone among the Rajput clans, the Sisodiyas of Mewar in southern Rajasthan, north India's pre-eminent warrior lineage, obstinately refused to negotiate with the Mughals. The ruler Rana Partap, undoubtedly, was admired yet no Rajput chief was willing to help him against the Emperor. Akbar in 1568 led a four-month siege of the Sisodiyas' principal stronghold of Chittor, which ultimately fell to the Mughals, but only after a spectacular *jauhar* in which the fort's defenders, foreseeing their doom, killed their women and gallantly sallied forth to meet their deaths. In all, some 30,000 defenders of the fort were killed, although its ruler, Rana Pratap, managed to escape. For decades, he and the Sisodiya house would continue to resist Mughal domination, whereas nearly every other Rajput lineage had acknowledged Mughal overlordship.

The Rajput friendship and matrimonial alliances made the Rajputs longlasting friends of Mughal Empire. The Rajputs supported the imperial cause whole heartedly and proved to be the stoutest defenders of the Emperor's person and crown in his struggles against his foes. The Rajput alliance was not merely the stroke of a diplomat to win the support of militant Hinduism; it was the beginning of a new orientation of state-policy, the first expression of that doctrine of Sulh-i-Kul (universal toleration) which his great Persian tutor Mir Abdul Latif Qazwini had infused into Akbar. He was not to be the head of a community but all people. No Muslim ruler before, not even Sher Shah, with all his benevolence, held this exalted conception of state and kingship so definitely and vividly.

Rajputs received high-ranking positions in Akbar's imperial service, which had the effect of transforming what had been parochial, regional clans into elite players empowered to operate on an all-India stage. To gain this new mobility and status, moreover, Rajputs did not have to sacrifice their autonomy within their native lands, as they were free to continue managing their own courts and internal affairs, a major concession. Moreover, whereas the land assignments, or *jagirs*, of other imperial officers were regularly rotated around the empire, Rajputs were allowed to continue administering their ancestral lands as "native" (*watan*) *jagirs*. Mughal support also gave those clans that entered the imperial orbit considerable bargaining strength with local rivals, which is what had induced Bhar Mal to ally himself with Akbar. Finally, Rajputs were guaranteed religious freedom; there was no pressure on them to convert to Islam.

These marriages and Rajput reations led Akbar to take a much more favourable view of Hinduism and his Hindu subjects. Military service, which had so far been confined to Muslims, was thrown open to them and the Rajputs, by their deeds and actions, justified the favour and confidence of the Emperor. Akbar's Rajput policy showed the people of India that Akbar was not content to remain the leader of a band of foreign conquerors, as his father and grandfather had been, but that he intended to be a really Indian ruler and to found an Indian dynasty.

Rajput princes were not only raised to high commands, but they were in all respects treated as near relatives of the imperial family and were advanced in their official careers in accordance with their merits. Some twenty Hindu chieftains, mainly Rajputs, were now admitted to the innermost parts of Akbar's palace, a privilege not allowed even to Muslim courtiers. A Rajput Prince Man Singh, the nephew of Raja Bhar Mal, was appointed Viceroy at Kabul on the death of Hakim Mirza, the younger brother of the Emperor.

Abolition of Pilgrim Tax

In the autumn of 1562, the year of the disappearance of Maham Anaga and her son, Akbar's mind seems to have undergone a change. He was no longer the youth intent on sport and amusements. He seems to have realized now what his responsibilities were as ruler of a great country. Previous events had taught him that those responsibilities must be borne by himself alone and that he could not trust others toshare them. Henceforth it was by his own efforts that the various reforms which he had conceived were to be carried out. One reform was introduced early in 1563. This was the abolition of the tax levied on pilgrims.

Before Akbar, Hindus were required to pay pilgrim tax on visiting or praying their holy places of public gathering. This type of tax was known to Akbar before 1563, when he was encamped at Mathura and a religious festival was going on at that time. While hearing the petition of the local people about the pilgrim tax, he ordered to stop the collection of the pilgrim tax. Akbar further removed all restrictions on the building of places of public worship as well.The abolition of the pilgrimage tax, it made it possible for the followers of all religions to worship their gods in their own way. But Akbar's generosity and justice did not stop here. He had destroyed the prevalent myth that the public celebration of the Hindu worship was a profanation to Muslim ears and eyes.[15]

Abolition of Jazia

Emperor Akbar was born in Hindu Rajput palace of Rana Vrisal in Umarkot or Amarkot in Sind. His early childhood in Hindu atmosphere and secular brotherhood left a deep impact on future policies of Akbar. When Akbar became Emperor of India in 1556 after his father's death, he adopted a very lenient policy, although he met a very tough resistance from Afghan commander and newly declared Samrat Hemchandra alias Hemu, a Hindu trader of Rewari (according to Persian writers—Mewati Bakkal). After occupying Delhi, Agra and rest of the Empire, Akbar fully established rule for public interest irrespective of cast, creed or religion. Akbar forbade the enslavement of war prisoners in 1562, abolished the pilgrim tax in 1563 and also abolished protection tax *jazia* in 1564.

This was the prelude to a more important reform the following year (1564), namely, the abolition of the *jazia*, the poll tax (protection tax) levied on the people not associated with service of the state, especially non-Muslims. As certain people, right from the time prophet (PBUH), especially non-Muslims were not at war against enemy of Islam or not in service of state, were allowed to live in the state by paying protection tax or *jazia*. By paying this tax the Islamic army or state was responsible for the protection on non-associates or non-Muslims. If these non-Muslims were in service of state they were considered as associates of the state and exempted from the tax of *jazia*. This tax, which had originally been imposed by the Caliph Omar, had been introduced into India in the eighth century by Mohammad bin Kasim, the conqueror of Sind. It seems to have been levied more or less spasmodically by vatious Sultans of Delhi who were strong enough to collect it. Its abolition was part of Akbar's definite policy of gaining the loyalty and support of his Hindu subjects.

In India the people felt humiliation on paying this *jazia* tax although same type of tax *zakaat* was levied only upon the Muslims whether they were associates of the state or not. In both cases only capable persons were bound to pay who were having paying capacity. Any how the tax *jazia* was humiliating to the Indian people and they considered it as symbol of inferiority and they began to demand for its abolition.

As per the demand of his subjects, Akbar abolished *jazia* in 1564 and its abolition was, undoubtedly, turning point of the Muslim rule in India. With its abolition Akbar created c6mmon citizenship for all his subjects, Hindus and Muslims alike. Akbar declared that the state is responsible for the protection of each and every subject whether they were in state service or not. By its abolition Akbar created common citizenship for all his subjects, Hindus and Muslims alike. It may be added here that *jazia* was abolished years before liberal courtiers Abul Fazl and Faizi were introduced to the Emperor Akbar.[16]

Akbar was of the view that Mughal Empire is an umbrella for its subjects which not only protects the lives, property and opportunity but also guarantees to provide the people food and job security without any discrimination of caste, creed and religion. He created job opportunity for his subjects as per their ability and qualifications and for the labour class Akbar gave them employment in his building works which were always under construction in different parts of empire at very low distances. Akbar was many steps ahead of his forefathers in maintaining peace and communal harmony. Abolition of the pilgrim tax, the abolition of *jazia* and commencing the practice of *jharokha darsrhan*, etc., were totally to appease his Hindu subjects of the country.

Ibadat Khana

Akbar was perhaps the first ruler of India who committed not only for the unification of India geographically but to unite the people of India culturally. He hoped that there should be a system under which the people of every faith should unite. He wanted to unite for the peace, unite for the country and nation. He thought that every religion profess the same truth in different way, worship the one truth with different names and habitats the same country with different name. In the process of uniting the people culturally Akbar wanted to assemble the religious leaders of every religion to discuss their religious truth and create common platform for all religions for peace, unity and integrity of the country. Akbar was sure that if all religions are true then a common platform must be created to eradicate the bitterness and animosity and to promote brotherhood. In order to materialize his ideas, Akbar established a religious assembly house called *ibadat khana* at Fatehpur Sikri. Here religious discussions were held every Friday evening. It was commenced in 1575 and came to an end in 1582.

Initially it was confined to Muslims and was divided into four sections, occupied by four classes of members: the nobles of the court, Shaikhs or ascetics, Sayyids or descendants of the Prophet and the '*ulama* (jurists). The violent intolerance of the orthodox party led by Shaikh Abdun-Nabi and Makhdum-ul-Mulk and bitter differences between the Sunnis and Shias disgusted the emperor and alienated him from orthodox Islam. Of course, he showed his interest in pilgrimage by arranging Gulbadan Begam's journey to Mecca (1975) and next year he himself intended to proceed on pilgrimage. But Akbar was passing through a mental crisis. In January 1578, he expressed his abhorrence of meat diet. In April at Bhera, on the bank of the Jhelum, while hunting his heart was changed and ordred to set free all animals.[17]

In October 1578, discussions in the Ibadat-Khana were revived with renewed vigour and started on on every Friday night (Thursday evening). Now the House of Worship had become a Parliament of religions where the Sufi, the philosopher, the orator, the jurist, the Sunni and the Shia, the Brahman and the atheist (Charvaka), the Jaina and the Buddhist, the Christian and the Jew, the sabaean and the Zoroastrian and others met and debated under the presidency of the Mughal Emperor Akbar. Besides them, the Sufis, doctors, preachers, lawyers, Sunnis, Shias, Brahmans, Jainas, Buddhists, Charvaks, Christians, Jews, Zoroastrians and learned men of every belief were gathered together in the royal assembly and were filled with delight. Each one fearlessly brought forward his assertions and arguments and the disputations and contentions were long and heated. Every sect, in its vanity and conceit, attacked and endeavoured to refute the statements of their antagonists. Even the theologians of the same sect fought and declare heretic to each other. One night the Ibadat Khana was brightened by the presence of Padre Radalf, who for intelligence and wisdom was unrivalled among Christian doctors. Several carping and bigoted men attacked him and the statements were torn into pieces. This prejudice and violence greatly annoyed the impartial mind of the Emperor.[18]

The bitter differences among the *ulama* in these debates, which revealed their shallow pride as well as the narrowness of orthodox Islam, further weakened his faith in it and he decided to take all religious matters in Islam into his own hands. The time had arrived when the king as the secular head of the state should be the head in spiritual matters as well. The exalted conception of sovereignty that he held necessitated it and the Timurid tradition pointed to it. On Friday 26 June 1579, emulating the Caliphs and his illustrious ancestor Timur, Akbar mounted the pulpit of the mosque at Fathpur Sikri and recited the *khutba* composed by Faizi in verse which ended with the words: Allahu Akbar. Some modern authors believe with Badauni that Akbar made ambiguous use of these words to mean both God is great as well as Akbar is God. But Akbar claimed that he was the agent of God, Khalifatullah; he never laid claim to divinity.[19]

Nurul Haq in his *Zubdatu-i-Tawarikh*, says that up to the time 1578, Akbar used to attend public worship at the five stated times, whether he was in the capital or in camp and the reciters of the Quran, who were on the royal establishment, used to read that sacred book both at prayer and at other times. Indeed, the king himself used to take the lead in worship. But on the strange incidents of Ibadat Khana was the king's abandonment of the national religion, which became a stumbling-block to many people weak in the faith. The cause of this dereliction was, that the court had become the centre of attraction to all sects, persuasions and people, to the learned of Khurasan, Iraq, Mawarau-n Nahr (Transoxiana) and Hindustan, to doctors and theologians, to Shias and Sunnis, to Christians and philosophers, to Brahmans and professors of every existing religion. The king used openly to say in the presence of his officers, doctors and chiefs:[20]

> "My sole object, oh wise Mullas, is to ascertain the truth, to find out and disclose the principles of genuine religion and to trace it to its divine origin. Take care, therefore, that through the influence of your human passions, you are not induced to conceal the truth; and say nothing contrary to the almighty decrees. If you do, you are responsible before God for the consequences of your impiety."

The annoying events in Ibadat Khana shattered the future plan of Akbar. The behaviour of Muslim theologians made an impression on Akbar that Islam is not the only true religion. By their discussions or rather their heating controversy over different issues maligned their position in the eyes of Emperor. From that time Akbar began to believe and respect all religions equally. However, Akbar didn't lose hope and began to think his plan afresh by different method.

In 1579, as Akbar was annoyed with the theologians, he displaced the chief *imam* or the regular preacher at the chief mosque in Fatehpur Sikri to emphasize his position as both the spiritual and temporal head of his realm. After few months Akbar issued the infallibility decree declaring himself the absolute temporal and spiritual head in his realm. Within a week he left for what turned out to be his last visit to Khwaja Moinuddin Chishti's tomb Ajmer.

Infallibility Decree

On 2 September 1579, Akbar issued the Infallibility Decree and became the *imam* and the *mujtahid* (highest authority on law) of the age. Akbar obtained the famous *mahzar* (declaration) or Infallibility Decree from the famous *ulama* of that time. This document was drafted by Shaikh Mubarak and signed reluctantly by five others, the principal *ulama* and prominent theologians of Hindustan. It made Akbar, who was the temporal head of the state, the Supreme Head of the Church or more properly the Islamic faith in India as well. The *mahzar* was really the funeral oration of the 'Ulama' as it overthrew the nimbus of their legal and spiritual power. It was the natural corollary to Akbar's ideal of royal absolutism. It led to the virtual assumption by Akbar of the title of the Caliph and is closely connected with the "pulpit incident". Some of his coins also bear the title of exalted Caliph and we are told by Arif Qandahari that in all the mosques of the Mughal Empire the *khutba* mentioned him as Amir-ul-Mominin.[21]

It determined the rank of just king as higher than that of *mujtahid* and declared that Akbar as the just ruler (Sultan-i-Adil) could decide between *mujtahids*, if they differed in opinion on any religious question, by accepting any of the conflicting views and that his decision was final and binding. Also it empowered him to issue new orders which the people must obey, provided they were in conformity with the Quran and were for the benefit of the people. The decree had its significance in the outer Islamic world as well. It was a vindication of Akbar's sovereign authority and a challenge to the Sultan-Caliph of Turkey, the juridical head of Islam in whose name the *khutba* was recited at Mecca and Medina. It was a reply to the Satavi Shahs of Persia as well, who posed as the perpetual patrons of the Mughal dynasty because both Akbar's father and grandfather had sought and obtained Persian help on condition of accepting the Shiah faith. Akbar's authority was now superior to that of the *mujtahids*, the highest ecclesiastical and juridical authorities of the Shias.[22]

The decree, however, did not at all involve Akbar's repudiation of Islam: it was as a Muslim king that Akbar could decide between the conflicting views of the *mujtahids*. Neither was Akbar invested with infallibility. The scope of the decree was limited: the king should accept one of the conflicting views and any new order he might issue must be in conformity with the Quran and for the benefit of the people. There can be no doubt that the declaration displeased the *ulama* and orthodox Muslims.

In 1579, Emperor Akbar issued the Infallibility Decree. By its declaration, Akbar became the supreme arbiter over all religious matters of his subjects. By this decree, Akbar became the Imam-i-Aadil and the sole arbitrator of Islamic Law.[23] The decree shows that though the laws were based on reason, the state itself was not separated from religion totally in the modern sense of secularism. However, it must be kept in mind that the above decree, especially in relation to Islam, was in order to prevent Islamic religious authority from tampering with the religious policies of Akbar. This decree prevented fundamental and communal forces from influencing in any way the Emperor's decisions. By positioning himself above the Islamic religious leaders, getting declared himself as a judge most beloved on the Day of Judgement and conditioning his laws to be in line with the Quran, Akbar was able to gain a religious backing for furthering his syncretistic and rational religious policies.

Din-i-Ilahi (Tauhid-i-Ilahi)

By the discussions and controversies in Ibadat Khana, it made clear to Emperor that every religion is right but the theologians or followers are unable to logically prove this fact. However, Emperor Akbar was sure that every religion professes only one truth or God with different names. To end the religious controversy, Emperor Akbar intended of founding a new religion suitable to Hindus and Mohammadans alike. He realized that hostilities among different faiths gave birth to political factions in the kingdom and he wished to introduce religious uniformity in the land. In 1582, Akbar introduced a new faith officially known as Tauhid-i-Ilahi (Divine Monotheism) which was later explained as Din-i-Ilahi (Devine Faith) and declaring himself to be the vice-regent of God on earth and the authorized exponent of His will.[24]

It is difficult to define the Divine Faith, for its author did not define it. It was neither inspired by Revelation nor based on any well-defined philosophy or theology. It was deism modified by Hindu and predominant Zoroastrian influence, a religion without priests and books, "an ethical rationalism leading to the ideal of mystic union of the soul with the divine", in which respect it was based on the Sufi idea of absorption of the soul in the Divine Being. It enjoined such ethical and social reforms as recommending alms-giving and sparing of animal life, permitting remarriage of widows, prohibiting child-marriage and marriage among close relations as well as forced *sati*, recommending monogamy, enforcing chastity and controlling gambling and drinking by restricting the sale of drink.[25]

In 1585, he ordered the minting of coins bearing only the words *allahu akbar jalla jalaluhu*, (God is great, splendid is His Glory)—an ambiguous legend that could also be read as 'Akbar is God', with the word for glory also matching part of the emperor's given name, Jalal. The Din-i-Ilahi was definitely an attempt at religious syncretism, as much a child of Akbar's spiritual development as a product of the age, following as it does the movement of Kabir and Nanak.

Botelho writing in 1648-54 declared that Akbar desired to found a new religion combining Islam and Christianity. Even Pinheiro, writing in September 1595, from the royal court, is doubtful about the religion Akbar followed. Pinheiro writes that it is the opinion of the many that he aims at making a new religion of which he himself is to be the head. All that Pinheiro can definitely say in the matter is that it is more or less certain that he has a strong desire to be looked upon and esteemed as a God, or some great prophet.According to Monserrate, the first Jesuit Mission when it left in 1583 had only suspicions that Akbar intended to found a new religion of his own.[26]

Tauhid-i-Ilahi or Din-i-Ilahi had no book, no priests, no ceremonies and practically no religious beliefs. According to the new belief there is only one God and all must bow in reverence to Him. All must subdue evil passions and practise virtues. All must bow to reason and not to the authority of any Man. It is claimed that out of the ten virtues enjoined by the Divine Faith nine were directly derived from the Holy Quran. It was an order rather than a religion and more akin to free masonry than any religious movement. Badauni in *Muntakhib-ut-Twarikh* and the author of *Dabistane Mazahib* are responsible for declaring Tauhid-i-Ilahi to a new religion Din-i-Ilahi. The infallibility decree of Emperor Akbar much before the promulgation of the new faith or sect Tauhid-i-Ilahi gave the rise of a belief that Akbar having founded a new religion called Din-i-Ilahi.[27]

At the head of this new sect Tauhid-i-Ilahi stood Akbar himself; next after him came Abul Fazal and Faizi. It had no book, no priests, no ceremonies and practically even no religious beliefs. The greeting or rallying call of the new faith—*allahu akbar*—was very serious pun, which could simply be the usual pious invocation affirming that "God (Allah) is Great (Akbar)". However, the opponents who have defined the new faith as Din-i-Ilahi explained the greeting *allahu akbar* with another possible meaning that "Akbar (Akbar) is God (Allah)". *Allahu Akbar,* was no doubt adopted by him for his coinageand even introduced asa form of salutation.[28]

Some of the courtiers of Akbar blindly accepted Akbar as supreme authority on earth and easily accepted the new faith. Badauni in *Muntakhib-ut-Twarikh* states that Mirza Jani, governor of Thatta and other apostates wrote their confession,

> "I who am so and so, son of so and so, do voluntarily and with sincere predilection and inclination, utterly and entirely renounce and repudiate the religion of Islam, which I have seen and heard of my fathers and do embrace the Divine Religion of Akbar Shah and do accept the four grades of entire devotion, viz., the sacrifice of Property, Life, Honour and Religion."[29]

While Akbar chiefly relied on the art of persuasion in inducing others to accept his faith, he sometimes used force and bribery also to intimidate or tempt others to follow him. Whatever the case may be, the new religion did not appeal to the masses, who could not comprehend it. Even some of his own trusted courtiers declared their dislike toit. The Rajput Raja Bhagwan Das was the first dissentient voice. Some years later his adopted son, Kanwar Man Singh, repeated the same sentiments:[30]

> "If discipleship means willingness to sacrifice one's life, I have already carried my life in my hand; what need is there of further proof? If, however, the term has another meaning and refers to faith, I certainly am a Hindu. If you order me to do so, I will become a Musalman, but I know not of the existence of any other religion than these two."

Emperor Akbar also introduced a new calendar with a solar year in the year 1586 (994 AH) and called the Ilahi Year. It is said that Ilahi Year was introduced because the lunar Hijri year was not suitable for revenue purposes as its months did not correspond with harvest seasons. On this account it was not possible to fix any dates in the era either for the issue of demand slips for revenue to the cultivators, or for the collection of revenue. It was not intended to and it did not, supersede the use of the Hijri era. The Ilahi era was intended to be used in official records, oftener than not, along with the Hijri dates. It did not involve the disuse of the Muslim era either by Akbar or his subjects.[31]

It must be cleared that even after promulgation of new creed Tauhid-i-Ilahi, Akbar never abstained from practising the religion Islam but declared himself as temporal head. However, his slight deviation from religion Islam could not ignored. Thus it is clear whatever Din-i-Ilahi was, Akbar was not very anxious to obtain adherents for it. He seldom used the resources of his empire for advancing the fortunes of those who were admitted thereto, still less did he force his subjects to adopt it. He had overthrown the conception of a state religion in India.It is said that Akbar on his deathbed acknowledged the Mohammadan creed, but the evidence on this point is unreliable.

Above all his religious system or religious policy had an important political bearing. His whole policy was the endeavour to unite with a bond of common interest to all the diverse social, religious and racial elements of his empire. Akbar's principal ideologue, Abul Fazl, implied that his patron did not oppose Islam or any other religion, but rather that, as the most sacred sovereign on earth, he was simply above all religions. He had fashioned himself not as a Muslim ruler, but as the ruler of all humanity.

Promotion of Hinduism

Akbar's ideal was to weld the different states of India into one compact Empire and he soon perceived that he could never hope to achieve this without the cooperation of the Hindus, who formed a large majority of his subjects. Circumstances operated to increase his natural tolerance. He was, from many points of view, the type of a modern ruler. He fully realized the important principle that to rule well and effectively, he must not make any distinction between people professing different religious views.

He was very prejudiced against the spirit of bigotry shown towards Hindus by doctors of Muslim law. In addition to his policy of religious toleration he was inclined for political reasons to favour the Hindus. He adopted some of their customs and encouraged others to do so. Akbar himself also endorsed much of Hinduism by participating in their festivals. Definitely, Akbar's Hindu policy was greatly influenced by the many Hindu wives that he had. He allowed his Hindu spouses to perform their religious rites in the palace. But in spite of all this, Akbar's toleration did not extend to countenancing inhuman and unjust religious practices.

Under Akbar Hindu-Muslim unity and idol worship were never discouraged. This pluralistic attitude also grew out of his comparative study of the various religions and people as well as his own belief in the power and value of reason in understanding and judgement. Akbar was also a regular audience of Hindu saints and philosophers. It is also said that Akbar learned Hindu doctrines from Hindu Brahmans, Jaina thought from Heera Vijay Suri, Vijaysena Suri, Bhanuchandra Upadhyaya and Jinchandra; Zoroatrian beliefs from Dastur Meherji Rana and Christian doctrines from the Pastors called in from Goa. Akbar had become acquainted with Sikhism and came into contact with its *gurus*, Amar Das (died 1974) and Ram Das (died 1581). He found in the *Granth* only Jove and devotion to God.[32]

Some consider that a probable influence behind Akbar's Hindu policy could be Sufism that is said to have inspired him towards a more liberal approach towards Hinduism. Before Akbar the conversion from Islam to other religions was not allowed but Emperor Akbar allowed the people to convert or follow whatever religion they liked. In the forty-fifth year of his reign Emperor Akbar issued order that the Hindus converted to against their will at any age, could return to the religion of their forefathers. Many scholars believe that Akbar's Hindu policy was politically motivated. However, Akbar's Hindu promoting policies encouraged the Hindus morale as high as they began to destroy the mosques and built the temples over there.

In Akbar's time, the eminent Islamic theologian Shaikh Ahmad Sirhindi complained that the Hindus were demolishing mosques and were building their own places of worship in their stead. In Thanesar, near the Kurukhet (Kurukshetra) tank, there was a mosque and the shrine of a saint. Both these have been destroyed by the Hindus and in their place they now have a big temple. Again, the Hindus perform their rituals and religious practices freely while the Muslims find themselves helpless and are unable to execute ordinances of the Sharia. On the day of Ekadashi (eleven days after the moonrise) when Hindus abstain from eating and drinking, they see to it that the Muslims also do not cook, sell or buy anything in the towns. On the contrary, in the month of Ramzan (the month of fast for Muslims), Hindus cook and sell bread in the market openly.[33]

Akbar also appeased the Hindus by forbidding the use of beef as the cow was considered a sacred animal by the Hindus. In his reign, the Hindus prospered greatly since most Rajputs were given high posts and Hindu warriors formed a large part of the Mughal army. Badauni in *Muntakhab-ut-Twarikh* records the fact that the Hindus kill good men if they kill cows. In 1583, Akbar forbade the killing of animals on certain days. In 1590-91, Akbar is said to have forbidden the eating of the flesh of oxen, buffaloes, goats or sheep, horses and camels. Fishing also was prohibited for some time when Akbar visited Kashmir in 1592. Akbar, however, respected the feelings of the Hindus enough to abstain from the use of some of these articles. Akbar started participating in some of the Hindu festivals. The Rakhi festival was celebrated in the court when the Brahmans came to tie strings of different types of threads to the imperial wrists. Akbar also started celebrating in the Dipavali, the festival of lamps and Holi, festival of the colours.[34]

Akbar made another attempt to maintain peace and tranquillity in India by reforming society. He conditionally abolished the cruel practice of *sati* in the Hindu society. *Akbarnama* mentions that in the interior of Hindustan it was the custom, when a husband dies, for his widow willingly and cheerfully to cast herself into the flames (of the funeral pyre). In 1583, Abul Fazl reports, Akbar decreed that if a Hindu woman wished to be burnt with her husband, they should not be prevented, but she should not be forced and women who had children were not allowed to burn themselves. Akbar appointed the inspectors in every city and district, who were to watch carefully over these two cases, to discriminate between them and to prevent any woman being forcibly burnt. Child marriage was also prohibited and widow remarriage was promoted during Akbar's rule.[35]

Promotion of Zoroastrianism

Zoroastrianism found its able exponent at the Ibadat Khana. In its theologian Dastir Mahyarji Rana whom Akbar had met in Gujarát in 1573 was arrived at the court of Akbar in 1578. His influence was so great that it was believed Akbar had become a convert. A sacred fire was established in the palace. In 1580 Akbar began to prostrate himself publicly before the fire and the sun. In this the emperor was influenced also by Birbal, who gave emphasis to sun-worship and by the Hindu ladies of his harem who performed homa. Persian festivals were revived and the solar Ilahi era, with Persian names for months and days, was adopted in 1584.[36] Akbar was venerating the rising sun every dawn from the highest point of his palace roof. Emperor Akbar had also memorized the 1,001 Sanskrit names of the sun.

Promotion of Christianity

In response to Akbar's invitation the first Jesuit mission from Goa arrived on 28 February 1580, at Fathpur Sikri and was received with gracious respect. It consisted of Father Rudolf Aquaviva, an Italian, Antony Monserrate, a Spaniard and Francis Henriquez, a Persian convert who acted as the interpreter. Akbar showed profound reverence for a copy of the Bible which the Fathers presented and made respectful salutation to a picture of the Madonna. He appointed Abul Fazl to translate the Gospel and Monserrate to give Murad a few lessons in Christianity.[37] The emperor built for them a chapel in the palace and held prolonged discussions with them on Christianity. Akbar was highly impressed by Christianity, though he was not convinced of the doctrines of the Trinity, of the Virgin birth of the Son and the Incarnation. The Fathers took part in the discussions at the Ibadat Khana where they used very strong words about Islam and its Prophet, so much so that Akbar had to give them mild warning.

Akbar twice invited Jesuit missionaries to his Court from Goa. Aquaviva came there in 1583 for the first time.[38] The Fathers hoped that they had discovered the Second Constantine in the Mughal Emperor, for in their zeal and bigotry they could not properly understand him and failed to notice the varied appeals to which he equally responded. As the Hindus and Muslims had freedom of religious practices Christians were also given the same rights and equal opportunities.

In 1603, a farman was issued permitting the Christians the right to preach, make converts and built churches in his empire. The freedom of conversion was never discouraged. A lot of Muslims freely converted to Hinduism and Christianity. Even three sons of Akbar's younger son Daniyal were christened, although this had been a political ruse, disqualify the boys from contending for the (Muslim) throne and they soon reverted to Islam. Mulla Shah Ahmad, a Shia, is known to have made some converts to his way of thinking.[39] The permission to make converts was a very great concession to the members of other faiths. These liberal policies of Akbar permitted his Muslim and non-Muslim subjects to live together in peace without any fear of their religious activities being checked.

Promotion of Jainism

Akbar invited and in 1582 received a Jaina delegation as well which consisted of Heera Vijaya Suri, Bhanuchandra Upadhyaya and Vijayasena Suri. Jainism, with its doctrine of non-violence, made a profound impression on him and influenced his personal life. He curtailed his food and drink and ultimately abstained from flesh diet altogether for nine months in the year. He renounced hunting which was his favourite pastime, restricted the practice of fishing and released prisoners and caged birds. Slaughter of animals was prohibited on certain days and ultimately in 1587 for about halt the days in the year.[40]

Persecution of Muslims

If Badauni and the Jesuit Fathers may be believed, Akbar subjected Islam to a severe persecution. At any rate, his conduct was such as to produce a widespread belief that he pulled down the turrets of mosques converting them into stables and storerooms, destroyed Quram and scandalized good Mohammadans by boar-fights and enamelled boar-tusks. Being Muslim Akbar's negligence of Islamic Theology (Sharia), religious toleration, promotion of almost all faiths under his rule, celebration of the Hindu festivals also made him convict of Muslim persecution. The Bengal rebellion of 1580 which began with the slogan of Islam in danger suggests the former. It is certain that Akbar must have received the greatest opposition to his religious beliefs from the orthodox Muslims. This affected to a certain extent the emperor's feeling towards them.

There has always been much discussion regarding the question of Akbar's persecution of the Muslims. V.A. Smith opines that Akbar showed bitter hostility to the faith of his fathers and his own youth and actually perpetrated a persecution of Islam.[41] Sir Wolsley Haig says that in the latter part of his life Akbar persecuted its followers and destroyed its places of worship.[42] Edwardes & Garrett says:[43]

> "Close observation of Akbar's religious policy indicates that his toleration was not equally shown towards all ...

> undue severity was shown to everything Muhammadan. People were not allowed to give the name of Muhammad to their children. The study of Arabic was discouraged. The practice of shaving the beard was introduced. The Muslim era was changed for a solar year. The custom of prostration before the King was also introduced, to the disgust of orthodox Muslims. No new mosques were built and the old ones were not repaired. Akbar's mode of life, on the whole, ceased to be that of a Muslim and constantly approached the Hindu ideal of *dharma*, as modified by himself. This intolerance towards the religion of his birth indicated the swing of his mind, to the other extreme."

These historians are based on two sets of authorities, the orthodox Badauni and his followers and the Jesuit missionaries who came to convert Akbar to their faith. Akbar's personal practices might have become objectionable but they do not and cannot prove that he persecuted Islam. The objectionable practices as alleged by Badauni and other historians are as follows:[44]

(i) Akbar made the wearing of silk dresses and ornaments obligatory at prayer times.
(ii) He forbade Islamic prayers.
(iii) He discontinued public prayers and the call to prayers in the Assembly Hall.
(iv) He forbade Muslim fasts.
(v) Pilgrimages to Mecca were stopped. Any one even mentioning the subject in 1595-96 (1004 AH) received capital punishment.
(vi) Muslim festivals were discontinued.
(vii) Akbar changed some names, wherein the name of the Prophet figured, in order to avoid using it.
(viii) Mosques and prayer rooms were turned into stables and given to Hindu *chaukidars*.

(ix) Akbar, when in need of money, would even plunder mosques.
(x) Shaving of the beard was allowed with the support of the unprincipled and scheming *mullas*.
(xi) The eating of the flesh of tigers and wild boars was permitted.
(xii) The king razed to the ground the towers built for the Muslim call to prayers,
(xiii) Mosques were turned into stables and those decaying were not repaired.
(xiv) Blochmann and Low have both interpreted a passage of Badauni's implying that good men were killed in place of cows presumably by Akbar.
(xv) Another passage has been translated as stating that killers of animals on certain days were either killed or their property confiscated.
(xvi) Besides, Akbar is generally credited with the design of annulling the statutes and ordinances of Islam. Badauni refers to Islam as having died in this reign and Mulla Ahmad described it as having become old and decrepit. He further adds that under Akbar many ceremonies of the Hindus had been introduced by the King.

Badauni, the contemporary chronicler severely criticizes the religious policy of Akbar in his *Muntakhab-ut-Twarikh* and proves through his writings that the policies of Akbar were anti-Muslim and anti-Islamic. Some other historians based on the contemporary record also opine the same but these charges are full of exaggerations.

Religious Beliefs of Akbar

Over the belief and activities of Akbar his reign may be divided into two parts, i.e. 1556-74 and 1574-1605. In the beginning of his rule and until the year of Abul Fazl's arrival in Akbar's court in 1574, Akbar had been a good Muslim, making pilgrimages and circumambulating the tombs of saints. The second period of his reign (1574-1605) is chiefly memorable for its peaceful triumphs, religious toleration and un-Islanmic activities and practices. The influence of Abul Fazl seems to have confirmed Akbar's disposition and to have stimulated definite inquiry.

During the first eighteen years of his rule Akbar was very religious and every year he bowed at the tomb of Shaikh Moinuddin Chishti at Ajmer, the holiest of Muslim shrines in India. As soon as the one dear wish of his heart, birth of Prince Salim, was accomplished, he vowed in all solemnity to make a pilgrimage on foot to that sacred spot in Ajmer. Repeatedly he visited and sojourned for weeks with Shaikh Salim Chishti at Fatehpur Sikri, the most renowned of contemporary Muslim sages in India. Shaikh Salim Chishti also raise his voice in prayer for an heir to the throne. In April 1572, died the venerable Shaikh Salim Chishti and over his remains rose a mausoleum which ranks among the finest pieces of Indian architecture. In his later years, Akbar belief was drained away from basic tenets of Islam or it was rather confusing that what the religioun or belief Akbar was practising.

Akbar's beliefs, views and policies regarding institutional religions evolved throughout his lifetime, swinging from one position to another in ways that puzzled or shocked contemporary observers. It was due to Akbar's problem that how to reconcile imperial and religious authority and perhaps, ultimately, how best to articulate his own sovereign identity. Several issues were now forcing a break with Sunni opinion. One of these was his multiple marriages, for which his Muslim jurists believed there was no legal basis. A particularly bitter controversy arose when one of his judges ordered the execution of a Brahman who had allegedly cursed the Prophet of Islam. Akbar was infuriated when he heard of this, especially when advised that Muslim rulers were legally obliged to protect their non-Muslim subjects, even if they committed the act of which the Brahman was accused. In response, the emperor exiled the judge to Mecca.

Both in his own day and in modern times he has been called everything from a strict Muslim to an apostate, from a free-thinker to a crypto-Hindu, from a Zoroastrian to a proto-Christian, from an atheist to a radical innovator, even a prophet. Each of these assessments contains a degree of truth, depending on which phase of his long forty-nine-year reign one considers. Akbar's history of religious beliefs may properly be divided into three parts:[45]

1. As a youth, Akbar had received a sound religious training by both Shi'i and Sunni tutors. Up to the year 1575 he was an acknowledged Musalman of the Sunni sect, regular in prayers, a zealous builder of mosques and a constant pilgrim to the tombs of the saints, particularly that of the saint at Ajmer.
2. For three years, from 1575-78, he was engaged in listening to the doctrines of Islam as expounded by orthodox teachers. Their constant quarrels convinced him that the law was not indubitable since there were so many differences between the doctors themselves. Instead of unity in the creed of Islam, he found a number of divisions. Abul Fazl, who had been introduced to him in 1574 by his elder brother Faizi, took a subordinate part in these discussions.
3. Emperor, who was acknowledged a just ruler, was given the title of "Imam-i-Adil" (a just leader).

Akbar had early come into contact with Sufi literature and thoughts: Hafiz and Rumi were read to him and he maintained this contact in advanced years. According to Abul Fazl, as early as 1557, when Akbar was barely fifteen, during the siege of Mankot he had experienced religious ecstasy when suddenly he broke away from the camp into a distance where he spent many hours in solitary meditation. Seventeen years later as he would often listen to Mir Sharif reading books on spiritual lore, tears would roll down his eyes. Badauni tells us that he passed whole nights in praise of God and "would sit many a morning alone in prayer and meditation on a large flat stone in a lonely spot". In his eager search for truth, Akbar imbibed a passionate love for philosophical discussions and only the pressure of duties forced him to abstain from them and "return from the errancy into the infinite". In the liberal Shaikh Mubarak and his two sons, particularly Abul Fazl, "the king's Jonathan", as the Jesuits call him, Akbar found his true spiritual companions.[46]

A mystic as well as a rationalist, Akbar was sincerely religious and an earnest seeker after truth. From early youth he was fond of the society of *fakirs* and *yogis*. Ever since 1562 to 1579 he made annual pilgrimages to the shrine of the founder of the Chishti Sufi tradition in India, Shaikh Moinuddin Chishti, located in Ajmer, 350 km west of Fatehpur Sikri. Some of those visits he made by foot across the scorching sands of Rajasthan. Around 1571, Akbar fell under the influence of the Spanish-Arab mystic Ibn al-Arabi, whose pantheistic doctrines seem to have led him to reject the narrow, scripturalist understandings of Islam as promoted by his own state-supported clerics. His commitment to the more liberal-minded Chishti school of Sufism also deepened. By 1577 he was practising arduous physical austerities unique to the Chishti order.[47]

Akbar was also fond of visiting the holy shrines in India due to his Islamic religious beliefs. He prayed fervently at the shrines of Ajmer and Delhi for an heir to his throne. He now approached the venerable Shaikh Salim Chishti who lived at Sikri, 23 miles to the west of Agra and was assured by him of the early fulfilment of his prayers. Early in 1569 the daughter of Raja Bhar Mal was found to be with child and she was sent to the Shaikh's hermitage at Sikri where, on 30 August 1569, she gave birth to a son who was named Salim in honour of the saint. In the course of a few years the royal nursery was enriched by new arrivals in succession: in November 1569, a daughter was born to him and on 7 June 1570, Prince Murad saw the light. Two years after, on 10 September 1572, was born a third son at Ajmer in the house of Shaikh Daniyal whom he named after the saint. Two daughters also were born after Daniyal. These three sons of Akbar all attained mature age.[48]

After Salim's birth and in pursuance of a vow, Akbar set out on foot on pilgrimage to Ajmer on 20 January 1570, to offer thanks for the birth of Salim. From Ajmer he returned to Delhi where he inspected the splendid mausoleum of his father which had been recently built. In September 1570, he set out again on pilgrimage to Ajmer where he repaired and enlarged the fortifications and began construction of buildings for himself and his nobles. On 3 November 1570, he left for Nagaur where he stayed a few months and received the homage of the Rajput states of Jodhpur, Bikaner and Jaisalmer as well as that discrowned fugitive Baz Bahadur of Malwa. From Nagaur he arrived at Pak Pattan in the Punjab to visit the shrine of Shaikh Fariduddin Ganj-i-Shakar in March 1571. From there he returned to Ajmer by way of Hissar and on 9 August 1571, arrived at Sikri which he now decided to make his capital as the auspicious place where his two sons Salim and Murad had been born. Sikri, which was named Fathpur after the conquest of Gujarat, remained the capital of Akbar's empire.[49]

Shaikh Mubarak, the father of Abul Fazl and Faizi, was meanwhile preparing the ground for the great step which he took in 1579. In that year the Shaikh introduced one evening in the discussions of the Ibadat Khana (the house of worship), a building specially used by Akbar for these meetings, a subject which led to along debate. His theme was that aking should be regarded not only as a temporal but also as the spiritual guide of his subjects. This doctrine struck at the fundamental principle of Islam, according to which the Quran is the highest authority. The orthodox doctors of religion, who had differed widely from one another during the past three years, could not wholly oppose this doctrine. A compromise was therefore, arrived at. A document was drawn up, in which the Emperor, who was acknowledged a just ruler, was given the title of "Imam-i-Adil" (a just leader). While the *ulama* were pacified by the insertion of a proviso that the Emperor Akbar should not alter the laws of Islam, the effect of the document was to constitute Akbar the supreme interpreter of those laws.

In May 1578, in the midst of a hunting expedition in the Punjab, Emperor Akbar suddenly fell unconscious, which his friend and adviser Abul Fazl attributed to some spiritual experience. Upon recovery, he halted the hunt and freed the animals that had been caught by the beaters. At about the same time he adopted a vegetarian diet and shortened his hair in the manner of religious ascetics. About a month after the hunting incident, informed that his ancestor Timur had occasionally read the Friday sermon in the Samarqand mosque, Akbar mounted the pulpit of Fatehpur Sikri's royal mosque and began to do the same. In the midst of the sermon, however, he suddenly broke into a fit of stammering and trembling. Unable to continue, he stepped down and handed over the duties to a cleric.[50]

The result of this was important and marks a turning-point in the life and reign of Akbar. Sages and learned men of all creeds began to be invited to the court. Akbar had definitely become estranged from orthodox Islam. The creed of his birth could no longer satisfy his enquiring spirit; and contact as well as acquaintance with diverse creeds made him a confirmed eclectic. The influence of the Hindu wives of his household had been strengthened by the Brahmans, particularly Devi and Purushottam, who participated in the debates of the Ibadat Khana and instructed the emperor in the secrets of Hinduism. Akbar was converted to belief in transmigration. He gave private interviews to several Hindu *yogis* from whom he made enquiries about the secrets and spiritual questions regarding Hinduism. Perfect toleration was openly established, so far as other religions were concerned, but orthodox Muslims were humiliated. The Emperor once displaced the regular preacher at Fathpur Sikri and himself mounting the pulpit recited verses composed by Faizi.

In early 1581, during that march to Afghanistan against his brother Mirza Hakim, Akbar's religious thinking made another sharp turn. When his army reached Peshawar, at the base of the Khyber Pass, he assured the son of Shaikh Bayazid, founder of the militant illuminationist Roshaniyya cult in eastern Afghanistan, that he was perfectly free to practise his religion. Yet Akbar was still seen publicly offering prayers in a mosque in the Khyber Pass and he still maintained his white tent where he supposedly performed his prayers in private. But on the return trip, after having driven his brother out of Kabul and reasserted his authority there, the white tent was nowhere to be seen. Akbar confided to Father Monserrate that he was not a Muslim, adding that he would allow his sons to follow whatever religion they might choose. Upon returning to his capital, Akbar once again overhauled his sovereign identity, combining a saintly and a messianic persona in ways that recall what Iran's Shah Ismail had done earlier in the century.[51]

Akbar's religious policy had resulted in fraternization of the learned in the two communities; as they were drawn together, their angularities were rubbed off, their hatred of each other decreased. The Hindus came to consider the Muslims less of a defiling influence, when they met them on terms of equality in the private audience-chamber, on the battlefield and in the administrative secretariat. The Muslims ceased to think of the Hindus as an offence against their religion when they stood shoulder to shoulder with them in the great enterprise of governing India.

Akbar's policy of toleration and promotion of Hindu and Christian ideology created confusion about the belief or religion of Akbar. From many centuries it was the long heated controversy among the medieval history scholars. Some scholars say Akbar as heretic, Hindu, Christian and some as unbeliever. In many cases it could be seen that Akbar adopted toleration towards all religions and communities. He also defended some practices of many religions and also criticized certain practices which were seemed illogical for him. These attitudes of Akbar created a confusion that what was his belief and which religion he followed. Emperor Akbar in certain spheres without abandoning his policy of toleration he preserved his liberty of action by refusing to be guided in all matters by the opinions of his theologians.

Other than the toleration with all religions of India, the infallibility decree of Akbar and promulgation of his Divine Faith Tauhid-i-Ilahi were also main reasons of controversy regarding the religious beliefs of Akbar. His Hindu promoting policies, Badauni's account and Jesuit Fathers' remarks further make Akbar religiously controversial. Vincent Smith is definite in his opinion that after 1582 Akbar ceased to be a Muslim. He holds Akbar, therefore, guilty of still another sin, hypocrisy. Akbar was not a Muslim presumably because he was not practising certain rites. The Jesuit Fathers' letters were full of emphatic declaration that at the time of the First Mission Akbar was not a Muslim. The entire above thesis make the Emperor as an unbeliever.[52]

Emperor Akbar is also accused of having violated the Islamic law because from 1591-92 (1000 AH) onwards. Akbar shaved his beard. He kept dogs and pigs in the palace yard and inspected them every morning. He discontinued keeping fasts. He gave up going to public prayers. Akbar laid aside "the Resurrection and Judgement and other details and traditions of which the Prophet was the repository". He ceased to believe in the evil spirits, angels, invisible beings, the Prophet's method of receiving revelation and miracles and the authority of the Prophets and the *imam*. He is further accused of acknowledging "reason to be the basis of all religion" and of possessing "a spirit of inquiry opposed to every principle". All doctrines of Islam, Akbar is said to have set down as "senseless". It has been asserted that Akbar examined some accounts of the Prophet's life and refused to believe certain incidents as related therein. Badauni's also specifies that till 1578-

79 (986 AH), Akbar was an earnest seeker after truth. But on account of the quarrels of the *mullas* themselves, "doubt was heaped upon doubt so that after five or six years (1584-85) not a trace of Islam was left in him".[53]

Akbar's pluralism is also reflected in the impact Zoroastrianism had on him. Emperor Akbar violated Muslim commandments he kept a perpetual fire burning and as he sat in the *jharokha Darshan* (the Salutation Balcony). In 1578, the Zoroastrian scholar Dastur Meherji declared to Akbar the specialties of this Parsee religion. Consequentially, from 1580 onwards Akbar began to worship the sun and fire before his subjects and his courtiers began standing up in respect on the lighting of the evening lights. He kept muttering 1,000 and more names of the sun which had been particularly strung together in Sanskrit verse for his special benefit. He had a peculiar regard for the sun and fire and had Zoroastrian priests brought to the court and explain the mysteries of their religion.

The Hindu scholars as well had been instructing him in their own mysterious ways and in his own fashion he had been learning from their teachings what he could. Badauni and men of his way of thinking had spread the vindication that Akbar ceased to be a Muslim. The orthodox Muslims spread tales of his straying from the true path throughout the empire. The courts of the independent kings in the Deccan rang with rumours of his apostasy. Even in Persia, Kabul and Turan these stories were often told.[54]

Some scholars opine that the policies of Akbar grew out of his pluralistic mind than his adherence to any particular religion. One Portuguese Jesuit of the group that Akbar had invited to teach him of Christianity when he was in search of truth reported that the Emperor was not a Muslim. The Jesuit also reported that Akbar had found Christianity more interesting than all other religions and that he was close to conversion. He said that there were some in the court who argued that Akbar was a Hindu who worshipped the sun; some believed that he was a Christian and others that he was starting a whole new religion (Din-i-Ilahi) himself. The Jesuit reporter said that there were differences of opinion even among the subjects: some said he was a Muslim; some, Christian; others, Hindu. The wiser men of understanding, the Jesuit continued, believe that he was neither a Muslim, a Hindu, nor a Christian; and that they only considered him a Muslim who was outwardly interested in gaining the approval of all religions.[55]

Ashirvadi Lal Srivastava considers Akbar to be a true rationalist who carried on his investigation into truth in a scientific spirit by which he concluded that sensible men and abstemious thinkers could be found in all religions and that if some true knowledge was thus everywhere to be found, why should truth be confined to one religion or creed like Islam which was comparatively new and scarcely thousand years old. Once the Emperor confesses that he is no longer a Muslim. He ignored revelation and rejected the Islamic doctrines of Resurrection and Judgement. He believed in the doctrine of transmigration of souls and in the worship of the sun which Islam does not admit.[56]

But in his letter to the Sharifs of Mecca, written not long before 1582 and in his two letters written in 1586 to 'Abdullah Khan, ruler of Bukhara, Akbar maintains that he is not only a good Muslim but a champion of Islam: he was not prepared to risk his empire for the sake of his personal religion. There was a tradition also that Akbar died a Muslim as Sir Thomas Roe states. The Jesuit writers record the truth when they say: Among the people there are various opinions regarding the emperor; some holding him to be a Christian, others a heathen, others a Mohammadan. The more intelligent however consider him to be neither Christian nor heathen nor Mohammadan and hold this to be the truest. Akbar went very far with Hinduism and Jainism as well as with Zoroastrianism and Christianity but everywhere he "stopped upon the threshold". In reality Akbar was born a Muslim but died, as he had lived, an eclectic.[57] On the basis of such rational attempts to understand truth, Akbar took to study of different religions and absorbed several ideas from them.

However, on the contrary of above thesis there are many other evidences which prove that Akbar was a Muslim. Du Jarric's account mentions that Akbar held many disputations with the Fathers of the First Mission in defence of Islam. When the *mullas* could not defend the Muslim conception of paradise, Akbar came to their help and tried to defend it. Similarly, he so earnestly tried to defend his *mullas* on another occasion that the Fathers were reluctantly compelled to conclude that they had no chance whatever of converting him to Christianity. Botelho writing in 1648-54 declared that "in spite of discussions the king remained as much a Moor as before". Peruschi writing in 1595 no doubt mentions rumours current about Akbar's religious beliefs. He comes to the conclusion that the more intelligent think him to be a Mohammadan who outwardly conforms to all religions in order to obtain popularity. Akbar's letter written in 1582 to the philosophers of Europe and entrusted to Monserrate speaks of the Prophet with all respect.[58]

Despite all the heretical charges recorded by Badauni, his belief in the Prophet remained unshaken and any one insulting the Prophet in his dominions was sure of having a dagger plunged in his breast even in 1598. He cautioned even the Christian Fathers of the first mission to take care not to slander the Prophet. The *Akbarnama* mentions the Prophet with all respect; Faizi's *Nal-o-Daman* presented to Akbar in 1595 contains a section on the Prophet's praise. Akbar's made his assertion in his letters to 'Abdulla Khan that he was a sound Muslim and a follower of the Prophet as well.[59]

These studies and discussions on religions of various hues confirmed the growing eclecticism of the emperor who, as Badauni points out, found truth in all religions and realized that it was not the monopoly of Islam. The idea gained ground among the people that "Akbar was the Sihib-i-Zamain who would remove all differences of opinion among the seventy-two sects of Islam and the Hindus." Above all there might be some liberality in following the religion Islam and granting concessions to the non-believers in his empire but as far as his personal leaning were concerned Akbar was a Muslim believing the basic tenets of Islam.

Appointment of Hindu Officers

Emperor Akbar abolished the humiliating distinctions between his Hindu and Muslim subjects. If a man served him well, it mattered little to him to what religion he belonged. This was the principle which underlay his inclination towards the Rajputs. This was the principle on which he married the Princesses of Jaipur and Marwar. This was the policy which allowed him to bestow honours upon men, irrespective of sectarian considerations.

By offering lenient terms to the conquered, by allowing them, in the case of Rajputs, to retain their territories as a fief from the Imperial government and by other generous measures, he made it easier for his opponents to submit to such a magnanimous foe. Romila Thapar pointed out that Akbar won the allegiance of the Rajputs, the most belligerent Hindus, by a shrewd blend of tolerance, generosity and force; he himself married two Rajput princesses. Rajput princes were given high government ranks and by 1583 all Rajput states had accepted Akbar as ruler.[60]

Akbar started appointing the Hindus on higher posts as they were fit for. Out of 137 *mansabdars* of 1,000 and above, 14 were Hindus at the time *Ain-i-Akbari* was completed. Out of 415 *mansabdars* of 200 or above, 51 were Hindus. Out of 415 *mansabdars* of the rank of 500 horses or above, 56 were Hindus. Todar Mal became Akbar's finance minister and for sometimes his prime minister as well. Man Singh, Bhagwan Das, Raj Singh and Todar Mal served at various times as governors of provinces. Raja Rai Sigh of Bikaner was another most trusted Rajput *mansabdar* of Akbar.[61]

In 1582, Akbar divided the work of the government into several departments. In all, forty-six public servants at the centre were appointed to look after the various affairs of the state. Out of these nine (Raja Todar Mal, Rai Shal, Rai Durga, Rai Surjan, Jagan Nath,

Lun Karan, Asakaran, Jagmall and Birbal) were Hindus. In 1586 Akbar appointed two joint governors, one *diwan* and one *bakshi* for every one of the twelve provinces of the empire. Of these, two *diwans* (Todar Mal, the Imperial *diwan* and Diwan of Lahore and Rao Pitri Das, Diwan of Bihar) were Hindus, besides nine *bakshi* (Tara Chand of Oudh) and six joint governors (Raja Jagan Nath and Rai Durga of Ajmer, Raja Asakaran in Agra, Raja Man Singh in Kabul, Raja Bhagwan Das and Rao Rai Singh in Lahore).[62]

Sri Ram Sharma says that the percentage of Hindu officers in Akbar's army was higher than the percentage of Indian officers holding the kings' commissions in the army in India before Second World War. Against four governors in Akbar's reign of half a century, there was only one Indian governor in India during a century and a half of the British rule till 1937. No one in British India ever rose to the high rank which Todar Mal held as the Vicegerent and finance minister. Of the twelve provincial finance ministers appointed in 1594-95, eight were Hindus. During Akbar's reign the Hindus, who ran the lower sections of the accounts and the revenue departments of the empire were promoted to higher ranks in the administration. Further, Akbar devised another channel for the utilization of the administrative talents of the Hindus. Akbar set up new courts under Brahman judges to decide Hindu cases under Hindu law.[63]

During the time of Akbar, there was no discrimination between Hindus and Muslims, regarded Hindus as his subjects, not the infidel. From the very beginning, Akbar had a Hindu impact on his mind as he was sheltered by a Hindu king of Amarkot when he had to flee from a powerful Muslim enemy. He married the daughter of the *raja* of Amber Bhar Mal and brought the *raja*, his son Bhagwan Das and the grandson Man Singh into the Mughal hierarchy as *amirs* (noble), his most trusted lieutenants, allowing them to retain their land, their Hinduism and their caste status. Besides them, another jewel of his court was Raja Birbal, a Brahman by caste. He was the only Hindu who joined Akbar's Divine Faith Tauhid-i-Ilahi.[64]

Another Hindu jewel of his court was Raja Todar Mal, a Kshatriya by caste. He was a leading general, finance minister and also the prime minister. It must not be forgotten that the same Todar Mal was a staunch Hindu and a devotee of Lord Krishna. He was famous for setting the image of Krishna and in 1572 and had gathered a group of Varanasi scholars to compose a giant Sanskrit compendium of Hindu culture and learning, the Todar-Ananda (Todar Bliss). In this gathering, Todal Mal openly criticized, in general, the "aliens" (*mlecchas*, surely meaning the Muslims) and in particular the rulers of darkness (*tamas*, possibly meaning his patron Akbar).[65]

Whenever there was any harm to the Hindus by the royal forces, Akbar always apologized and duly compensated. During the royal campaign under Raja Birbal to the Nagarkot near Kangra, the soldiers slaughtered 200 cows and many Hindus and also damaged the temple. Akbar compensated it by repairing the temple and sending golden umbrella to cover the idol. On another occasion, Akbar ordered the reconstruction of the Hindu temple in Kurukshetra when it had been demolished and a mosque built on its debris. This was perhaps the unique example under Muslim rule when a mosque was destroyed and the temple was built over it. Due to his pro-Hindu policies, Akbar was equated with Lord Rama in some of the bardic traditions of Rajasthan.[66]

Harbans Mukhia writes that a Persian-language text composed in 1025 H/CE 1614, less than a decade after Akbar's death, records the written instruction sent by Akbar to his son Danial, after appointing him Governor of the Deccan and Khandesh in 1601, that "he should demolish the Jama mosque at Asir and raise a temple along with the pattern of the Hindus and Kafirs on its site". The prince, though, wisely sidestepped the implementation of the order.[67]

Burning of the widows in the Hindu society greatly annoyed his mind and on the consultation of the Brahmans and his Hindu courtiers, he practically banned the forced *sati* system which was actually a murder and highest level of gender discrimination.

Akbar was much careful even to his meanest subjects such as beggars. An attempt was made by him to deal with the beggar by setting apart three colonies for beggars where arrangements were made to maintain them by the royal charity. Khair Pura for the Muslims, Dharm Pura for the Hindus and Jogi Pura for the Hindu *jogis* were the main organized centres. He always primarily looked at the interest of the Hindus more than his forefathers. Akbar died in the Fort at Agra on 13 October 1605, in the fifty-first year of his reign, aged 63. He was buried at Sikandra, in the mausoleum commenced by himself and finished by his son and successor, Jahangir.

Translation of Hindu Scriptures

Emperor Akbar tried to break through the barriers which were keeping the two communities apart. He organized a department of translation for the translation of Hindu texts into the Persian language, towards building a common ground for unity between the two cultures. He ordered that the *Atharvaveda*, the *Mahabharata*, the *Harivansa* and the *Ramayana* be translated into Persian. Badauni in *Muntakhib-ut-Twarikh* tells us that several of *Atharvaveda*'s precepts resemble the laws of Islam. He further says that several Brahmans became Muslim because they found in the *Atharvaveda* many passages which were contrary to current Hindu beliefs.[68]

Akbar also ordered for translation of many Sanskrit Hindu religious books including *Ramayana* and *Mahabharata* which promoted the liberalism and tied the Hindu Muslim knot closer. In the reign of Akbar, all the Hindus were fairly treated in the court, in the appointment, in the beneficiary policies of the government and opportunities of the state. There is no trace of a single event which shows that there had been any discrimination in providing justice from top to bottom.

Building and Architecture

Like his son and grandson, Akbar was a great builder and at this date he initiated a number of schemes, the earliest of which was a country retreat near Agra, to which he gave the name of Amanabad. Like nearly all Mughal buildings, it was surrounded by beautiful gardens. This earliest work has disappeared, but part of his next work stands today (the great fort at Agra). This was begun in 1565 and took some fifteen years to complete. Akbar employed nearly 1,500 stonecutters at Agra. Most of it was pulled down by Shah Jahan, but parts of Akbar's building still remain. Fatehpur Sikri Fort and Buland Darwaza were another marvelous important building works of Emperor Akbar. The building of the city took about fourteen years and it continued to be Akbar's capital till 1585. If he had not been succeeded by two kings with a passion for architecture, like Jahangir and especially Shah Jahan, Akbar would have been famous as a builder also.

Akbar adopted Indian style of architecture in almost all his buildings, particularly, Rajput and Jaina style in building the forts and other similar buildings in all over his dominion. The eclectic architecture of Fatehpur Sikri combined Persian with Hindu and Jaina forms. Akbar permitted Man Singh to erect several temples in Vrindavana, built of red sandstone, the material usually reserved for Mughal official architecture. These Hindu temples also had many Mughal architectural features.[69]

Temple Building

Emperor Akbar ordered the building of numerous public temples in the famous places of Hindu pilgrimage. The *raja*s made most of their opportunities and built temples dedicated to their favourite gods. During the reign of Akbar the land of Braj including Vrindavana and Mathura were considered as the place Krishna worship. Akbar had granted land of Braj to Raja Man Singh who patronized and constructed major monument in this region. Man Singh built Govinda Deva Temple in Vrindavana at a cost of half a milion rupees. Akbar instituted a grant that maintained the Govinda Deva Temple at Vrindavana.

Govinda Deva Temple in Vrindavana was dedicated to Krishna and completed in 1590, this was the largest Hindu structure built in north India since the thirteenth century. Its long barrel vault, dome, squinches, cross-vaulting and intersecting arcuated corridors not only employ distinctly Persian architectural features, but create a sense of open space not previously seen in Mughal architecture. At the same time, by patronizing the construction of this temple, Man Singh was acting like a traditional Hindu king, even though he had no administrative or juridical authority in Vrindavana, since both taxation and justice were handled by local Mughal officials. Man Singh also built another famous temple at Benares same as Vrindavana at the cost half million rupees. These temples were so beautiful and fortunately they were built in the service of Islam. A Christian church was built at Agra, another at Lahore, while permission build churches at Cambay and Thatta was also sought and given. Several Jaina temples seem to have been built at Satrunjaya and Ujjain.[70]

Local tradition credits Akbar with the presentation of a golden umbrella to the shrine of the fire Goddess of Jwalamukhi in the modern district of Kangra in the Himachal Pradesh. Bhavani's temple below the Kangra Fort which had been desecrated by the imperial soldiers in 1572-73 and the idol carried away was allowed to be repaired and the idol restored to its place of honour. Akbar allowed the Hindus of Thanesar to rebuild the temple in the sacred tank at Kurukshetra which had been demolished earlier by Muslim zealots who had built a mosque at the site. Similarly he had the temple at Achal Makani near Batala rebuilt after the Muslim *fakirs* had demolished it during a fight with the *sannyasis* there. The permission to build temples and churches implied toleration of public worship after the Hindu and the Christian fashion.[71]

Religious Rebellion against Akbar

In August 1579 Akbar issued an order proclaiming his own ultimate authority in interpreting all matters pertaining to Islam, adopting for himself such grandiose titles as "commander of the faithful", "shadow of God" and "king of Islam". For many of his Muslim subjects this was simply too much. In 1580, with rumours of

Akbar's religious excesses circulating throughout the realm, one disgruntled cleric urged the emperor's half-brother Mirza Hakim in Kabul to seize the throne, which triggered the emperor's long and eventful expedition to the north-west frontier. Akbar's religious policy and his religious beliefs caused a most alarming rebellion which rose almost simultaneously from three quarters: Bengal, Kabul and Gujarat.

The Bengal revolt came first and it was the most serious of the three. It was primarily and in reality a a challenge of aristocratic force against centralized government but the Bengal rebellion assumed a cloak in which it appeared as a conflict between orthodox Islam and Akbar's heterodoxy. The rebellion obtained support from the Afghan chieftains of Bengal who regarded Mughal occupation as nothing but usurpation. The rebellion did not remain confined to Bengal; it spread like infection to Bihar, Orissa, Ghazipur, Benares, Allahabad, Awadh and Katehr (Rohilkhand).[72]

The Bengal officers openly raised the standard of revolt on 28 January 1580 and raised Mirza Hakim to the throne. Mulla Mohammad Yazdi, issued a decree enjoining on all Muslims to rise in revolt against the crowned infidel of Fathpur Sikri who had assumed the title of *imam*. Thus the rebellion of the malcontent party of Bihar and Bengal assumed the garb of a struggle between Islam in danger and heresy in triumph. The Bengal mutineers crossed the Ganga at Rajmahal and joined with the Bihar rebel force at Teliyagarhi where they defeated and captured Muzaffar in Tanda and put him to death. The *khutba* was recited in the name of Mohammad Hakim and Baba Khan Qaqshal was appointed viceroy of Bengal. Bengal and Bihar were lost to the empire.[73]

Imperial army under Todar Mal met the rebels at Monghyr and defeated but on arrival of fresh reinforcement under Khan Azam raised the siege and forced the rebels to flight. The imperialist force recovered Bihar by the end of 1580. Qutla Khan Lohani, a lieutenant of Daud, defeated several Mughul officers and set up an independent principality in Orissa for the time being. Rebels were badly defeated by Shahbaz Khan in Awadh (January 1581), while

Allahabad, where the infection had spread, was recovered from the rebels under Niyabat Khan and the rebellion in Katehr was suppressed by Ain-ul-Mulk who defeated the leader Arab Bahadur. On 10 August 1581, the rebels at Kabul were defeated by imperialist army and made their triumphant entry into Kabul and drove the pretender to the hills.[74]

With the return of Shahbaz Khan to Bengal in January 1586, he won over most of the Afghans by diplomacy and thus isolated Isa Khan who was obliged to make peace. Mastim Kabuli sent his son to the emperor's court and proceeded to Mecca and the last flame of the Bengal revolt was put out in 1587.[75] The *de jure* authority of Akbar over all Bengal was acknowledged. In Kabul, until the death of Mohammad Hakim in 1585, it was the plague-spot of Akbar's Empire.

Battle of Haldighati (1578) and Rana Pratap

When Sisodiya dynasty ruler Rana Pratap (1572-97), the successor of Rana Udai Singh, became the king of Mewar (although Chittor and larger part of Mewar was in the Imperial hand), the larger part of India and almost the whole of northern India acknowledged Emperor Akbar as its sovereign and master. From Kamrup to Ahmedabad, from Kashmir to Gwalior and Khandesh, almost every square inch of territory owed allegiance to this mighty ruler Akbar. Of the Rajput rulers, the Rathors of Jodhpur and Bikaner, the Bhatis of Jaisalmer, the cachhwahas of Jaipur, the Deoras of Sarghi, the Hadas of Bundi, had all been made to feel the presence of this great ruler on the throne of Delhi. All these states except Mewar, Bundi and Sirohi confirmed their submission to the Emperor by matrimonial alliances.

In June 1573, Raja Man Singh of Amber, the topmost lieutenant of Akbar, visited Udaipur to pay respect to Rana Pratap, the head of the Rajput clans, after his ascending to the throne. Rana received Man Singh very warmly, donned the royal robes of honour and then put off Man Singh with pliant excuses. The Rana arranged a feast to be held in honour of Man Singh on the Udai

Sagar Lake. Thither all the chiefs went and Amar Singh began to do the honours of the table as the host when the time for partaking of the feast came. Man Singh wanted to have the honour of sitting at dinner with Pratap who, however, profusely excused himself on the plea that some trouble in the stomach indisposed him from the pleasure of Man Singh's company at dinner. Man Singh saw through this thinly veiled excuse and at once guessed that the marriage relations between the house of Amber and Akbar constituted the real cause of Pratap's keeping away. Man Singh rose leaving the meal untasted and replied rather curtly hinting at a probable invasion of Mewar. Rana also reported that Man Singh would always be welcome whether he came on his own account or under orders from his maternal uncle, the Emperor. After Man Singh's departure, Pratap gave orders for the purification of the site of the feast. Every dish that had been served was thrown into the tank along with the gold and silver plate that had been used. Emperor Akbar again tried to persuade Pratap and send another two deputations under Raja Bhagwan Das and Raja Todar Mal to Pratap after a gap of few months. But all persuaders returned empty-handed.[76]

After all persuasions, it was finally decided to wage war against Pratap. In April 1576, Man Singh was appointed to command the expedition against Pratap. He was ably assisted by Sayyad Hashim Barha, Sayyad Ahmad Khan Barha, Man Singh's uncle Raja Jagannath Kachhwaha, Mehtar Khan, Rai Madho Singh Kachhwaha, Ghazi Khan Badakshi, Rai Lunkaran Kachhwaha of Sambhar, Sakat Singh, a renegade brother of Pratap, etc. They marched through Mandalgarh towards Gogunda, but were opposed by Rana Pratap at Haldighati. Here, near the pass, the memorable battle was fought on 21 June 1576. Pratap also had prepared a huge army with the assistance of the Bhils and youth Rajputs. His commanders were Hakim Khan Sur, Chandavat Krishna Das, Ram Das Rathor son of Jaimal of Chittor fame, Bhim Singh, Man Singh Jhala, Man Singh Sangora, Raja Ram Shah of Gwalior, Bhama Shah, Rana Punja, Purohit Gopi Nath, Mehta Ratan Chand, etc. Badauni says that Man Singh was having a force of 5,000 and

Pratap was also having a strong force of 3,000 Rajputs besides a good number of Bhil archers.[77]

The battle raged from early morning till midday. Pratap lost the battle with a considerable loss. Gogunda fell into the Mughal hands. Both the armies met in a village Khamnor (Haldighati—the place was called Haldi because the soil was yellow like turmeric), near Goganda in 21 June 1576.[78]

On 21 June 1576 (according to some 18 June), the Rajputs under their Pathan leader and Rajput chiefs attacked the Imperial army and pushed back the Imperial line. But soon Mehtar began to beat the drum to convince the army that Emperor Akbar was himself arriving in the battlefield and once more the battle raged furiously. Rana's *mahavat* killed and he rode his famous steed Chetak. Rana also killed the *mahavat* of Man Singh and Man Singh made a blow upon Rana that led to the injury in the Chetak's leg. Raja Ram Shah saved the Rana and died along with his three sons. Ram Das and Man Singh Jhala also played important role in saving the life of Pratap. Pratap fled from the battlefield to the hills and the Imperial army won the battle. Badauni in his book *Muntakhibu't-Tawarikh* puts the number of the men engaged at 5,000 Imperialists and 3,000 Rajputs declares that 120 Imperialists and 310 Rajputs fell dead. *Akbarnama* puts the casualties on the sides of the Mughals at 160 and 500 Rajputs were reported dead.[79]

Pratap had left the battlefield earlier, his army had been routed, but Man Singh did not order a pursuit. If Rana was pursued, he would have, definitely, been captured as his horse was lame. Two Mughals chased him but in the way, Man Singh's ally Sakat Singh joined Pratap and both killed the chaser. Man Singh with his army came back to rest for the evening in their camps.[80]

The whole episode shows that Pratap was badly defeated in the battle of Haldighati, but the Rajputs forces of Mughal didn't make the pursuit. Perhaps Man Singh didn't want to kill Pratap due to his relationship but only to chastise him for the dishonour of some years before in dining hall. On the other hand, Sakat Singh the brother of Pratap and ally of Man Singh also favoured his brother Rana Pratap and saved him from the two Mughal chasers while he was fleeing. The Haldighati episode was full of treachery for Mughals and rather loyalty for Rana Pratap. Here the blood proved thicker than water. But as far as the defeat of Rana Pratap was concerned, no doubt that he was badly defeated.

Akbar regretted the escape of the Rana and even suspected loyal Man Singh of connivance. He was, however, able to establish effective Mughal authority in the southern part of Rajasthan. Sirohi was occupied, the principality of Idar was reduced to obedience and Akbar received the submission of several minor chiefs: the rulers of Banswara and Dingarpur, the latter offering the emperor the hand of his daughter. In 1577 the chief of Bundi was subdued and next year Madhukar, the Bundela chief of Orchha, who had been defying the imperial authority, surrendered and acknowledged Akbar's sovereignty.[81]

Akbar was determined to overthrow the Rana of Mewar. In October 1578, a considerable force under Shahbaz Khan was despatched against Pratap Singh. The Mughals seized Kelwira, defeated the Rajput garrison at Kumbhalgarh and captured Gogunda and Udaipur. The Rana retired to the remote fastness of Chavand and from that base began to recover his territories. Kumbhalgarh was recovered and the chiefs of Banswara and Dungarpur acknowledged the Rana's sovereignty. Shahbaz Khan made a renewed attempt at suppressing the Rana who retired to the hills, but the Mughals returned unsuccessful. Six years later another expedition was sent by Akbar under Zafar Beg and Jagannatha Kachhwaha, which met with the same fate. Before his death in 1597 the Rana had recovered all his territory except Ajmer, Chittor and Mandalgarh. In 1600, Akbar made another attempt against Mewar when the expedition led by Prince Salim and Raja Man Singh defeated Pratap's successor, Amar singh and devastated the country; but the expedition came to an abrupt end due to the recall of Man Singh whose services were urgently required in Bengal.[82]

Purushottam Nagesh Oak and the other Hindutva historians forged the facts and declared Maharana Pratap as the winner of the

Haldighati battle. Chandrashekhar Sharma, the author of *Rajasthan ka Itihas aur Sanskriti* also writes, as in the battle of Haldighati the purpose of Emperor Akbar was not solved, it was the victory of Rana Pratap.[83]

It was the purely a political affair of two Rajput *raja*s in which Man Singh wanted to chastise Pratap for his dishonour during his visit in Udaipur. From the Haldighati episodes it also becomes clear that Raja Man Sigh never wanted to finish or kill Pratap who was his near relative. When Pratap fled from the battlefield Man Singh's aim was solved and he returned to his camp. The Hindutva historians, unfortunately, brand this battle by the communal eyes and call this battle as the war of Hindus and Muslims. Although it is well known that this battle was fought between Raja Man Singh of Amber and Rana Pratap of Mewar in which Pratap was defeated by Man Singh. It is another matter that Rana Pratap was wounded, fled from the battlefield but never surrendered in his lifetime.

Purushottam Nagesh Oak mentions the fight between Rana Pratap and Akbar and says that both were sworn deadly enemies of one another. If then Rana Pratap is to be admitted as a patriotic, brave and righteous son of his soil who fought, back-to-the-wait to save Hindustan from foreign domination, does it not follow that Akbar was an alien villain who wanted to murder Rana Pratap like many others, for self-aggrandizement and for enslaving Hindustan? Oak says that after the titanic battle of Haldighati, it was Akbar who, ultimately, withdrew from the struggle while Pratap emerged triumphant and invincible though with a reduced realm.[84]

Here Purushottam Nagesh Oak proves Rana Pratap as an immortal hero and Akbar as aggressive villain whereas Akbar was the emperor of Hindustan and Rana as petty chieftain of Mewar principality. It also must be remembered that it was not a direct fight between Rana and Akbar but between Man Singh of Amber, the commander of the Imperial forces and Rana Pratap in which Rana was defeated and retired to the jungles. Oaks remark is out of the skill that how he could save the whole Hindustan by saving his own principality Mewar.

A new controversy in the Vasundhara Raje's government in Rajasthan arose when it decided to change the history of the school textbooks in 2017. The Rajasthan government decided to teach the school students that Rajput warrior Maharana Pratap defeated the decorated army of Mughal Emperor Akbar in the Battle of Haldighati in 1575. But most of the academicians ridiculed at this idea because historical evidence shows that Pratap, the ruler of the erstwhile Mewar region, was fled from the battlefield, although in the later years he continued his guerilla war against the Mughals.

The storied military campaign is among several historical events that Hindutva historians are accused of trying to rewrite as part of efforts to promote its vision of Indian culture and way of life. D.N. Jha, a former member of Indian Council of Historical Research says about the event,

> "In fact all heroes ... from Pratap to Prithviraj Chauhan ... that the RSS is projecting had lost conclusively. By twisting facts one cannot re-write history."

Irfan Habib, refused to even comment, saying it would be senseless to argue with the RSS. But Rajasthan education minister Vasudev Devnani told that students will not read "distorted history" and questioned, "If Akbar's armies won the battle then why did they return to the battlefield six times? There has been an attempt to downplay the role of our heroes." The state government is believed to have got its idea of rewriting the history of Haldighati from a book of K.S. Gupta titled *Maharana Pratap: Kumbalgarh se Chavand.*[85]

K.S. Gupta, a retired professor of history from Udaipur's Mohanlal Sukhadia University, says that his book examined contemporary Persian records, contemporary Rajasthani sources and studied the circumstances to conclude that the dominant view that Maharana Pratap lost the battle is not correct. On his thesis, most of the historians from Rajasthan disagreed. Reema Hooja, author of *History of Rajasthan* said,

> "If the Mughals lost the battle, they should have left but the fact is they never left for several years and Pratap didn't give up fighting. So if there was any winner in Haldighati, it was the Mughal army which was left standing in the battlefield".

K.G. Sharma, head of the history department at the University of Rajasthan said,

> "Initially the Rajputs were overpowering in the war but then somebody spread the rumour that Akbar himself had arrived with a large contingent. The rumour caused Maharana Pratap and his men to retreat into the hills."[86]

No doubt the Handighati's new episode was the creation of state government of Rajasthan only to glorify Rana Pratap on the cost of Emperor Akbar. The Hindutva elements wanted to pose Rana Pratap as hero and Akbar as a villain of past historical episodes. It has nothing to take with the reality and no doubt the history will not be changed by any nefarious mentality. Emperor Akbar was, as proved by the historian, so kind to his subjects irrespective of races, religion or caste.

Patron of Learning

Akbar never learned to read and write. However, it was neither the fault of Humayun nor Akbar. It was due to the situations and shortage of time that Akbar couldn't find time to study and even to play. Although Akbar was not able to read and write but he had thurst for seeking knowledge. Even his bitterest enemies were forced to admire his unquenchable thirst for knowledge, his insatiable passion for inquiry and investigation, his ceaseless search for truth, his exquisite delight in learned discussion, his unstinted patronage of merit.

It is not too much to regard him as one of the first and greatest students of comparative religion. There is nothing in history like the Ibadat Khana, the great debating hall at Fatehpur Sikri, with professors of orthodox and heterodox Islam and Hinduism, Christianity and Judaism, Jainism and Zoroastrianism, presided over by the emperor, keenly discussing theology and morality through long hours of the night. Nature had dowered Akbar with intellectual gifts of the highest order and a memory singularly retentive and accurate. Diligent, incessant exercise sharpened the natural powers which ranged over the whole field of human knowledge.

His mechanical inventions alone would make him a remarkable figure. His interest in historical truth alone would entitle him to an honourable place in historiography. He inspired Gulbadan Begam's charming *Humayun Nama*, Jauhar and Bayazid's *Memoirs*, Nizamuddin Ahmad's *Tabaqat-i-Akbari* and the *Tarikh-i-Alfi*. He was responsible for the Persian version of Babur's *Memoirs* and Kalhana's *Rajatarangini*. The *Ain-i-Akbari*, a veritable Imperial Gazetteer, was an absolutely unique administrative and statistical record till the nineteenth century. *Lilavati*, the famous Sanskrit work on mathematics, was translated into Persian. The *Ramayana*, the *Mahabharata*, the *Harivansha Purana*, the *Panchatantra*, *The Story of Raja Nala* appeared in a Persian garb. Religious literature received its fair share of attention. *Atharvaveda* was rendered into Persian. Xavier, nephew of the great St. Francis, was prevailed upon to compose a life of Christ in Persian.[87] Many other works were translated from Sanskrit, Hindi, Arabic and Greek into Persian. It is hardly needful to remark that hundreds of poets and scholars, scientists and artists, basked in the sunshine of royal favour at Fathpur Sikri and Agra.

In 1562, after the assasination of Bairam Khan, his four years' infant son Abdur Rahim was taken under royal protection and given a varied and splendid education, which, acting on his native intellectual vigour, made him one of the first minds of the age. A master of Persian, Arabic, Turkish, Sanskrit and Hindi, he was reputed to be the greatest linguist in India. Later writers gravely asserted that he could converse freely in most of the languages of the world. A vigorous prose-writer and a facile versifier, he perpetuated his name in contemporary literature. His Persian translation of Babur's memoirs was a remarkable service to the cause of historical scholarship. His Persian verses flow with natural ease and sparkle with wit and humour. His Hindi stanzas have always been prized for their elegance of diction, weight of thought and elevation of sentiment and will be read so long as the language endures. As a patron of literature, he stands at the head of the Mughal nobles. The *Maasir-i-Rahimi* has preserved the biographies and specimens of the composition of some thirty Persian versifiers who found shelter with him.[88]

Not only Abdur Rahim but many of the scholars were taught and patronized in the court of Akbar. Moreover, Akbar was a man of versatility and complexity, a genius of rare intellectual vigour and a Socratic temper. Akbar kept his children under his immediate care and imparted to their infant brains such direction and guidance as they were capable of receiving. Every prince ought to read books on morals, arithmetic, the notation peculiar to arithmetic, agriculture, mensuration, geometry, astronomy, physiognomy, household matters, the rules of government, medicine, logic, the *tabii*, *riyazi* and *ilahi* sciences and history.

Akbar's Harem

Almost all the kings and emperors maintained a large *harem* (ladies apartment) in his fort but in the Mughal reign in India Akbar was the first to maintain a large *harem* in a much organised way. Abul Fazl writes that there is, in general, great inconvenience arising from a number of women, but his majesty, out of the abundance of his wisdom and prudence, has made it subservient to public advantage; for by contracting marriages with the daughters of the princes of Hindustan and of other countries, he secures himself against insurrections at home and forms powerful alliances abroad. The *harem* was an enclosure of such immense extent as to contain a separate room for each one of the women, whose number exceeds 5,000. They are divided into companies and a proper employment is assigned to each individual. Over each of these companies a woman is appointed to rule. And one is selected for the care of the whole, in order that the affairs of the *harem* may be conducted with the same regularity as the other departments of the state.[89]

The *harem* was thus a state bureau; its chief was Maham Anaga, who had been Akbar's nurse and faithful attendant during the perivious adventures of his childhood and who was, in fact, his prime minister in the early years of his reign. Each one receives a salary equal to her merit. Abut Fazl writes that the pen cannot measure the extent of the emperor's largesses; but here shall be given some account of the monthly stipend of each. The ladies of the first quality received from Rs. 1,610 down to Rs. 1,028. Some of the principal servants had from Rs. 51 down to Rs. 20 and others were paid from Rs. 2 up to Rs. 40. Whenever any of this multitude of women wanted anything, they could apply to the treasurer. The inside of the *harem* is guarded by women and there were eunuchs, porters and military guards at different distances outside, each in a prescribed position. The equipages for journeys and encampments were as complex as a town. It must be remembered that when the emperor moved from a city, the inhabitants moved with him; merchants, families, servants and slaves. The camp was simply the city under tents.[90]

Akbar's Death

By 1601, just four years before his death, he had evidently backed off from anti-Muslim or un-Islamic measures. In fact, he seems to have resumed practising the external rites of Islam, if only to silence his conservative critics. On 3 October 1605, Akbar fell ill with dysentery and the efforts of his best physician Hakim Ali failed to cure him. The majority of nobles decided in favour of Salim. The Sayyeds of Barha supported his cause and the Rajputs of Raja Ram Das, the Kachhwaha, guarded the treasury in his interest. On 21 October when at last Salim visited his dying father, he could not speak; he made a sign asking his son to place the imperial turban on his head and gird himself with Humayun's sword. At midnight on 25-26 October the great monarch passed away and next morning his body was borne in state to the garden of Bihishtabad (Sikandra), some 6 miles from Agra, where he had commenced to build his own mausoleum.

Akbar's Critics

Like most of the rulers Akbar also had been criticised by contemporary as well as writers of the later periods but they all were prejudiced over certain state of affairs. The authority of the Jesuit Fathers is tainted because of the fact that though they were always ready to see him baptized, they never succeeded in bringing him into their fold. They took his spirit of inquiry as willingness to be converted. Accustomed to the horrors of the Inquisition, they were dazzled by the sight of a king, who allowed them full liberty of opinion. As he did not gainsay them, they thought he agreed with them. Their statements about his readiness to be converted are all an indication of their desire to see him admitted into their church and so are their statements about his having ceased to be a Muslim.[91]

The next bitter critic of Akbar was his contemporary writer Badauni who wrote *Muntakhibu't-Tawarikh.* In order to understand his criticism it is necessary to understand him first. He was an ultra-conservative in religious matters for whom the beaten path was the only path to salvation. When Akbar sent Prince Daniyal to learn Portuguese from the Fathers, Badauni distorts this to mean that he sent him to learn the elements of Christianity. Thus if Badauni describes Akbar as having founded a new faith, we should be rather cautious in accepting his word too literally. If he says that Akbar had ceased to be a Muslim, it only amounts to the fact that he ceased to be an instrument for perpetuating the fantastic distinctions between his Muslim and non-Muslim subjects.[92]

Unfortunately some writer in connivance with the Hindutva element have targeted Akbar like a ruler and branded him as a Muslim icon. A Hindutva historian Purushottam Nagesh Oak

(P.N. Oak), who had a contract of defaming Turks and Mughal rule in India, has left no ground to defame Akbar who had been branded by the contemporary historians as no more a Muslim. He asks a very layman or rather ridiculous question that when his third-generation Aurangzeb was intolerant and barbarous then how Akbar could be fare to his subjects?[93]

Oak branded Akbar as a foreigner and his invasion on Indian rulers not as the unification of India but the enslavement of India but the fact is that Akbar and his predecessors as well as ancestors spent the whole of their lives in serving the country and loved it as much as any ancient Indian ruler. Their buildings are still benefitting the country even after passing the many hundred years. Oak even puts a question mark on the kind, merciful and benevolent attitude of Akbar. Without referring Ashoka and his bloody Kalinga War, Oak gives the example for Akbar that if an invading gang of dacoit claims that it looked after the children of a village with tender filial care better than their slaughtered parents could, will any man endowed with reason pay any heed to that claim? Likewise when histories claim that Akbar who killed or conquered one Indian ruler after another did so only to lavish more loving care on the Indian people than those slaughtered or conquered Indian rulers ever could one must at once declare the claim as nonsensical.[94]

Hindutva historian P. N. Oak raises the question mark on some buildings constructed during the reign of Akbar. About the Red Fort, Oak says that it was an ancient fort built by Hindu *rajas* but it was mere speculation as he never mentions that who originally built the Red Fort. No doubt there may be a ruined fort but it was Akbar who built this fort for his new abode in Delhi, which was given final shape by Shah Jahan by using red sandstone. Oak also questions on the Humayun's Tomb which was built by Akbar in 1570 after continuous masonry work of eight or nine years. Its architect was Mirak Mirza Ghayas. Oak reiterates it as canard and says that Humayun's tomb was a Hindu palace in which Humayun was living and after his death, he was buried there. It's very much clear that Humayun was living in the Old Fort of Delhi and died after slipping from the stairs of the library building in the fort. Oaks remarks is based on the hatred and prejudices against Muslims and misguiding Hindutva conception.[95]

Surely the hundreds of such cases are there in the political and military history of India but Oak claims only Akbar as dacoit and the leader of invading gang. Such biased writings of Hindutva historians would certainly lead to the knowledge of the past to an ashtray. On the contrary of these self claimed and biased scholars like Oak, Akbar by his policies emancipated India from the domination of the religion of the minority. Akbar emancipated the state from its thraldom to the Muslim theologians in order to create a common citizenship in India.

Whatever the Hindutva historian says is only the foolish and baseless remarks miles away from the reality. If they do not spare Akbar who was a pro-Hindu ruler, it is a matter of concern that how will they treat the other rulers of India. Emperor Akbar was a kind-hearted and true lover of the Hindu-Muslim unity. His Hindu queens enjoyed the full freedom of practising their own religion. He allowed his Hindu spouses to perform their religious rites in the palace. The Hindutva historians should note that if idol worship was tolerated in the palace, it would have looked rather unreasonable to prohibit it outside. During the time of Akbar there was only one belief and only one religion that was the loyalty to the state and Emperor. Whoever, either Hindu or Muslim, raised against state and Emperor was brutally crushed and who obeyed them was rewarded and awarded.

Among the rulers of India Akbar occupies a very high place for having attempted to bring Hindus and Muslims together with some success. If he did not succeed in creating a nation, it was because of the greedy subordinate rulers and some hardliner theologians of every religion of India. His policy of inclusivism, religious tolerance and interreligious respect and endeavour towards an empire based on unity and equality led to Jawaharlal Nehru calling him the "the

Father of Indian Nationalism".[96] It can be stated that though Akbar's policies did not totally conform to all the elements of modern secularism, they contained the secular seeds of state-sanctioned religious freedom and dignity. Undoubtedly, Emperor Akbar was the first and almost the greatest experimenter in India, who may be credited for trying to create a nation by his toleration policies, unity, brotherhood and common citizenship.

Akbar, thus, came to be surrounded by Hindu influences at home which must have worn away the natural repugnance of a Muslim for Hindu practices. Under Akbar Hindu-Muslim unity and idol worship were never discouraged. It is worth remembering that at a time when Europe was plunged into strife of warring sects, when Roman Catholics were burning Protestants at the stake and Protestants wore executing Roman Catholic, Akbar guaranteed peace not only lo "warring sects" but to differing religions. He had full trust and faith in his Hindu officers and deployed them on many important battles in which Hindu and Muslims contingents fought together and celebrated the victory together. They were never having even the feeling that they belong to such and such races and religion.

Akbar's religious policies of religious freedom and religious tolerance flowed out of his syncretistic, liberal, rational and pluralistic way of looking at things. His integrative perspective prevented him from siding with any particular community and thus helped him to inculcate in his subjects a spirit of mutual respect and goodwill. The Hindus came to consider the Muslims less of a defiling influence, when they met them on terms of equality in the private audience-chamber, on the battlefield and in the administrative secretariat. The Muslims ceased to think of the Hindus as an offence against their religion when they stood shoulder to shoulder with them in the great enterprise of governing India.

Notes

1. Edwardes & Garrett, *op. cit.*, p. 22.
2. *Ibid.*, p. 23; Majumdar, *op. cit.*, p. 105.
3. Edwardes & Garrett, *op. cit.*, pp. 23-24.
4. *Ibid.*, p. 24.
5. *Ibid.*, p. 25.
6. Majumdar, *op. cit.*, pp. 107-08.
7. *Ibid.*
8. *Ibid.*
9. *Ibid.*
10. Edwardes & Garrett, *op. cit.*, pp. 25-26.
11. *Ibid.*, pp. 26-27.
12. Majumdar, *op. cit.*, p. 111.
13. Edwardes & Garrett, *op. cit.*, pp. 30-31.
14. *Ibid.*, pp. 29-30, 37 & 41. Though Akbar had several wives, none of his children so far had survived. In order to secure a son, he was in the habit of constantly visiting the shrines of famous saints at Ajmer and other places. Among others he visited Sikri, at a little distance from Agra and the residence of the holy Shaikh Salim. The latter assured the Emperor that his prayers would be heard and that he would have ason. In August 1569 this promise was fulfilled by the birth of his eldest son, who was named Salim, after the Shaikh. In the following year a second son, Murad, was also born there.
15. Sri Ram Sharma, *op. cit.*, pp. 36-37.
16. *Ibid.*
17. Majumdar, *op. cit.*, pp. 133-34.
18. H. Beveridge (1939). *The Akbarnama of Abul Fazl*, (tr. *Akbarnama* of Abul Fazl, vol. III, Calcutta, pp. 865-69. (Akbar's marriages with Hindu princesses and his relations with the Hindu *rajas* provided the means for bringing Hindu teachers of all shades of opinion to the religious discussions in the Imperial presence. These meetings were thrown open to the adherents of other religions as well. Akbar's relations with the State of Bikaner procured for him the services of Jaina minister Karam Chand. The presence of the Portuguese on the western coast enabled the emperor to request for and receive at his court three representatives of their religion. The Parsis were also invited. The discussions in the Ibadat Khana had their immediate influence outside as well. When the Hindus could dispute with

impunity with the Muslim scholars' nice points of their respective theologies in the palace, some sort of freedom of views was naturally secured outside its walls as well. Sri Ram Sharma, *op. cit.*, p. 35.)

19. Majumdar, *op. cit.*, p. 134.
20. Elliot & Dowson (1877). *History of India as Told by its Own Historians: The Mohammadan Period*, vol. VI, London, p. 190.
21. Majumdar, *op. cit.*, pp. 135-36.
22. *Ibid.*, p. 136.
23. Vidyadhar Mahajan (1979). *Muslim-Kalin Bharat*, Delhi, Part II, p. 110.
24. Sri Ram Sharma, *op. cit.*, p. 60; Oak, P. N. (2000). *Who Says Akbar Was Great*, New Delhi, pp. 36 & 37.
25. Majumdar, *op. cit.*, p. 137.
26. Sri Ram Sharma, *op. cit.*, p. 60
27. *Ibid.*
28. Wendy Doniger (2009). *The Hindus: An Alternative History*, New Delhi, p. 533. (*Allahu akbar*—God is very great. This expression is called the *takbir* (magnifying) and is often used at the commencement of undertakings. Blochmann says (p. 166n.): 'The words *allahu akbar* are ambiguous; they may mean, 'God is Great', or 'Akbar is God'. There is no doubt that Akbar liked the phrase for its ambiguity; for it was used on coins, the imperial seals and the heading of books, farmans, etc." He then translates from Badauni (II, 210) as, "It was during these days (AH 983=1575-76) that His Majesty once asked how people would like it, if he ordered the words *allahu akbar* to be cut on the imperial seal and the dies of his coins. Most said, people would like it very much. But Haji Ibrahim objected and said, the phrase had an ambiguous meaning and the Emperor might substitute the Koran verse *lazikru allahi akbaru*—To think of God is the greatest thing—because it involved no ambiguity. But His Majesty got displeased and said, it was surely sufficient that no man who felt his weakness would claim divinity; he merely looked to the sound of the words and he had never thought that a thing could be carried to such an extreme." However, it also must not be ignored that in Faizi's *diwan*, there is a long poem in praise of Akbar, every couplet of which ends with the words, *allahu akbar*. (*The Akbarnama of Abul Fazl*, vol. III, *op. cit.*, p. 1.)

29. George S.A. Ranking (1924). *Muntakhbu-t-Tawarikh,* (tr. *Muntakhbu-t-Tawarikh* of Al-Badauni, Abdul Qadir Ibn Muluk Shah), vol. II, New Delhi, p. 216.
30. Edwardes & Garrett, *op. cit.*, p. 45.
31. Sri Ram Sharma, *op. cit.*, pp. 44-45.
32. Mahajan, *op. cit.*, p. 110; Majumdar, *op. cit.*, p. 136.
33. Harbans Mukhia (2004). *The Mughals of India,* Malden, pp. 26-27.
34. Sri Ram Sharma, *op. cit.*, pp. 40-42.
35. *Ibid.*, p. 39; *The Hindus,* op. cit., p. 533.
36. Majumdar, *op. cit.*, p. 136.
37. *Ibid.*
38. *Ibid.*
39. *The Akbarnama of Abul Fazl,* vol. III, *op. cit.*, pp. 595-98; Sri Ram Sharma, *op. cit.*, pp. 42-43.
40. Majumdar, *op. cit.*, p. 136.
41. Vincent A. Smith (1917). *Akbar The Great Mogul 1542-1605,* Oxford, p. 257.
42. Edward James Rapson, Sir Wolseley Haig, Sir Richard Burn, Henry Dodwell (1962). *The Cambridge History of India: The Mughul Period,* Cambridge, p. 378.
43. Edwardes & Garrett, *op. cit.*, pp. 45-46.
44. Al-Badauni, vol. II, p. 215; Sri Ram Sharma, *op. cit.*, pp. 53-54.
45. Edwardes & Garrett, *op. cit.*, p. 43.
46. Majumdar, *op. cit.*, pp. 132-33.
47. *Ibid.*
48. *Ibid.*, pp. 123-24.
49. *Ibid.*
50. Rosalind O'Hanlon, "Kingdom, Household and Body: History, Gender and Imperial Service under Akbar", *Modern Asian Studies,* 41, No. 5 (2007), pp. 902 & 905; W.H. Lowe (1899), *Muntakhabu-t-Tawarikh* (tr. *Muntakhabu-t-Tawarikh* of Abdul Qadir Badauni), Delhi: Idarah-i-Adabiyat-i-Dehli, 1973, vol. 2, pp. 276-77.
51. John Hoyland (1922). tr., *The Commentary of Father Monserrate, S.J., on his Journey to the Court of Akbar,* London: Oxford University Press, pp. 142, 155-56 & 173.
52. Sri Ram Sharma, *op. cit.*, p. 56.
53. *Ibid.*, pp. 58-59.
54. *Ibid.*, p. 59.
55. Mahajan, *op. cit.*, p. 139.

56. Ashirbadi Lal Srivastava (n.d.), *History of India (1000-1707)*, Agra, p. 471.
57. Majumdar, *op. cit.*, p. 139.
58. Sri Ram Sharma, *op. cit.*, p. 57.
59. *Ibid.*, pp. 59-60.
60. Romila Thapar, *Akbar*, Microsoft Encarta Encyclopaedia (Microsoft Corporation, 2001).
61. Sri Ram Sharma, *op. cit.*, pp. 39-40 & 78-80; Sri Ram Sharma (1954). *Maharana Pratap*, Udaipur, pp. 25-26. (*Prominent Hindu Mansabdars of Akbar: Haft Hazari* (7,000). 1. Man Singh of Jaipur. Panj Hazari (5,000); 2. Bhagwan Das of Jaipur; 3. Bhar Mal of Jaipur, Chahar Hazari (4,000); 4. Todar Mal, Finance Minister; 5. Rai Singh of Bikaner; 6. Jagan Nath, son of Bhar Mal of Jaipur, Do Hazari (2,000); 7. Birbal; 8. Ram Chandra Baghela of Bandhav; 9. Kaiyan Mall of Bikaner; 10. Surjan of Bundi; 11. Bhao Singh; 12. Ram Das Kachhwaha; 13. Maha Singh. Yak Hazar Panj Sadi (1,500); 14. Durga Sassodia of Rampur (in Rajputana), Yak Hazar Do Sadi (1,200); 15. Rai Shal, Yak Hazari (1,000); 16. Rupsi, brother of Raja Bhar Mal; 17. Udai Singh of Jodhpur; 18. Jagmal, brother of Bhar Mal, 19. Asakarn; 20. Kalyan Das, Nav Sadi (900); 21. Pratap Singh; 22. Jagat Singh, son of Man Singh; 23. Raj Singh, son of Asakarn Kachhwaha; 24. Bhoj of Bundi, Haft Sadi (700); 25. Bihari, son of Todar Mal; 26. Rao Pitri Das; 27. Medni Pat Chohan; 28. Babu; 29. Salahadi, son of Bhar Mal, Panj Sadi (500); 30. Parmanand; 31. Jagmall; 32. Bhim of Jaisalmer; 33. Arjun Singh, son of Man Singh; 34. Sahal Singh, son of Man Singh; 35. Ram Chandra Bundela; 36. Ram Chandra of Orissa; 37. Dalpat, son of Rai Singh of Bikaner, Chahar Sadi (400); 38. Shakti Singh, son of Man Singh; 39. Manohar, son of Lun Karan; 40. Ram Chandra Kachhwaha; 41. Balaka Kachhwaha, Sih Sadi (300); 42. Bal Chandra Rathor; 43. Keshav Das, son of Jayamall; 44. Tulsi Das Yadav; 45. Krishna Das; 46. Man Singh Kachhwaha; 47. A Raja of Orissa, Do Sad Panjahi (250); 48. Jagat Singh, son of Raja Man; 49. Mathra Das Khatri; 50. Sanwal Das Yadav; 51. Mathra Das; 52. Keshav Das Rathor; 53. Udand, *zamindar* of Orissa; 54. Sundar, *zemindar* of Orissa.)
62. Sri Ram Sharma, *op. cit.*, p. 80.
63. *Ibid.*
64. *The Hindus*, *op. cit.*, p. 534.
65. *Ibid.*

66. *Ibid.*, pp. 534-35.
67. Harbans Mukhia, *op. cit.*, pp. 19-20.
68. Al-Badauni, *op. cit.*, p. 216; Sri Ram Sharma, *op. cit.*, p. 38.
69. *The Hindus, op. cit.*, p. 550.
70. Sri Ram Sharma (1992). *op. cit.*, pp. 36-37; Catherine, B. Asher, "The Architecture of Raja Man Singh: A Study of Sub-Imperial Patronage", in Barbara Stoler Miller (ed.), *The Powers of Art: Patronage in Indian Culture*, New Delhi: Oxford University Press, pp. 184-85.
71. *Ibid.*
72. Majumdar, *op. cit.*, pp. 139-40.
73. *Ibid.*, p. 40.
74. *Ibid.*
75. *Ibid.* p. 41.
76. *Maharana Pratap, op. cit.*, pp. 44-53.
77. *Ibid.*, pp. 61-67.
78. *Ibid.*, pp. 69-70.
79. *Ibid.*, pp. 71-77; *Akbarnama*, vol. III, *op. cit.*, pp. 245-47.
80. *Ibid.*, pp. 87-89.
81. Majumdar, *op. cit.*, pp. 131-32.
82. *Ibid.*
83. Sharat Kumar (25 July 2017). indiatoday.in.
84. *Who Says, op. cit.*, pp. 13 & 35.
85. *Hindustan Times*, 10 March 2017.
86. *Ibid.*
87. Beni Prasad (1940). *History of Jahangir*, Allahabad, pp. 15-16.
88. *Ibid.*, p. 18.
89. Holden, *op. cit.*, pp. 135-36.
90. *Ibid.*, p. 136.
91. Sri Ram Sharma, *op. cit.*, p. 63.
92. *Ibid.*, p. 64.
93. *Who Says, op. cit.*, p. 12.
94. *Ibid.*
95. *Ibid.*, pp. 27 & 31.
96. Laxminarayan Gupta (1973). *History of Modern Indian Culture*, Agra, p. 24.

Chapter 3

Religion and Justice Under Jahangir

Mughal Emperor Nuruddin Mohammad Salim Jahangir (1605-27) was born, after many prayers, on Wednesday, 30 August 1569, at Fatehpur Sikri to Emperor Akbar and Mariam-uz-Zamani or Harka Bai, the princess of Amber (but no chronicler mentions the Rajput name of Jahangir's mother). At that time his father Akbar had completed twenty-seven years of his age, thirteen of his reign and nine of his personal rule. After the birth of Salim, the emperor did not forget the vow he had taken in Ajmer. Leaving the capital on Friday, 20 January 1570 and walking on an average 14 miles a day, he reached Ajmer on Sunday, 5 February and straightway went to bow and pray at the shrine. The journey of 228 miles prompted by love and piety made a profound impression on contemporaries and posterity. After his return Akbar made Fatehpur Sikri his new capital on the occasion of Salim's second birthday and continued his rule at that seat from 1571-85.

The child was christened Mohammad Sultan Salim, but Akbar always addressed Salim as Shaikhu Baba. Of his three sons, Salim, Murad and Daniyal, Akbar always favoured his firstborn Salim. On 22 October 1573, the three princes were circumcised and nearly a month later began the education of Salim. It was the time-honoured Mughal custom that the princes were placed under the charge of tutors as soon as they were four years, four months and four days old. Jahangir's early education was entrusted to a famous Muslim divine, Maulana Mir Kalan Harvi and later to Shaikh Ahmad, the prince's foster-father and to Qutbuddin Mohammad Khan Atga. In 1582, Akbar put him in charge of the famous Abdur Rahim Khan-i-Khanan, son of Bairam Khan. Jahangir acquired proficiency in Persian and Turkish and became an excellent calligraphist. He also showed considerable interest in history, geography, botany, zoology and art. As was customary with the Timurid princes of those days, Prince Salim was placed in nominal charge of large detachments of the army in the important Kabul campaign of 1581, when he was only 12 years of age. In the following year, he was placed in nominal charge of the departments of justice and public celebrations.[1]

At the age of 15 in 1585, Salim was betrothed to his cousin, Man Bai, daughter of Raja Bhagwan Das of Amber. The marriage settlement was fixed at two crores of *tankas*. The Emperor himself, accompanied by all his nobles, went to the *raja*'s mansion and on 13 February 1585 celebrated the wedding in the presence of Muslim *qazis*, but with certain characteristic Hindu ceremonies. The dowry bestowed by Bhagwan Das included 100 elephants, several strings of horses, jewels, numerous and diverse golden vessels set with precious stones, utensils of gold and silver, "and all sorts of stuffs, the quantity of which is beyond all computation". The Imperial nobles were presented with Persian, Turkish and Arabian horses, with golden saddles, etc. Along with the bride were given, a number of male and female slaves, of Indian, Abyssinian and Circassian origin.[2]

Salim had created a veritable harem. Second to Man Bai, Jahangir married Jodha Bhai or Jagat Gosain daughter of Udai Singh, the Mota Raja in 1586. His third marriage was with daughter of Raja Rai Singh of Bikanir and fourth was the daughter of Said Khan Ghakhar. During the next ten years Salim married sixteen other wives of various nalionalities and religions. In these sixteen wives the most important were daughter of Jagat Singh, eldest son of Raja Man Singh and daughter of Ram Chandra Bundela. In the last but not least, Mehrunnisa, better known as Nur Jahan. The number of concubines raised to the harem of Jahangir was 300.[3]

Jahangir in his early age was influenced by his father's personality, by religious teachers of various persuasions, by Christian missions and, above all, by the spirit which pervaded the court. During his boyhood, he took some lessons from the Jesuit teachers, the best schoolmasters of the age and formed a close friendship with Father Rodolfo Aquaviva, the head of the first Jesuit Mission to Akbar's court. Jahangir often appeals to God, but never mentions the name of the Prophet. If he observed the Shab-i-Barat or Eid, he celebrated the Hindu festivals, Diwali, Dussehra, Rakshahandhan and Shivaratri with the regularity. His heresy gave rise to the rumour that he was an atheist at heart. In short, there is not the slightest reason to suppose that Jahangir was an ardent Mussalman. Wine and women destroyed his natural vigour and blasted all his prospects in life.

Jahangir as a Ruler

After the death of his father Akbar, Jahangir ascended to the throne in the fort of Agra on 3 November 1605, at the age of 36.[4] After Jahangir's accession to the throne, the friends and political opponents were all alike recipients of favours. Bir Singh Bundela, the murderer of Abul Fazl, was raised to the dignity of a commander of 3,000. The sons and relatives of his patron saint, Shaikh Salim Chishti, were given ranks and offices beyond their hopes and abilities. Jahangir began to win the hearts of all the people and officers and to rearrange the withered world. Jahangir followed his father Akbar's non-religious and secular outlook and liberal policy. Jahangir was even more secular than his father and due to his association with his Rajput mother, Rajput prince and nobles, he was not inclined to any religion. Like Akbar, Jahangir also asserted that there was not much difference between the Sufi traditions in Islam and the Vedantist school of Hindu philosophy. He gave equal status to all religions under his rule.

There was no war of succession at the time of Jahangir's accession to the throne because Jahangir's brothers Murad and Daniyal were destined to a miserable death from alcohol in 1599 and 1605. In his young age, Jahangir was also habituated of wine and opium. Till his seventeenth year he never tasted wine except as an ingredient in an infantile medicine. In 1585 he was induced by a royal servant to take a cup to drive away the fatigues of a hunting expedition. When he started drinking wine it increased day to day. Even wine made from grapes ceased to intoxicate him and he took to drinking *araq* (spirits). Matters went from bad to worse by 1594, when he consumed twenty cups of doubly distilled spirits, fourteen during the daytime and the remainder at night.[5]

At Jahangir's accession in 1605, the Muslim theologians, who had not been pleased very much with Akbar's attempt at secularizing the state, seem to have tried to win back their lost influence. Jahangir never took back the concession provided to Hindus and other communities. Jahangir would not go back on the path of toleration which his father had opened. Jahangir was in the influence his beloved queen Nur Mahal or Nur Jahan, the daughter of Mirza Ghiyas Beg (Itmad-ud-Daulah) to who he married in 1611.[6] During the latter part of his reign he became a nerveless tool in the hands of his wife Nur Jahan and her ambitious family.

Jahangir as ruler was most benevolent, tolerant, justice loving and always attached to the problems of his subjects. One of Jahangir's earliest orders, which he mentions with pardonable pride in his *Memoirs*, was the setting up of a chain of justice made of pure gold, 30 *gaz* long, with 60 bells upon it. One end was attached to a battlement of the fort of Agra and the other to a stone column on the bank of the River Jamuna.[7] Anyone who failed to secure justice might pull the end outside the fort in order to draw the attention of the Emperor so that the latter might redress his grievances. The chain was a symbol of Jahangir's determination to dispense justice fairly and firmly without fear or favour. By the chain of justice, he removed the rust of oppression from their hearts. The chain of justice was an emblem of his accessibility and of his desire to redress wrongs.

Another of his important acts was the issuing of the twelve orders to be observed as rules of conduct (*Dasturul Amal*) or Ordinances for the better government of the country. These ordinances are as follows:[8]

1. Forbidding the levy of cesses under the names of *tamgha* and *mir bahri* (river tolls) and other burdens which the *jagirdars* of every province and district had imposed for their own profit.
2. On roads where thefts and robberies took place, which roads might be at a little distance from habitations, the *jagirdars* of the neighbourhood should build *sarais* (public rest-houses), mosques and dig wells, which might stimulate population and people might settle down in those *sarais*. If these should be near a *khalisa* estate (under direct state management), the administrator (*mutasaddi*) of that place should execute the work.
3. The bales of merchants should not be opened on the roads without informing them and obtaining their leave.
4. In my dominions if anyone, whether unbeliever or Musalman, should die, his property and effects should be left for his heirs and no one should interfere with them. If he should have no heir, they should appoint inspectors and separate guardians to guard the property, so that its value might be expended in lawful expenditure, such as the building of mosques and *sarais*, the repair of broken bridges and the digging of tanks and wells.
5. They should not make wine or rice-spirit (*darbahra*) or any kind of intoxicating drug, or sell them; although I myself drink wine and from the age of 18 years uptil now, when I am 38, have persisted in it. When I first took a liking to drinking

I sometimes took as many as twenty cups of double-distilled spirit; when by deerees it acquired a great influence over me I endeavoured to lessen the quantity and in the period of seven years I have brought myself from fifteen cups to five or six. My times for drinking were varied; sometimes when three or four sidereal hours of the day remained I would begin to drink and sometimes at night and partly by day. This went on till I was 30 years old. After that I took to drinking always at night. Now I drink only to digest my food.

6. They should not take possession of any person's house.
7. I forbade cutting off the nose or ears of any person and I myself made a vow by the throne of God that I would not blemish anyone by this punishment.
8. I gave an order that the officials of the Crown lands and the *jagirdars* should not forcibly take the ryots' lands and cultivate them on their own account.
9. A government collector or a *jagirdar* should not without permission intermarry with the people of the *pargana* in which he might be.
10. They should found hospitals in the great cities and appoint physicians for the healing of the sick; whatever the expenditure might be, it should be given from the *khalisa* establishment.
11. In accordance with the regulations of my revered father, I ordered that each year from the 18th of Rabt-ul-Awwal which is my birthday, for a number of days corresponding to the years of my life, they should not slaughter animals (for food). Two days in each week were also forbidden, one of them Thursday, the day of my accession and the other Sunday, the day of my father's birth. He held this day in great esteem on this account and because it was dedicated to the sun and also because it was the day on which Creation began. Therefore it was one of the days on which there was no killing in his dominions.

12. I gave a general order that the offices and *jagirs* of my father's servants should remain as they were. Later, the *mansabs* (ranks or offices) were increased according to each one's circumstances by not less than 20 per cent to 300 per cent or 400 per cent. The subsistence money of the ahadis was increased by 50 per cent and I raised the pay of all domestics by 20 per cent. I increased the allowances of all the veiled ladies of my father's *harem* from 20 per cent to 100 per cent according to their condition and relationship. By one stroke of the pen I confirmed the subsistence lands of the holders of *aimas* (charity lands) within the dominions, who form the army of prayer, according to the deeds in their possession. I gave an order to Miran Sadr Jahan, who is one of the genuine Sayyids of India and who for a long time held the high office of *sadr* (ecclesiastical officer) under my father, that he should everyday produce before me deserving people (worthy of charity). I released all criminals who had been confined and imprisoned for a long time in the forts and prisons.

A careful analysis of these ordinances shows Jahangir's genuine desire to ensure to his subjects freedom of person and security of life and property and his solicitude for their material and moral welfare. The fact that these regulations did not in effect serve the purpose they were intended for, at least to the degree desired by Jahangir, does not detract from his honest and sincere desire to promote the happiness and prosperity of his subjects without distinction of class or creed. The regulations are "remarkable for the humanity, justice and political sagacity which pervade them".

Jahangir and Islam

Jahangir was a secular ruler protecting every faith under his rule but still was a Muslim by faith and at the beginning of his reign he attempted to act as the protector of the true faith and tried to defend it against attacks from other religious preachers. There are certain cases are cited as evidence of Jahangir's orthodoxy and fanaticism born of the fear and suspicion of the times. For example, it is asserted that Jahangir allowed daily allowances to new converts. When he learnt that in certain localities Muslim girls were converted to Hinduism and married to Hindus, he put a stop to it and punished the guilty. From this it is inferred that Jahangir attempted to stand forth as a protector of the true faith. In this he was only following an old custom, for Muslim law does not permit the marriage of Muslim girls to non-Muslims. The protection of the Muslim minority obviously was a source of strength and vitality to the Mughals. In spite of all these Jahangir issued order to provincial governors in the sixth year openly declared that they were not to convert anyone forcibly to Islam.

The Jesuit Fathers defamed Jahangir and tried to prove Jahangir as protector of Islam and avoided the toleration policy of his father. According to Jesuit Fathers, converts to Islam were given daily allowances. In the beginning of his reign in 1605 Jahangir forcibly converted an Armenian Christian Zulqarnain to Islam but finding him steadfast in his religion he left him alone. In the tenth year of his reign Roz Afzun, son of Raja Sangram, was honoured by admission into Islam and given the status of his father. A Hindu who had been circumcized during Akbar's reign, is said to have been converted to Islam by Jahangir. A Goanese was admitted into the "true faith" in 1606. Some prisoners were offered pardon if they turned Muslim. Jahangir in fourth year of his reign had whipped and imprisoned two Muslim young men Qutub and Qumar Khan because they had been frequenting the house of a *sannyasi* and seemed inclined towards Hinduism. Kalyan kept a Muslim dancing girl. Further, when Jahangir discovered in his fifteenth year that the Hindus at Rajauri converted and married Muslim girls of the locality, he gave orders that this practice be put a stop to and the guilty be punished.[9]

Some of the events might have happened during the reign of Jahangir but almost all events mentioned by Jesuit mission are full of exaggerations or were mere less important events which happened without the proper knowledge of Emperor Jahangir. The most important events of his rule that non-Muslims were as free as before to practice their religion publicly or built the temples anywhere in India as they desired. However, this practice was followed only in the empirical regions and not fully followed in the enemy country or during the war. Above all Jahangir fully followed the toleration policy of his father Akbar except the few exceptions.

Emperor Jahangir was a ruler believing a pluralistic culture of India and protected it like his father Akbar. His orders, policies and behaviour, all witness for the same. Jahangir was never a devout Muslim and like his father, his religious tendencies were distinctly deistic. He delighted in hearing disputes between the Jesuits who visited his court and the *mullah*s. Always a lover of art, he surrounded himself with a number of religious pictures, mostly of a Christian nature, which gave offence to many of his courtiers. He even went so far as to employ a seal inscribed with Christian emblems.

Some time Jahangir pose himself as a devout Muslim, some time more secular than his father Akbar and sometimes more inclined towards various faiths of India. His pluralistic policies had confused the Christians and Hindus and they began to claim the Emperor as follower of their own religion. As Christian scholar claims, Jahangir was more inclined towards Hinduism and Christianity than Muslim religion. All the events and policies during his rule show him a secular and national forebearer.

Jahangir was accused for the persecution of some Muslim saints and many honourable Muslims felt insecure during his reign. A Muslim contemporary writer asserts that things had become so difficult that no other way was left for honourable men (Muslims) but to leave the country. Jahangir was not at all orthodox or true follower of all tenets of Islam but as a Muslim ruler he claimed a protector of "the true faith" like his father Emperor Akbar. This policy of Jahangir persecuted many of the theologians, scholars and saints. Soon after his accession it was reported to him that Shaikh Ibrahim had set himself up as a religious leader in Lahore. He had gathered together a large number of Afghans as his followers. Jahangir ordered that he be brought before him. On being unable to satisfy the Emperor, Shaikh Ibrahim imprisoned in the fortress of Chunar. In another case Shaikh Nizamuddin Faruqi of Thanesar was driven out of India partly on account of his showing Khusrau in rebellion a little more than usual courtesy due to a prince visiting a Chishtiyya hospice. Another scholar Qazi Nurullah was flogged to death by Jahangir on account of his being an effective Shia writer.[10]

Shaikh Ahmad Sirhindi, a significant and influential theologian of Akbar's and Jahangir's time, lamented the deplorable state of Islam in India. The law of God, which Mohammad (PBUH) had preached, was, in the Shaikh's view, no longer honoured in India and unbelief was openly propagated even in the Persian language.[11] Shaikh Ahmad Sirhindi met the same case of persecution. He was the leader of the Chishtiyya, Qadariyya and Naqshbandiyya sects of Muslims and had followers in every part of the country. Some Muslim theologians complained to Jahangir that in some of his writings Ahmad Sirhindi claimed to have risen to a status higher than that of the Caliphs. Jahangir thereupon called him from Sirhind and asked him to explain his position. Shaikh Ahmad Sirhindi unsuccessfully tried to explain his position but by not performing *sijdah* to the Emperor, he was imprisoned in the Gwalior Fort. Mulla Ahmad was released in the fifteenth year when Jahangir realised that he had been a tool of rival theologians in ordering Shaikh Ahmed's imprisonment. In an open court he was given a robe of honour and R. 1,000 and released.[12]

Niccolao Manucci, the Italian traveller who came to India in 1656-1717, observes of Jahangir that of all his subjects, he was kind to everyone except the Muslims. Francois Bernier, the celebrated French doctor who travelled to India in the mid-seventeenth century, announced that Jahangir "died, as he had lived, destitute of all religion". Manucci, also, tells the story of Jahangir's fondness for pork and wine, growing more intense during the holy month of Ramazan—when devout Muslims observed strict fast from sunrise to sunset! Implored by the theologians to abstain from pork, at least, both in everyday life and more determinedly during the Ramazan, for if Christianity allowed its consumption, for Muslims it was a mortal sin, he resolved to turn to Christianity instead! He did not convert, but such was the casualness of his regard for Islam.[13]

The remarks and judgement of the Christianity scholars and preachers are due to the confusion to understand the pluralistic policy of Emperor Jahangir. They were unaccustomed to religious liberty as they had been in Europe, seem to have been as much dazzled by the toleration granted by Jahangir as they had been under Akbar. To them, if a man believed in the truth of a religion, he could only prove it by persecuting the non-believers. If Jahangir listened to their statements of the merits of the Christian religion, he lost caste among Muslims. Although Jahangir was a Muslim and remained as a Muslim but patronized almost all religions of India.

The claim of the Christian scholars proved false and full of confusion because in his time the Muslim magistrates and judges remained as heretofore in office. The Sadr-us-Sadur remained in-charge of justice and charities. He punished heresy and suppressed conversions to Hinduism.The pig hunting and pork eating statement of Christianity preachers is also confusing because Emperor Jahangir was fond of hunting and he also hunted wild pigs or boars and presented their meat to Rajputs and Christians. Pigs are not sacred to Muslims, pork is unlawful to them. The hunting of pigs therefore is not an unlawful act according to Islam.

Jahangir and Christianity

Portuguese were very powerful in the Mughal court during Jahangir. Although Portugal was absorbed in Spain during 1580-1640, the Portugal Christian missionaries were much influential and under Albuquerque they had acquired Goa from Bijapur kingdom. Jahangir came into contact with the Jesuits during the lifetime of his father. He always treated the Jesuit Fathers with great courtesy. Jahangir followed the policy of his father in contributing large sums for the erection of churches and showing general toleration for the Christian faith. Jahangir desired to maintain friendly relations with Christian Fathers and he sent an embassy to Goa in 1607 and another in 1610.[14]

He was, however, thoroughly annoyed with the Portuguese when in 1613 they seized four imperial vessels near Surat. Failing to get satisfaction, Muqarrab Khan, the governor of Surat was ordered to chastize the Portuguese. The Mughal commander wisely and skilfully managed to come to terms with Downton, the English sea-captain. This enabled the Mughal commander to inflict a naval defeat on the Portuguese. So, the privileges granted to the Portuguese were withdrawn, the churches at Agra and Lahore were forcibly closed and the Portuguese living in the empire were arrested, wherever they could be found. However, Portuguese became successful in restoring their position in the Mughal court.[15]

The Portuguese Jesuit Fathers were challenged by British diplomats who arrived at Surat under Captain William Hawkins in 1608. He was armed with a letter from James I to Jahangir, 25,000 gold pieces with the object of securing trading privileges for the East India Company. and a present of. In spite of the opposition of the Jesuit Fathers, Hawkins was well received by Jahangir. His mission, however, was a failure and he left in 1611. Paul Canning appeared at the court in 1612 and was followed in 1615 by William Edwards. Both of them met with the same difficulties which Hawkins had to face.[16]

The most important and the best known English plenipotentiary who came to Jahangir's court was Sir Thomas Roe. Sir Thomas Roe was a veteran soldier and diplomat. He bore formal credentials from James I and a number of ceremonial presents for the Emperor. Roe remained in India for three years but did not succeed in achieving his object. Jahangir gave Sir Thomas Roe an official appointment and a salary.[17]

Although Portuguese and the British had the political rivalry but they all were Christian and sought enough concession to profess Christianity by their missionaries. During the reign of Jahangir forcible conversion was banned otherwise the people of every faith were free to convert where they wish. The annual Jesuit letter from Goa, dated 1 February 1621, stated that Jahangir didn't withdraw his earlier permission granted to the Christians to make converts to their faith. Besides the needy, the Jesuits were able to convert the dying or to buy slaves and convert them. Some twenty persons, most of them whilom Christians, were baptized at Agra. A Brahman and a Moor were converted at Lahore, but in secret.[18]

However, the most sensational of the conversions was the public baptism of Daniyal's sons and a grandson of Jahangir in 1610. Christian Fathers were overjoyed. Even the English Protestants participated in the public procession that marched through the streets of Agra in order to celebrate their baptism. To the Jesuits it seemed that grace was at last settling on the princely house of Timur and they were waiting for the time when it would be possible for them to number the Emperor himself among their followers. The three were given Portuguese names: Tahmurs became Don Felipe; Baisangar, Don Carlos; and Hoshang, Don Henrique. Four years later, "they had rejected the light and returned to their vomit", observes Maclagan in utter disgust.[19]

Sir Thomas Roe, King James I's ambassador to India during Jahangir's reign, also tells the story of two princes' conversion to Christianity only to enable Jahangir to demand a Portuguese wife for himself; on not obtaining one, "the two Princes came to the Jesuits and surrendered up their crosses and all other rites, professing they would be no longer Christians". Roe, however, reinforces the emperor's image of indifference towards Islam: "His religion is of his own invention; for he envies Mahomett and wisely sees no reason why he should not be as great a prophett as he and therefore professed himself so...." Other European Terry, the English traveller, mentions that when the recitation of the *azan*, the call for prayers, began in the mosques in Agra his companion Coryat would go up to the turret and substitute "Hazrat Isa ibn-Allah" (Christ the son of God), for "Mohammad Rasul-Allah".[20]

Over the conversion of Daniyal' sons, Jahangir disqualified them for the imperial throne. Ultimately, the three princes renounced Christianity and re-embraced Islam in 1611. This led to the Jesuit castles in the air shattered. Jahangir was broad-minded or cynical enough to tempt Hawkins to his service by offering to procure a Muslim wife for him and to allow him to convert her to Christianity. Jesuit accounts of their success in making converts seem to be more hopeful than true. Some of these assert that Muqarrab Khan, Customs Officer at Cambay, was secretly converted to Christianity in 1611 when on a mission to Goa. It is difficult to believe this story for various reasons. Further Maclagan, on the authority of the Annual Letter from Cochin, dated 1621, asserts that Muqarrab Khan's son fell ill, was cured by Christian spells and prayers and converted to Christianity. But Guerreiro as translated by Payne stops short at the child's recovery and mentions no conversion.[21]

The Fathers claim of conversion is full of exaggeration and they were only successful in their mission to convert only the poor, needy and greedy people of the lower strata in the society. There might me the conversion in the upper class but it was very rare, although, Fathers were allowed freely to convert people according their wish. Jahangir not only tolerated Christianity, he maintained it as well. The Christian Fathers were paid from Rs. 3 to Rs. 7 daily; occasionally he would give them money for their religious services and once at least he tried to relieve the distress of the Christian poor by a monthly grant of Rs. 50.[22]

Jahangir and Sikhs

Guru Nanak (1469-1539), belonged to rural Punjab's upper-caste Khatri community, had initiated a movement or a religious tradition called Sikhism. According to one tradition, a holy man came to him and so "subdued his mind" that he gave away all his granary's assets, together with his personal property and abandoned his wife and children. He settled at Kartarpur, on the banks of the Ravi River and famously declared his distance from both Hindu and Islamic institutions, gathering a group of followers who would hear and accept his message. He started the institution of Guruship in the Sikhism and himself became first Guru of Sikh religion.

Third Guru Amar Das (1552-74) established festival days and distinctive ceremonies for a Sikh's birth, marriage and death. Guru Amar Das built a well of eighty-four steps in his village of Goindwal, which became the Sikhs' first pilgrimage centre. Before his death in 1574, he had begun excavating a great tank on a plot of 500 *bighas* (a unit of land area) given to him by Akbar. Completed by the next *guru*, Ram Das (1574-81), the tank would become known as Amritsar, "the nectar of immortality". Eventually the town that grew up around the tank would be known by that name, too, as it became the primary seat of Sikh authority.

The fifth *guru*, Guru Arjan (1581-1606), updated the *Adi Granth* by adding his own verses and those of Guru Amar Das to the two-volume body that had been collected by Guru Ram Das. He then supervised the compilation of an authoritative text, completed in 1604. The result was to stabilize the scriptural foundation of the Sikh religion. To strengthen its institutional and ritual basis, Guru Arjan enlarged Amritsar's great tank, paved it with bricks and most prominently in 1589 built in its middle the famous Harmandir, popularly known as the Golden Temple. Apart from being one of India's greatest architectural triumphs, the Harmandir made Amritsar the Sikh faith's primary ritual focus, since it was here that the *Adi Granth* was placed for continuous reading, highlighting that scripture's role as the heart and soul of Sikhdom.[23]

Jahangir's attitude towards the Sikhs has been a matter of controversy. A careful perusal of contemporary evidence shows that the Sikh religious leaders suffered because they interfered with politics, which was a dangerous game and might have constituted a menace to the state unless suppressed in time. There is no evidence to show that he persecuted the Sikhs as such. Punishment of fifth Guru Arjan has been represented by Sikh tradition as the first of the long series of religious persecutions which the Khalsa suffered from the Mughal emperors. In reality, it is nothing of the kind. The whole affair amounts to a single execution due primarily to political reasons. No other Sikhs were molested. No interdict was laid on the Sikh faith. Guru Arjan himself would have ended his days in peace if he had not espoused the cause of a rebel Prince Khusrau.

During Jahangir's reign, his son Prince Khusrau rebelled against his father and fled towards Punjab and reached Tarn Taran, a settlement south of Amritsar, which Guru Arjan had established. Guru Arjan was the contemporary head and the fifth *guru* of the Sikhs and the author of the *Granth Sahib*. The *guru* responded favourably to Khusrau's call for supporters, notwithstanding the fact that the emperor was advancing towards the Punjab in hot pursuit of his rebellious son. Khusrau was well received by the Guru Arjan who felt compassion for him and gave him Rs. 5,000. Jahangir himself relates what took place next:[24]

> "Khusrau happened to halt at the place where he (Guru Arjan) was and he came out and did homage to him. He behaved to Khusrau in certain special ways and made on his forehead a fingermark in saffron, which the Indians (Hinduwan) call *qashqa* [*tika*] and is considered auspicious. When this came to my ears and I clearly understood his folly, I ordered them to produce him (Arjan) ... and having confiscated his property commanded that he should be put to death."

After the suppression of this rebellion, Jahangir called the *guru* to his presence and awarded him capital punishment for countenancing treason. Some influential Hindus, however, intervened and it was decided that the *guru* might be let off if he paid the heavy fine of Rs. 1,00,000 but *guru* never agreed and died in imprisonment. Guru Arjan's execution posed a major crisis for the Sikh community. The late *guru* had personally acquired both spiritual and temporal authority and had done more to institutionalize the Sikh religion than anybody since Guru Nanak. Prince Khusrau was also ordered to be blinded, after an insurrection was attempted in his favour. But Jahangir afterwards relented and, under the treatment of a Persian physician, Khusrau regained the sight of one eye.[25]

It is also claimed that Guru Arjan incurred Jahangir's displeasure on account of his proselytizing activities. Some Muslims were reported to have accepted him as their religious leader and thus renounced Islam. Jahangir offered Guru Arjan to either convert him to Islam or take steps to close his "religious shop".[26] Though Jahangir declares it to have been his intention to close the shop of the Sikh *guru* for religious reasons, the actual facts contradict him. However, the persecution of Sikh religion by Jahangir is not proved either by the Sikh traditions or Muslim accounts. Jahangir ordered the execution not out of any animus against Sikhism, which in any event he failed to recognize as a separate religion, but because of the *guru*'s apparent support for a state rebel. So, this was not an act of religious persecution, but a punishment for aiding the rebellion.

Guru Arjan's son Guru Hargobind (1606-44) girded himself with two swords that symbolized spiritual and temporal authority. He also built a fort to defend Amritsar, another sign of the community's more militant profile. Finally, he adopted the trappings of royalty, building opposite Amritsar's Harmandir a high platform called the Akal Takht (immortal throne), where he conducted worldly business in a court-like atmosphere. When suspicious officials reported these activities to the imperial court, Jahangir ordered that the guru be detained in Gwalior Fort in 1616, where the Mughals' political prisoners were held. After twelve years of imprisonment Hargovind was released probably during the usual clemency that followed Shah Jahan's accession to the throne in 1627.[27]

The execution of the Guru Arjan was not an act of religious persecution, but it was politically unwise and the Mughals paid a heavy penalty for it. However, the death of the *guru* sowed the seeds of hatred between the Sikhs and the Muslims which the passage of time did not diminish. Undoubtedly, the motif was political but who suffered was a religious *guru* the Sikh religion and naturally his followers curse fell upon the Mughal Emperor Jahangir. The same Sikh community during the Revolt of 1857 crushed the rebellion in Delhi and started genocide of Mughals in particular and Muslim as a whole in the Red Fort and entire Delhi area. The Sikhs fought with the religious zeal of revenging the death of their Guru Arjan.

Jahangir and Jainas

Like Sikhs, the Jaina religion also faced displeasure and persecution of Emperor Jahangir. Before the confrontation Man Singh and Bal Chandra, the leaders of the two Jaina schools of thought had enjoyed royal hospitality under Akbar. Under Jahangir prince Khusrau rebelled his father and Man Singh became guilty of an act of indiscretion. Rai Singh of Bikaner consulted Man Singh in order to shape his own conduct during those troublous days. Jaina Guru Man Singh told Rai Singh that Jahangir's reign would not extend beyond two years. Believing in the prophecy of the Jaina monk, Rai Singh rebelled, threw up his command under Jahangir and repaired to Bikaner.[28]

Soon the Khusrau's rebellion was crushed and Rai Singh also was defeated. Jahangir pardoned Rai Singh and restored to his former position in the royal service.Now Man Singh's prophecy seems to have been reported to Jahangir. He could, however, take no action against him as Rai Singh had been pardoned and Man Singh was living under his protection at Bikaner. Moreover, the Emperor was still having the distrust for Jaina community.

In the twelfth year, when Jahangir visited Gujarat, he saw that the Jainas having built temples and other buildings which were reported to be centres of disturbance. Their religious leaders were accused of immoral practices (probably of going about naked). It seemed that Jaina monk Man Singh was behind the disturbances and immoral practices. It also may not be ignored that Jahangir's displeasure for Man Singh over Rai Singh's rebellion was still alive in Jahangir's chest. Whatsoever might be the reason but Jaina monk Man Singh was summoned to the court. Afraid of meeting a mere ignominious fate he took poison on his way from Bikaner to the Emperor.[29]

Jahangir issued orders thereupon for the expulsion of the Jainas from the imperial territories. These orders do not seem to have applied to the territory of the Rajput *rajas* where the Jainas were driven to seek protection. The *Intikhab-i-Jahangir Shahi* gives the following account of Jahangir's treatment of the Jainas of Gujarat:[30]

> "The Emperor ordered them to be banished from the country and their temples to be demolished. Their idol was thrown down on the uppermost steps of the mosque that it might be trodden upon by those who came to say their daily prayers there. By this order of the Emperor the infidels were exceedingly disgraced and Islam exalted."

Jahangir and Hindus

Jahangir remained tolerant in religious matters like his father. In his *Memoirs* he says that an "audacious speculator" suggested to him the reimposition of the *jazia*. Jahangir repudiated this suggestion and punished the speculator. In the subsidiary regulations issued some time after his accession, he ordered his officials not to enforce Islam on anyone. Like his father he was fond of religious discourses, though he did not give as much time to them as Akbar had done. Roe and Terry testify to the fact that he accorded equal welcome to Christians, Jews and Muslims. Hindu festivals like Rakhi, Dussehra, etc. were celebrated as in old days. The *tula dan* (weighing of the emperor against gold) was also observed.

Jahangir continued the practice of allowing non-Muslims to build public places of worship. His friend, Bir Singh Bundela, built a magnificent temple at Mathura, which was now once again rising into prominence as the sacred city of the Vaishnavas. He raised another magnificent place of public worship in his own state as well. More than seventy new temples were built in Benares alone towards the end of his reign. They were, however, not yet complete when Jahangir died. He allowed the Christian Fathers to open a church at Ahmedabad in 1620 and another at Hughly. At Lahore and Agra public cemeteries for the Christians were allowed to be set up.

As it has been mentioned earlier when Jahangir made war on the Hindus and the Christians these considerations were sometimes given up. Because most of the Mughal army, which included both Hindus and Muslims, in order to chastise and inflict more harm to the enemy generally targeted worship places. When Mewar was invaded, many temples were demolished by the invading Mughal army.[31]

One of the important military achievements of the Mughal armies under Jahangir was the capture of Kangra. The fort of Kangra, perched on the crest of a lofty hill, had long defied all earlier attempts against it. Tradition declares that it had been attacked no less than fifty-four times. In 1615, Murtaza Khan and Suraj Mal were commissioned to capture the fort. Suraj Mal was accused of hampering the operations and recalled. On the death of Murtaza Khan, Suraj Mal was again placed in command, but this time he broke into open revolt, allied himself with the hill chiefs and plundered the imperial territory. Raja Bikramajit was next sent into the valley and he succeeded in recovering the lost imperial prestige. The Raja of Chamba, who had helped Suraj Mal, submitted and Suraj Mal's property was confiscated and given over to Jagat Singh. The siege of Kangra now began in right earnest and, after a stout resistance of fourteen months, the garrison surrendered on 16 November 1620.[32]

Jahangir visited the fort a year later with some Muslim divines and to celebrate the occasion a mosque was built in the fortress. Jahangir writes in *Tuzuk-i-Jahangiri*:[33]

> "On the 24th of the month I went to pay a visit to the fortress and I gave orders that the Kazi, the Chief Justice and others learned in the law of Islam, should accompany me and perform the ceremonies required by our religion. After passing over about half a kos we mounted to the Fort and by the grace of God, prayers were said, the *khutba* was read, a cow was killed and other things were done such as never had been done before from the foundation of the Fort to the present time. All this was done in my presence and I bowed myself in thanks to the Almighty for his great conquest, which no previous monarch had been able to accomplish, I ordered a large mosque to be built in the fortress."

Whatsoever Jahangir writes but it is rather proved by the historians and analysts that at the time of Jahangir's visit of Kangra fortress he never hurt the sentiments of the Hindus and his visit was purely a military and political. The Bhawani[34] Temple below the fort walls was, however, left untouched, though not unnoticed. Also left untouched was the Jawalamukhi[35] Temple in the neighbourhood, after testing the priests' claim that the fire there was divine and eternal and could not be extinguished by water. Indeed, Jahangir allowed not only repairs to it but also extensions. Prince Khurram was the formal victor at Kangra, earlier attempts to conquer the fort had been led by Raja Bikramjit and Jauhar Mal, son of Raja Basu, among others.[36]

Harbans Mukhia says that Jahangir writes of the conquest in hyperbolic terms in his memoirs, the *Tuzuk-i-Jahangiri*. In the fort, a Durga Temple was demolished and a bull was slaughtered.[37] The above statement that "no previous monarch had been able to accomplish" is also not strictly true. Although a fortress of very great natural strength, it had fallen both to Mahmud of Ghazni and to Firoz Shah Tughlaq. It is also seems not very true the fact that these high-ranking Hindu nobles were commissioned to reduce a fort, where victory was ultimately celebrated by demolishing a

Hindu temple and erecting a mosque, lends a degree of irony to the enterprise, although it was far from unusual.

Fury of the Emperor on certain points also caused negative effect to that particular community. At the time of Jahangir's reign differences with Portuguese, a church at Agra was closed and the churches elsewhere also suffered similar indignities. These exceptions apart, Jahangir usually followed the path shown by his father. It is interesting to note that some of the Hindu shrines of Kangra and Mathura continued to attract a large number of Muslim pilgrims besides their Hindu votaries.

Jahangir also continued to allow, as Akbar had done, Hindu pilgrims to visit without hindrance their holy places. New temples and Christian churches were freely built during his time, though now and then, during a campaign, religious places suffered at the hands of zealous or fanatical soldiers. Hindu pilgrims freely visited their shrines. Coryat puts the number of persons visiting Hardwar at 4,00,000 while Roe puts it at 5,00,000. Roe was prepared to take it even to half a million visitors. Of course, there must have been other similar places of pilgrimages in other parts of the country as well. It appears that the open celebration of Hindu religious customs and festivals was continued, just as in Akbar's time. In some places, at least certain days of Hindu fasts were observed as public holidays when no buying or selling, even of foodstuffs, was allowed.[38]

Jahangir himself was in the influence of a Hindu hermit Yogi Jagrup and Jahangir had the most profound respect for him. Jahangir paid several visits to his hermitage and considered "association with him a great privilege". The Yogi too was effusive in his compliment to the Emperor:

> "In what language can I return thanks for the gift of God, that in the reign of such a just King I can be engaged in the worship of my own Deity in ease and contentment and that from no quarter does the dust of discomposure settle on the skirt of my purpose?"[39]

As for the celebration of the festivals in the court and rest of India, it was freely allowed and even Emperor frequently participated in such festivals. In the seventh year, Jahangir celebrated the Rakhi festival for the first time and had auspicious threads bound on his wrist. He met the *yogis* on the night of the Shivaratri in his eleventh year, when he was staying the night at Sangor, renamed by him Kamalpur, in Bengal. Dussehra was celebrated by the Emperor by holding reviews of troops and elephants. On the Dipavali, Jahangir allowed gambling to go on in his presence. There was no restriction whatever on the public celebration of religious festivals. It was not Jahangir alone who thus took part in the celebration of Hindu festivals but many Mohammadans, men and women, participated in the festivities that accompanied these celebrations.[40]

As far as admissions of the Hindus to the higher public services, his father Akbar's practices were continued. Under Jahangir, out of forty-seven *mansabdars* holding the rank of commanders of 3,000 horses or above, mentioned by Hawkins, six were Hindus. During Jahangir's reign of 22 years, there were three Hindu governors of provinces. A Hindu, Mohan Das, is mentioned as serving as a *diwan* under Jahangir.[41]

Jahangir continued Akbar's work of bringing the intellectuals of the two communities together by having translations of Hindu sacred books made under his patronage. Girdhar Das, a Kayastha of Delhi, rendered Valmiki's *Ramayana* into verse, called it *Ram Nama* and dedicated it to Jahangir. Masihi made another Persian translation of the *Ramayana* and took pains to prove by inserting a section in praise of the Prophet. Some of the scholars of Jahangir's time acted as a link between the two communities. Abdur Rahim Khan-i-Khanan (one of the nine jewels of Akbar) under his Hindi pen-name of Rahim wrote all sorts of Hindi verse including many in praise of Hindu gods and a description of the feelings of a devotee towards God in his various incarnations. Jahangir is said to have patronized Sur Das whose *Sur Sagar* is reputed to have been compiled under Jahangir's patronage. The emperor is said to have given Sur Das one gold coin for every verse.[42]

So the Emperor Jahangir patronized Hinduism and allowed full freedom and religious conversion without force or greed. During Jahangir's reign, many Hindu sacred places such as Mathura and Varanasi were the centre of conversions. Muslims were allured by money and women to convert into Hinduism. Mahmud bin Amir Ali Balkhi, a Central Asian traveller in Jahangir's reign, was horrified to see a group of 23 Muslims in Benares (Varanasi) who had deserted their religion and turned Hindu, having fallen in love with Hindu women. Balkhi says that for some time he held their company and questioned them about their mistaken way, they pointed towards the sky and put their fingers at their foreheads. By this gesture, he understood that they attributed it to Providence.[43]

Jahangir and Rajputs

Akbar had succeeded during his lifetime in befriending the proud Rajput rulers and acknowledging the supremacy of the Mughals. But the Rajput State of Mewar continued to wage an unequal fight against superior Mughals. During the first six years of his reign Jahangir repeatedly sent armies into Mewar against Rana Pratap's son and successor Amar Singh. But the results were inconclusive, if not outright failures. The first military expedition undertaken by Jahangir was against Rana Amar Singh of Mewar. An army of 20,000 horses was despatched under the command of Prince Parvez and Asaf Khan. A battle was fought at *Dewar* or *Dewair* but its issue was doubtful as both sides claimed victory. The rebellion of Khusrau, which occurred during the course of this war, necessitated the withdrawal of the army.[44] A second expedition was sent in 1608 under the command of Mahabat Khan, but in spite of some initial success the Mughals made no effective headway against the Rajputs. In 1609, Mahabat Khan was replaced by Abdullah Khan. However during the course of operations, Abdullah Khan was sent as governor of Gujarat and the command given to Raja Basu.

Finally, in 1614 the emperor dispatched the veteran general Aziz Koka into Mewar, assisted by the 22-year-old Khurram, his first major military assignment. However, the two had a falling-out that ended with the prince placing the senior general in confinement. Having a free hand, Khurram prosecuted a vigorous campaign against Amar Singh, who, with his forces thinning and famine threatening, finally offered peace negotiations. The agreement concluded in 1615 between Khurram and Amar was exceptional in the history of Mughal-Rajput relations. The Sisodiyas were exempted from entering into matrimonial relations with the Mughals; they were not obliged to send their ruling head to the imperial court; and no Sisodiya territory was placed under Mughal administration. In addition, Jahangir made two gestures of goodwill towards these ancient adversaries. First, he returned the historic fort of Chittor to the Sisodiya house, on the condition that it never again be fully inhabited. And, second, he ordered that two life-size equestrian statues of Amar Singh and his son Karan Singh be carved from marble and placed in Agra's most important palace garden.[45] With a view to integrating this last major Rajput holdout and hereditary enemy of the Mughal family into the Mughal system, Khurram treated his adversary with dignity and respect.

Nur Jahan

The daughter of high-ranking Iranian immigrant Mirza Ghiyas (Itmad-ud-daula), Mehrunnisa (Nur Jahan) was born in 1577. Itmad-ud-daula had served Akbar and was now in Jahangir's court, together with his son Asaf Khan. At the age of eighteen, Mehrunnisa was married to Ali Quli Beg Istajlu, better known as Sher Afghan the governor of Bengal. It was reported to Jahangir that Sher Afghan was insubordinate and disposed to rebellion. As a result Qutbuddin was sent to Bengal as governor in 1606, but Sher Afghan slew Qutbuddin during an interview and was killed by the followers of Qutbuddin. Mehrunnisa was sent to the capital and entrusted to the care of Jahangir's mother. Jahangir has been accused of complicity in the murder of Sher Afghan, but there is no evidence in contemporary records to substantiate the charge.

The course of Jahangir's life was changed for ever in March 1611 when the emperor met a striking woman named Mehrunnisa. He was immediately fell in love, notwithstanding that his *harem* was already stocked with seventeen wives and numerous concubines. Mehrunnisa was a capable, independent and intelligent woman of uncommon beauty. She was already a mature woman of thirty-four and the mother of a young girl from an earlier marriage. Four years after the death of her former husband, Mehrunnisa was married to Jahangir. She received the title of Nur Mahal and later on of Nur Jahan, by which title she is most popularly known.

Emperor granted Nur Jahan the rights of sovereignty and government. Sometimes she would sit in the balcony of her palace, while the nobles would present themselves and listen to her dictates. Coin was struck in her name, with this superscription: "By order of the King Jahangir, gold has a hundred splendours added to it by receiving the impression of the name of Nur Jahan, the Queen Begum". On all *Farmans* also receiving the Imperial signature, the name of "Nur Jahan, the Queen Begum", was jointly attached. At last, her authority reached such a pass that the king was such only in name. Repeatedly he gave out that he had bestowed the sovereignty on Nur Jahan Begum and would say, "I require nothing beyond a sir of wine and half a sir of meat".[46]

Within months of her marriage, Nur Jahan began to exercise considerable influence at court, arranging high positions for her family members and associates. A powerful clique soon formed around her, consisting of herself, her father Itmad-ud-daula, her brother Asaf Khan and Jahangir's third son, Khurram. Nur Jahan accelerated their promotion and the Mughals gained greatly by the ability and the devotion of these two highly gifted and talented officers. In 1612, Arjumand Banu Begum, better known as Mumtaz Mahal, daughter of Asaf Khan, was married to Prince Khurram. Since Nur Jahan had no children with the emperor, it was Khurram on whom the clique fixed their sights to succeed Jahangir, in preference to the disgraced and partially blinded Khusrau, the dull and incompetent second son Parvez, or the much younger and totally untested Shahryar. In 1620, Ladli Begum, Nur Jahan's daughter by her former husband, was betrothed to prince Shahryar.[47]

In the last five years of his life, from 1622 to his death in 1627, the emperor became so incapacitated by drink and opium that Nur Jahan took many administrative matters into her own hands. The extent of her influence in this latter phase of Jahangir's reign is suggested by Francisco Pelsaert, a Dutch East Company commercial officer serving in Agra from 1621 to 1627. He wrote:[48]

> "When the King comes home in the evening from hunting, he takes his seat in his *ghusalkhana* (private audience chamber), where all the lords come to present themselves and where strangers who have requests to make are received in audience. He sits here till a quarter of the night or more has passed and during this time he drinks his three *piyala*, or cups, of wine, taking them successively at regular intervals.... Everyone leaves when the last cup has been drunk and the King goes to bed. As soon as all the men have left, the Queen comes with the female slaves and they undress him, chafing and fondling him as if he were a little child; for his three cups have made him so 'happy' that he is more disposed to rest than to keep awake. This is the time when his wife, who knows so well how to manage him that she obtains whatever she asks for or desires, gets always 'yes' and hardly ever 'no' in reply."

Her father Itmad-ud-daula, for years the pillar of the empire, died soon after the marriage ceremonies. After the marriage of Shahryar with Ladli Begum, Nur Jahan changed her stand in favour of Shahryar but Asaf Khan's stand continued favouring Khurram. With brother and sister now backing different princes and Nur Jahan's new son-in-law by far the weaker of the two, the queen became ever more isolated.

Death of Jahangir

Due to excess drinking, Jahangir was suffering from asthama and usually spent some time in Kashmir to ease his illness. In 1627 he started back to Lahore from his usual visit of Kashmir. In the way, while engaged in hunting, a fatal accident overtook one of his *shikaris*, who fell over a precipice and was killed before the Emperor's eyes. The fate of the poor man greatly affected the Emperor. It seemed as though he had thus seen the angel of death. From that time he had no rest or ease and his state was entirely changed. The journey was continued two days. On the next day at Bhimbar where he was staying, he called for a glass of wine but when it was placed to his lips he was unable to swallow. Towards night he grew worse and he died early on the following day in the 22nd year of his reign. His remains were brought to Lahore and buried in a beautiful tomb at Shahdara, on the banks of the Ravi.

Due to his liberal policy and religious toleration the Christians as a whole and to some extent Hindus also have misquoted Jahangir's religion and belief. They believe that Jahangir was not a Muslim at all. They also claim that Salim was not circumcized, whereas there is the definite statement of Arif Qandahari that Salim had undergone this Muslim rite. They do not stop short even of making him a baptized Christian, without at the same time showing how they overcame the obstacle presented by his vast *harem*. It seems that the Jesuits were in these matters concerned with sending in good reports of their labours rather than with truth.

Thus Jahangir ordinarily continued Akbar's toleration. He experimented in the simultaneous maintenance of several religions by the state. He did not, in most cases, make any distinction between Muslims and non-Muslims in public employment. Emperor Jahangir ruled the country peacefully, respected all the religions of India and even of abroad. He never tried to sentimentally tease any community of his dominion. Except for Kangra, no religious building was harmed and no forcible conversion was allowed for any community.

All the communities of India, Hindus, Buddhists, Jainas, Muslims and even Christians had the freedom to profess their religion but not at any cost allowed to force the people to accept their religion. Jahangir was the ruler and he wanted his subjects happy and prosperous. Hindutva historians blame for conversion and destruction of the temple is baseless based on their hatred towards the Indian Muslim community. Even the rulers of independent India never learned a lesson from these Mughal rulers and continued the oppression of the Muslims, destruction of the mosques and conversion of the Muslims into Hindu fold.

Notes

1. Majumdar, *op. cit.*, p. 174; Beni Prasad, *op. cit.*, pp. 11-12.
2. Beni Prasad, *op. cit.*, p. 24.
3. *Ibid.*, pp. 25-26.
4. During the last days of Akbar, his relations with Salim was strained and in 1599 when he was campaigning in the Deccan, Salim gathered supporters and made an impetuous strike on Agra, where the imperial treasure was stored. When Akbar's mother scolded the wayward prince, Salim, ashamed and unable to challenge his dear grandmother, dashed back to his base in Allahabad. In 1601 Salim followed the urgings of his advisers and set up his own court in Allahabad. He even assumed imperial titles. Fearing Abul Fazl's advice Akbar to barring his succession to power, Salim took the drastic step of assassinating Abul Fazl by Bir Singh Bundela, the Rajput chieftain of Orchha in August 1602. A deeply anguished Akbar now sent another senior Mughal female, Salim's stepmother Sultana Salima Begum, to Allahabad to persuade his son to return to court. Due to her efforts a temporary reconciliation took place in April 1603. In 1603, when Akbar sent Salim to reduce the Sisodiya chieftains of Mewar, the last major

Rajput lineage to resist partnership with the Mughals, he refused to advance far from the court, fearing that, should his ageing father die, his brother Daniyal would be in a better position than he to claim the throne. Akbar finally relented and allowed him to return to his base in Allahabad, which he did in November 1603, only to set up an independent court once again. Four months later, when Salim was in Agra for the ceremonies after the death of Akbar's mother, the emperor reprimanded him for his many acts of disloyalty, even humiliating his 35-year-old son by confining him in a room for ten days without access to wine or opium, for both of which he had developed a fondness, if not a dependency. In September 1605, during an elephant fight that the emperor staged for courtly entertainment, Salim and his son Khusrau had an ugly quarrel as after death of Daniyal, Khusrau was emerged as the main contender of the throne. Consequently, when the emperor died a month later, Salim ascended the throne without a struggle, adopting as his imperial title Jahangir, "world-conqueror".

5. Beni Prasad, *op. cit.*, p. 23.
6. When Jahangir was prince Salim, the beauty of Nur Mahal attracted his attention, but Akbar disapproved her as a daughter-in-law, gave her in marriage to Sher Afghan, a nobleman of Burdwan. After his accession, having treacherously procured the death of her husband, Jahangir had Nur Mahal removed to Agra and placed under the care of his mother. For many years she repulsed all Jahangir's overtures, but when at last she consented to be his queen she became his most devoted wife. She accompanied him on all his travels and Jahangir consulted her in all important affairs of state. (E.B. Havell (1904), *A Handbook to Agra: The Taj, Sikandara, Fatehpur Sikri and the Neighbourhood,* Calcutta, pp. 26-27.)
7. Majumdar, *op. cit.*, p. 175.
8. Alexander Rogers, edit. Henry Beveridge (1909). *Memoire of Jahangir,* (*Tuzuk-i-Jahangiri* of Nooruddin Jahangir), 2nd edn., vol. I, London, pp. 7-10.
9. Sri Ram Sharma, *op. cit.*, pp. 82-83.
10. *Ibid.*, p. 89.
11. *Ibid.*
12. Harbans Mukhia, *op. cit.*, p. 24.
13. Sri Ram Sharma, *op. cit.*, p. 90.
14. Harbans Mukhia, *op. cit.*, p. 24.
15. Majumdar, *op. cit.*, p. 189.
16. *Ibid.*

17. *Ibid.*
18. Sri Ram Sharma, *op. cit.*, p. 85.
19. Harbans Mukhia, *op. cit.*, p. 24.
20. *Ibid.*, p. 20.
21. Sri Ram Sharma, *op. cit.*, pp. 85-86.
22. *Ibid.*, p. 86.
23. Gurinder Singh Mann (2001), *The Making of Sikh Scripture,* New York: Oxford University Press, p. 19. *Guru Granth,* the holy book for the Sikhs is also known as *Adi Granth* or *Granth Sahib.* Guru Arjan Dev wished to lay down the exact hymns to be sung and correct rituals to be performed by the Sikhs. He also desired to raise the status of Sikhism from a sect to a religion. He therefore decided to record the hymns of all the *gurus* in the form of a book. The *Granth,* written in verse in Gurmukhi script, was completed in 1604. It contained 974 hymns of Guru Nanak, 62 of Guru Angad, 907 of Guru Amar Das, 672 of Guru Ram Das, 2218 hymns and 116 Shabads of Guru Arjan, including his famous *Sukhmani,* sayings of 16 *bhaktas* both Hindu and Muslim such as Farid, Kabir, Namdev, Dhanna, Surdas, Pipa and Ramanand and songs of minstrels including those of Mardana, Satta and Balwand. One hundred and fifteen hymns of Guru Tegh Bahadur and one verse of Guru Gobind Singh were added later. The discourses of Guru Nanak as *Japji, Sodar* and *Kirti Sola* were given in the beginning. (Majumdar, *op. cit.*, pp. 163-64.)
24. *Tuzuk-i-Jahangiri,* vol. I, *op. cit.*, p. 72.
25. Sri Ram Sharma, *op. cit.*, p. 86-87. Majumdar, *op. cit.*, pp. 178-79.
26. *Ibid.*, pp. 86-87.
27. *Ibid.*
28. *Ibid.*, p. 87.
29. *Ibid.*, p. 88.
30. Edwardes & Garrett, *op. cit.*, p. 58.
31. Sri Ram Sharma, *op. cit.*, p. 83.
32. Majumdar, *op. cit.*, p. 182.
33. Edwardes & Garrett, *op. cit.*, p. 62.
34. Harbans Mukhia, *op, cit.*, p. 24. (The Bhawani Temple below the fort walls was, however, left untouched, though not unnoticed. His forebearance might have been inspired by the tales of the supernatural power of the Goddess. It was common belief that if a dumb person cut his tongue in two as an offering to the Goddess, after some time the broken pieces would join together and the devotee would start speaking. If a devotee, it was believed, cut his head as an offering to the Goddess, it would be carefully preserved and after some time

when it was placed on his body, the devotee would come alive. Sri Ram Sharma, *op. cit.*, pp. 82-83.)

35. Jahangir paid visit to Jawalamukhi Temple in the neighbourhood. He was at first persuaded that the ever burning flame in the temple was a trick of the priests. To confound them, he had a stream of water poured over the fire. This failed to extinguish the flame. He left the temple unharmed and gave order that the adjoining buildings be not only repaired but also added to. Sri Ram Sharma, *op. cit.*, pp. 82-83.)
36. Harbans Mukhia, *op. cit.*, p. 24.
37. *Ibid., op. cit.*, p. 19; Sri Ram Sharma, *op. cit.*, p. 83.
38. Sri Ram Sharma, *op. cit.*, p. 84; Majumdar, *op. cit.*, p. 192.
39. Harbans Mukhia, *op. cit.*, p. 24.
40. Sri Ram Sharma, *op. cit.*, p. 91.
41. *Ibid.*, pp. 92-93.
42. Harbans Mukhia, *op. cit.*, pp. 38-39.
43. Sri Ram Sharma, *op. cit.*, pp. 95-96.
44. Majumdar, *op. cit.*, pp. 179-80.
45. *Tuzuk-i-Jahangiri*, vol. I, *op. cit.*, p. 332.
46. Majumdar, *op. cit.*, pp. 185-86.
47. *Ibid.*
48. W.H. Moreland and P. Geyl (1972). tr. of *Jahangir's India: The Remonstrantie of Francisco Pelsaert,* Delhi: Idarah-i Adabiyat-i-Dehli, p. 53.

Chapter 4

Religion and Culture Under Shah Jahan

Shahabuddin Mohammad Khurram Shah Jahan (1592-1666) was born to Nuruddin Mohammad Jahangir and Jagat Gosain (Jodha Bai—a Jodhpur Princess) at Lahore on Thursday, 15 January 1592. He was brought up by Akbar's childless wife Ruqaiah Begum. During the lifetime of his father, he won his laurels as a successful organiser of victories in Mewar, Deccan and Kangra campaigns. He was a favourite of his grandfather, Akbar and his early education was no doubt carried on under liberal teachers of Sufist leanings. The rule of Shah Jahan was very peaceful, although sometimes he showed a little intolerance in the racial or religious affairs. Unfortunately, his reign, which opened with the execution of Shah Jahan's brothers and nephews was destined to close in circumstances, similarly tragic, finally ending in the death and disgrace of Shah Jahan's sons and grandsons and even his own confinement in Agra Fort until his death in 1666.

At the time of his father Jahangir's death Prince Khurram was in Deccan and Asaf Khan took matters into his own hands and put his sister Nur Jahan under detention. He also sent a courier down to the Deccan to fetch Khurram to north India. While marching to Agra, the prince sent a return courier ordering the execution of other princes who might contest his claim to the throne: his younger brother Shahryar, the two sons of his late brother Khusrau and two sons of his late uncle Daniyal. In January 1628 his grisly order was carried out and soon he triumphantly entered Agra where he was hailed with the title of Abul Muzaffar Shahbuddin Mohammad Sahib-i Kiran-i Sani. On 4 February 1628, at an hour precisely fixed by his astrologers, he was formally crowned emperor. Shah Jahan ruled India from 1628 to 1658.

Upon his coronation, he doled out generous sums to his immediate family: 2,00,000 gold coins (*ashrafi*) and Rs. 6,00,000 to his favourite wife, Mumtaz Mahal, 1,00,000 *ashrafis* and Rs. 6,00,000 to his favourite daughter, Jahanara and Rs. 1,50,000 to each of his first three sons. He made Asaf Khan the wazir of the empire, with a rank of 8,000/8,000. Mahabat Khan was made governor of Ajmer, with the even higher rank of 9,000/9,000. Nur Jahan was compelled to live her remaining eighteen years in Lahore with her daughter, Shahryar's widow. She was buried next to Jahangir in the magnificent tomb that she had built for her husband outside the city.

Due to some of his exceptional intolerance as told by some hardcore authors, Shah Jahan is known not as moderate and lenient as his ancestors. If Akbar was liberal in his religious views and Jahangir indifferent to nicer questions of theology, Shah Jahan was considered as an orthodox Muslim. Although born of a Rajput mother to a father whose mother was also a Rajput princess, Shah Jahan does not seem to have been much influenced by these factors. For Hindutva historians the period of Shah Jahan is considered a crucial period as he was more a Muslim than his forefathers.

Shah Jahan was himself fond of the Indian culture and his homeland Hindustan. He took a verse that the Sufi poet Amir Khusro (1253-1325), son of a Rajput mother and Turkic father, had originally composed in praise of India (Khusro's motherland). He had ascribed the words of the verse around the roof of the audience Hall in his Delhi palace: "If there is a heaven on earth, it is here, it is here, it is here".[1]

Under Shah Jahan, the whole empire enjoyed comparative peace and prosperity. Shah Jahan's just and liberal government continued his father's and grandfather's policy of tolerance towards the Hindus and in matters of administration. Shah Jahan although a practising Muslim, had no religious commitment at the time of his accession to the throne. But unlike his father and grandfather, he married no Hindu princess and thus that mellowing influence was lacking in his *harem*.

Shah Jahan and the Christians

During the last days of Jahangir and the biginning of Shah Jahan's rule, the Christian missionaries under Portuguese had become very strong and powerful in their religious activities. The Portuguese had made them even politically and economically more strong in Hughli in Bengal. The town of Hughli had of late risen to importance and the Portuguese had erected large and substantial buildings, which they had fortified with cannons and other implements of war. On one side of it was the river; on the other three sides was a ditch filled from the river. They had created their own strong military base. Along with their trade and commerce activities, the Portuguese were indulgence in the slave-trade and the religious conversion which had inflamed the wrath of the Emperor.

Abdul Hamid Lahori in his *Padshah-Nama* writes:[2]

> "Some of the inhabitants by force and more by hopes of gain, they infected with their Nazarene (Christian) teaching and sent them off in ships to Europe. ...These hateful practices were not confined to the lands they occupied, but they seized and carried off every one they could lay their hands upon along the sides of the river. ... After his accession, he appointed Karim Khan to the government of Bengal and impressed upon him the duty of overthrowing these mischievous people."

Preparations were accordingly made and towards the close of the month of June 1632 the siege of Hughli began. A large army, said to number 1,50,000 men of all arms, was sent by Qasim Khan, under the command of his son, assisted by Allan Yar Khan, the ablest officer in the Bengal Mughal army. Qasim Khan planned the campaign carefully and with 600 boats, 1,400 horsemen, 90 elephants and a large force of infantry blocked the passage to Hughli, both by land and sea. The siege lasted for nearly three months and it says much for Portuguese military discipline that this small garrison of 1,000 men made so heroic a resistance and defended the town and their factory against such heavy odds.[3]

Further resistance became impossible and the Portuguese left Hughli in a body by boats and the place was occupied by the Mughal forces. 14,400 Indians from Hughli and the neighbouring *parganas* were set free. The number of casualties on the imperial side is recorded as 1,000 but the Portuguese suffered heavy losses. Ten thousand persons lost their lives and more than 4,000 Christian were made prisoners. The Christian prisoners were brought to Agra to the presence of the "faith-defending Emperor". They were offered the choice between conversion to Islam and confinement or slavery under abjectly severe conditions. Few of them cared to save their bodies at the cost of their souls and, as the author of the *Padshah-Nama* remarks, "many of them passed from prison to hell".[4] Their religious images were broken up and thrown into the River Jumna. Shah Jahan's treatment was severe, but the Portuguese richly deserved their fate.

Shah Jahan and the Muslims

Shah Jahan never gave up the basic policy of toleration and forbearance, which had stood the test of time. However, in religious matters Shah Jahan was more uncompromising than Akbar or Jahangir and his policy was comparatively more straight, firm and bold than that of his predecessors. Shah Jahan's education had been carried on under liberal teachers of the Sufi (mystic) school, but later on, he became more orthodox and less tolerant. He married no Hindu princess and was thus free from the mellowing influence of the *harem* in the matters of religion. Shah Jahan started his reform of Muslim society by eradicating un-Islamic practices.

Shah Jahan abolished *sijda* practices in the court as it involved prostration which, according to the Islamic tradition, is due to Allah alone. This practice was very common in Akbar's reign and during Jahangir the religious officers, the *qazis*, the *mir adals* and the *sadrs* were exempt from paying respects to the emperor in that fashion. Shah Jahan allowed *chahar taslim* in place of *sijda*. This involved bowing and touching one's forehead, eyes and arms four times. But an exception was made in favour of the theologians of various degrees. They were excused *chahar taslim* and were to salute the emperor by using the common Muslim formula of "wishing peace".[5]

Shah Jahan was anxious to give his court a Muslim colouring. All the Muslim festivals were now regularly celebrated with imperial grandeur. Rs. 70,000 a year was set apart for distribution in charities, Rs. 30,000 was given away during the month of Ramazan, Rs. 10,000 was distributed during the months of Muharram, Rajab, Shaban and Rabi-ul-Awwal. These festivals were court festivals; Hindus and Muslims alike attended them, made presents to the emperor who, in his turn, gave gifts to the Amirs. The Eids and Shab-i-Barats were occasions of great rejoicings. Raja Jaswant Singh and Raja Jai Singh were both given an elephant each on the occasion of the Eid in the twelfth year of his reign.[6]

Shah Jahan did not reimpose the *jazia* but he revived the pilgrim-tax for a short while. He forbade the completion of certain temples and prevented the building of new temples. This policy was also reviewed later on. Certain temples were destroyed, but this was due to local prejudices and to the fact that some of them were utilised against the state. Prohibition of conversion to Hinduism and Christianity was justified as a defensive measure; inquiries made in Bhambar, an adjoining area, revealed that 4,000 Muslim women had keen converted to Hinduism: Laws against blasphemy were made more stringent.[7] On the whole, Shah Jahan was more anxious than his predecessors to uphold Muslim religion and to exalt Muslim society, but his orthodoxy was neither militant nor narrow-minded. He tried to hold the balance between the policy initiated by Akbar, on the one hand and the demands of the fanatical and orthodox Muslim divines, on the other.

When he despatched a mission to Qutb-ul-Mulk of Golconda in 1635-36, he definitely proclaimed himself ordained by Allah not only as the leader of the Sunnis but the destroyer of all those who did not conform to his ideas of Islam. In his letter to the ruler of Golconda, Shah Jahan spoke of himself as the leader of the Sunnis and the destroyer of all those who did not conform to his ideas of Islam. Hard pressed by the Mughal armies, Qutb-ul-Mulk had to proclaim himself a Sunni and inaugurate Sunni rites in his state. Shah Jahan also acted as the champion of the true faith, the Sunni variety of Islam.[8]

Abdul Hamid Lahori in his *Badshah Nama* says that in 1632, during the sixth year of his reign, it had been brought to the notice of Shah Jahan that during the late reign of his father many idol temples had been begun, but remained unfinished, at Benares. The Hindus were now desirous of completing them. Shah Jahan gave orders that at Benares and throughout all his dominions in every place all temples that had been begun should be cast down. It was now reported from the province of Allahabad that seventy temples had been destroyed in the district of Benares.[9]

These seventy temples were built during Jahangir's reign and were the place of great attraction for Muslims and conversion of Muslims to Hindu fold as well. Due to these large scale conversions from Islam to Hinduism enraged Shah Jahan against the Varanasi *pandits*. During Jahangir's reign, twenty-three Muslims were converted to Hinduism. All these incidents provoked Shah Jahan to order for demolition of these seventy temples in Varanasi. Shah Jahan had also destroyed the temples which were built by the rebel *rajas* such as Rajput *raja* of Orchha in Madhya Pradesh. Royal forces attacked the temples after subduing the rebellious chiefs to hurt them sentimentally and also teach a lesson for revolting the chiefs and subjects.[10]

During the early years of Shah Jahan, some unfinished or newly-built temples were destroyed on the logical basis. Throughout the Mughal period, Varanasi and Mathura were the centres of blasphemy and the Brahmans of these cities intrigued against the government and converted many of the Muslims into Hindu fold. They also had some prejudice, rigid and were adamant in this regard and flouted the rule for temple construction without permission. Moreover, the local *raja*s had made it the fashion to build the temples as their religious duty as well as the path of salvation. These *raja*s and traders, at the instigation of the Brahmans of sacred cities, usually build the temples in thousands of numbers as they thought it the only source of salvation. Shah Jahan thought that the sufficient numbers of temples were already for the worship and there is no further need of the temples for worship.

Shah Jahan and the Hindus

In the reign of Shah Jahan, some contemporary Muslim writers declare, the arrogance and boldness of the Hindus increased and in several places mosques were converted into temples and Muslims were converted to Hinduism; and there was a challenge even to the representation of Musalmans in the services, particularly in the revenue department. This awakened the fears of the Musalmans and Muslim public opinion was organised by Muslim divines. Shah Jahan was unable to resist the pressure of Muslim opinion or the influence of the divines. However, Shah Jahan was a pure Muslim following the tenets of Islam but continued the religious tolerance policy of his father and grandfather.

Shah Jahan followed many of his father and grandfather's old court practices which were undoubtedly Hindu customary practices to appease the Hindu subjects and nobility. Under his rule some of the older practices were preserved as being expedient and less harmful. He continued the balcony salutation (*jharokha darshan*) practice. He also maintained customary annual ceremony of *tula dan*, twice in a year on solar and lunar dates. It was a custom of weighing the emperor against different commodities and giving them away. He kept astrologers at court. He was a patron of painting, even of portrait-painting and many great paintings of his court are still preserved. The emperors used to make the *tika* sign on the forehead of the Hindu *raja*s when they acceded to their titles. Shah Jahan, though he would not discontinue it, delegated this task to his prime minister. Music and dancing regained in fashion at the court and the emperor kept court musicians who sang daily at regular intervals.[11]

During the reign of Shah Jahan, there were many examples of Muslim conversion to Hinduism. There were also many cases of conversion through marriages. There was a case in Kashmir where Muslim girls in Kashmir were married to Hindu boys and became Hindus. Even the Mughal officials were in the influence of the Hindu *pandits*. There were also many reports of participating the Mughal officials in Hindu festivals such as Jagannath festival. Besides them, the Hindu Brahmans thought that there was a need for conversion back to Hinduism. They evolved ceremonies for reconversion called purification (*shuddhi*), usually involving both the payment of money and a ritual. The Sikh Guru Hargobind reconverted a large number of Muslims into Sikh fold. *Dabistan* records this with an unusual trace of hyperbole: “Not a Muslim was left between the hills of Kiratpur in Punjab and the frontiers of Tibet and Khotan”. Shah Jahan, as a ruler, adopted harsh policies to control this blasphemy. Shah Jahan was worried about this and established a department to deal with it and forbade any proselytizing by Hindus.[12]

Shah Jahan revived the pilgrimage tax for the time being but did not re-impose the *jazia*. He remitted this tax when a Hindu scholar of Benares, Kavindaracharya led a deputation to the emperor against pilgrimage tax. Shah Jahan also allowed his Hindu subjects all religious liberty as enjoyed by the Muslim subjects.[13]

Shah Jahan never encouraged conversion to Islam among the general population and honoured Hindu law in some of his provinces. Jahangir had punished one Mughal official for converting the son of a defeated Hindu *raja*. Everywhere, there was an atmosphere of freedom of liberty and religion. However, Shah Jahan was unable to control the conversion among the high-class people who were converting for money, punishment, marriage and because they liked it. Some Hindu wives of the Muslim rulers were sometimes converted and built mosques.[14]

Hindu Mansabdars

During his reign, Shah Jahan promoted the Hindus on the very high ranks in the Mughal administration. In Shah Jahan's reign the number of *mansabdars* was very much increased. When Aurangzeb rebelled against his father, Maharaja Jaswant Singh of Jodhpur was the premier noble of the empire holding the status of a *hakim* and 7,000 horses out of which 5,000 was Do Aspa and Sih Aspa (having two or three horses). He, thus, held the highest office which was open to an imperial subject. In the revenue department Rai-i-Rayan Raghu Nath was the imperial revenue minister at the time. Thus when Aurangzeb challenged his father's right to the throne the Hindus occupied a very important position in the public services of the empire.[15]

In the thirty-first year of Shah Jahan's reign there were fifty-two Hindus in a total of 241, serving as *mansabdars* commanding 1,000 to 7,000. At the end of the tenth year there were 189 *mansabdars* of 1,000 and above and out of them 35 were Hindus. At the end of the twentieth year out of a total of 231 living *mansabdars* of 1,000 and above, 51 were Hindus. If we include the number of the *mansabdars* of 500 and above, the position revealed is almost the same. At the end of the tenth year, the number of the Hindu *mansabdars* of 500 and above was 76 out of a total of 419. At the end of the twentieth year there were 97 Hindus out of a total of 453.[16]

Under Shah Jahan Hindus counted among them the mightiest subject and the highest public servant, the Imperial finance minister and several provincial ministers of finance besides several military commanders of great time. The Hindutva scholars' complaint for Shah Jahan of being Muslim promoter is quite baseless and biased. No doubt Shah Jahan was a Muslim by faith and fully followed the Muslim religious practices but as a ruler he was most tolerant and lenient for all his subjects.

Shah Jahan's Temple Policy

There was a logic behind the Shah Jahan's temple policy of forbidding the completion of certain temples that had been started during his predecessor's reign and repairing to old temples were prohibited and the building of new temples was forbidden. This policy of Shah Jahan was based on the complaints against the Hindus on the frontiers of the Punjab that they had rebuilt seventy temples using the material of the mosques. All these temples were ordered to be destroyed and mosques built in their place. Shah Jahan now embarked on a campaign of complete destruction of the new temples of the Hindus. Three temples were destroyed in Gujarat, seventy-two temples in Benares and its neighbourhood and probably four temples elsewhere in the province of Allahabad. The materials of some of the Hindu temples were used for building mosques.[17]

In 1632, the Hindus of Benares also suffered heavy losses on religious grounds. It had been brought to the notice of His Majesty,writes Abdul Hamid Lahori, in the *Padshah-Nama*, that

> "during the late reign many idol temples had been begun, but remained unfinished, at Benares, the great stronghold of infidelity. The infidels were now desirous of completing them. His Majesty, the defender of the faith, gave orders that at Benares and throughout all his dominions in every place, all temples that had been begun should be cast down. It was now reported from the province of Allahabad that seventy-six temples had been destroyed in the district of Benares."[18]

The above order was naturally the result of the fury of Shah Jahan when he heard the destruction of the mosques but his order was very soon reverted and he applied policy of tolerance towards his Hindu subjects. No doubt there were also some instances of temple destruction by the Mughal army but it were only the symbolic act of the victorious army against the defeated *raja*s and religious shrines of rebel chiefs and enemies. In many of the cases the Mughal army was of Hindus who destroyed the Hindu temples of the defeated *raja*s. Thus these activities were mostly not the result of the Hindu-Muslim feelings but the feelings of the victory and superiority.

In later years Shah Jahan fully promoted the Hindus interests and religious tolerance policy. Prince Dara presented a stone railing to the temple of Kesho Rai at Mathura. Shah Jahan wrote a letter in 1643-44 to Jai Singh, Raja of Jaipur, conceded to him full liberty to appoint the presiding priest at the temple of Brindaban built by Man Singh. Man Singh's mother had died in Bengal and by a letter dated August 1639, Shah Jahan granted 200 *bigha*s of land to be attached to her mausoleum in order to ensure its upkeep. The restoration of their temples to the Hindus of Gujarat, however, also took place after 1647.[19]

Conversion under Shah Jahan

Shah Jahan also stopped the prevailing practice of allowing the Hindus and the Christians to make converts to their religion. The permission granted to Christians was withdrawn as the result of the war against the Portuguese. Christians had never been able to convert a large number of Hindus and Muslims to their faith. Their efforts had mainly been confined to keeping within the Christian faith such Armenians, Europeans and others of their faith who happened to take service at the Mughal court. Before the establishment of the Jesuit Missions at Agra and Lahore, the Christians entering the Mughal service usually adopted non-Christian modes of life from which they were rescued by the Jesuit missionaries. Now that the missionaries were established at Agra and Lahore, such cases became rare.[20]

Like the Christians, the Hindus also were very much involved in conversion activities. They had been actually absorbing a number of Muslims conversions to Hinduism. Shah Jahan while returning from Kashmir through Jammu, he discovered, as Jahangir had discovered before him, that the Hindus of Bhadauri and Bhimbar accepted daughters of Muslim parents and converted them to their own faith. These women were cremated at their death according to Hindu rites. Jahangir had tried to stop this practice but to no avail. Shah Jahan not only issued order making such marriages unlawful henceforward, but ordered that these converted Muslim girls be taken away from their husbands, who in turn were to be fined. They could escape the fine if they accepted Islam. So widespread was this practice of converting Muslim girls to Hinduism that these orders discovered more than 4,000 such women.[21]

Shah Jahan discovered that his orders had not completely stopped this source of conversion to Hinduism. During the course of the same journey Shah Jahan came across the same source of uneasiness to his orthodoxy in Gujarat. Here again some seventy such converts were discovered. General orders were issued to scour the Punjab and put down these practices by force. Four hundred cases were further reported in consequence. However, in spite of his orders to ban on conversion, his orders were being openly flouted by hardcore Hindus in all around his dominion.[22]

A large number of Muslims were converted to Hinduism by the vairagis. The author of the *Dabistan-i-Mazahib* speaks of these conversions as if from his own personal knowledge. Two Muslim nobles are mentioned among these converts, Mirza Salih and Mirza Haidar. *Dabistan-i-Mazahib* also mentions that when the Sikh Guru Hargobind, took up his residence at Kiratpur in the Punjab, he succeeded in converting a large number of Muslims some time before 1645. Not a Muslim was left between the hills near Kiratpur and the frontiers of Tibet and Khotan.[23]

Shah Jahan also noticed that Muslim war prisoners were openly sold in the market and they were purchased as slaves by wealthy Hindus and even Muslim army chiefs. In these sale-purchase and process of enslavement many Muslim war prisoners were forcibly converted to the Hindu fold. Shah Jahan now issued an order that Muslim prisoners of war were not to be sold to the Hindus as slaves. Hindu soldiers were also forbidden from enslaving Muslims.[24]

Shah Jahan tried to ban on conversion but he promoted conversion into true faith or Islam. There was a practice during Shah Jahan's rule that any crime could be expatiated if a man was willing enough to become Muslim. The Hindus of the Punjab, Bhimbar, Bhadauri and Sirhind, who were guilty of the offence of abetting apostasy, were all offered remission of their sentences provided they accepted Islam. When the war with the Portuguese started, many of them were made prisoners and condemned to slavery or death. But they too were offered their freedom and life if they accepted Islam. Of the 400 who were brought before the emperor, very few, however, accepted the offer, the rest were imprisoned but orders were issued that whenever they should express their willingness to be converted they should be liberated and given daily allowances.[25]

Shah Jahan as a Builder

Basically, Shah Jahan is known as a great builder and because of this his period is generally known as golden period in building and construction works. His period was one of the greatest epochs of Indian architecture. Shah Jahan had full architectural knowledge and interest. He built many world fame buildings such as the Shalimar Gardens in Kashmir, the white marble palace in Ajmer and the high-carat golden, jewel-encrusted Peacock Throne. When his beloved wife Mumtaz died, Shah Jahan built the Taj Mahal in her memory on the bank of Jamuna River near Agra fort. His son

Aurangzeb detained him in the Agra Fort, where he could gaze at the Taj Mahal until his death eight years later.[26]

His other most popular buildings were Grand Mosque of Delhi, Red Fort of Delhi, the Agra Fort, Lahore Fort, etc. In the first decade of his reign, Shah Jahan remodelled the forts of the empire's two primary capitals, Lahore and Agra. At both sites, nearly all the structures built by Akbar and Jahangir were dismantled to make room for new palaces. Prior to his reign, imperial *mansabdars* simply stood in the open courtyards before the emperor's *jharokha*. Shah Jahan, however, built covered audience halls, whose forty evenly spaced columns enabled a precise positioning of courtiers in the imperial hierarchy. Shah Jahan resolved to build an entire city-fort complex from scratch. This is Shahjahanabad, today's "Red Fort" and its adjoining walled city—now Old Delhi—built between 1639 and 1648 at a cost of six million rupees.[27]

It was in the fort's ornate Hall of Private Audience that Shah Jahan placed his famous Peacock Throne, which took craftsmen seven years to assemble and whose precious stones were valued at ten million rupees. The French traveller Jean-Baptiste Tavernier visited the court in the winter of 1640-41 and as a gem merchant, he described a dazzling throne 1.8 m in length and 1.2 m wide inlaid with numerous emeralds, rubies, pearls and diamonds, with a canopy surmounted with a peacock, its tail made of blue sapphires, its gold body inlaid with precious stones and an enormous pear-shaped pearl suspended from a large ruby fronting its breast.[28]

Besides these buildings, he built hundreds of beautiful, magnificent, architecturally rich mosques all over India. These include the most famous Lahore's mosque of Wazir Khan (1635), the mosque at Shaikh Muinuddin Chishti's shrine in Ajmer (1636) and the congregational mosques at Agra (1648), Shahjahanabad (1656) and Thatta (1657). In most of the buildings he used marbles and it was first time in the history of building architecture such a large scale marbles were used. Due to the building construction, his reign was known as the golden period of medieval India.

Shah Jahan's construction works provided the jobs to earn bread and butter for his subjects as he spent lavishly in his buildings. More interestingly, after his expenditure in the building projects, he left more wealth in the royal treasure than he received from his predecessors. In his reign, his subjects were happy and the atmosphere was peaceful. Fortunately, his buildings are still the source of high income for central and state governments in independent India. Undoubtedly, Shah Jahan raised the status of India by his building projects, which still attracting lakhs of foreign tourists to see his adventurous buildings including the Taj Mahal, one of the Seven Wonders of the World.

Taj Mahal

Taj Mahal is situated in Agra on the bank of Jamuna River. It is believed that the name Agra is derived from "Agur", a local word for a "salt-pan", the soil being brackish and much salt having been once made here by evaporation. Agra is said to have rebuilt by Sikandar Lodi in 1505 and Sikandara known after his name became his seat of government. Babur made Agra as his capital in the old fort build by Lodi rulers and tried to inhabit the city with his nobility and their relatives. Agra gained more importance when Akbar visited the place in 1558 and founded the modern city of Agra, popularly known as Akbarabad, opposite to the old city on the left bank of the River Jamuna. The present Agra Fort was commenced by Akbar in 1566, on the site of an older one constructed by Salim Shah Sur, the son of Sher Shah. Later on, Emperor Shah Jahan extended the Agra Fort and also built the world-fame Taj Mahal.[29]

Taj Mahal was built in Agra by Emperor Shah Jahan, which completed in 17 years (1632-48) (Tavernier says twenty-two years probably including all the accessory buildings—1632-53), to house the tomb of his favourite wife, Arjumand Bano Begum or Aliya Begum popularly known as Mumtaz Mahal (ornament of the palace). Arjumand Bano Begum was the daughter of Nur Jahan's brother, Asaf Khan and granddaughter of Mirza Ghiyas Beg (Itimad-ud-Daulah, father of Nur Jahan). She was married to Shah Jahan (then Prince Khurram) in 1612. The bridegroom was then twenty years and three months old and the bride just fourteen months younger. The youthful couple enjoyed a happy married life for about nineteen years.

Mumtaz Mahal died at Burhanpur after delivering her fourteenth child on 17 June 1631 at the age of 39, plunging the king into a state of unremitting grief. Keene says that she bore seven children to Shah Jahan and died in childbed of the eighth. On her death, Emperor Shah Jahan was much grieved and wept bitterly. For a week he refused to appear in public. No business was transacted. From constant weeping he was forced to wear spectacles, so his chronicler reports and within a matter of days a third of his beard and moustache had turned white. Abdul Hamid Lahori records that before this tragedy he did not have even twenty grey hairs in his beard, but after this incident, the majority of the hair in his beard turned grey. For two years he remained aloof from tasty dishes, gorgeous robes, music and merriment and other recreations.[30] Shah Jahan, who loved her both for her personal charms and for her moral virtues, faithfully cherished her memory and never married again, though he survived her by 35 years.

Mumtaz Mahal was buried in Burhanpur but after six months her dead body was transferred to Agra in January 1632 and buried temporarily in the garden of the Taj while the foundations of the building were being laid. It was then placed in the vault where it now lies. The land where Taj was build belonged to Raja Jai Singh, grandson of Raja Man Singh. Lahori mentions that another plot was given to him from the crown-land in exchange for this piece of land. In Agra, she was buried in a spot in a garden which could be still pointed out, close by the mosque until the mausoleum was ready for her reception. In the same month of her burial in Agra in January 1632, the Taj Mahal began to be constructed on the bank of River Jamuna.[31]

Emperor's aim was to create an earthly replica of the house of Mumtaz Mahal in the Garden of Paradise. For this purpose he took to a monumental scale the kind of riverfront style that was already prevalent among Agra's residential gardens, while also building upon the tradition of Mughal tomb design. After completion of the Taj Mahal, her body again shifted to the present position in the Taj. Taj Mahal also houses the tomb of Shah Jahan himself. It is said that Shah Jahan had intended to construct a mausoleum for himself opposite to the Taj, on the other side of the Jamuna and to connect the two by a great bridge. The project was interrupted and never completed, owing to the usurpation of Aurangzeb, shortly after the foundations were laid.

The Taj rises a total height of 243 ft and 6 inches including central dome surrounded by four smaller domes with four slender towers or minarets stood at the corners of the 19 ft high plinth. The verses from the Holy Quran were inscribed in calligraphy on the arched entrances to the mausoleum. Inside the mausoleum, an octagonal chamber adorned with carvings and semi-precious stones housed the cenotaph or false tombs of Mumtaz Mahal and Shah Jahan. The real sarcophagus containing their actual remains lay below at garden level. The rest of the Taj Mahal complex included the main gateway of red sandstone and squire garden divided into quarters by long pools of water, as well as a red sandstone mosque and an identical building called a *jawab* (mirror) directly across from the mosque.[32]

More than 20,000 workers and artisans from India, Persia, Europe and the Ottoman Empire were engaged in the construction. White marbles, red sandstone and other stones were supplied free by vassal states. The state treasury supplied 40,000 tola or 466.55 kg gold and other materials such as semi-precious stones including jade, crystal, lapis lazuli, amethyst and turquoise used for Pietra Dura technique. Besides the lavish expenditure on the building, lakhs of rupees were spent in providing the richest of Persian silk carpets, golden lamps and magnificent candlesticks. According to the local accounts, the total expenditure amounted to rupees nearly

Rs. 185 lakh. Colonel Anderson in a paper in *Calcutta Review* states the cost to have been Rs. 4,11,48,826. Keene quotes the statement from a guide to the Taj:[33]

> "The native account of the cost of the Taj gives 98,55,426 rupees as having been given by the Rajas and Nawabs. And out of the Emperors private treasury 86,09,760 rupees. There are said to have been two silver doors at the entrance of the Taj, which are stated to have cost 1,27,000 rupees and were studded with 1,100 nails, each having a head made of a Sonat rupee; these gates were taken away and melted down by the Jats when they attacked and sacked Agra."

The tomb of Humayun (1556) seems to have been the chief model of the elevation. It is believed that the chief architect of the Taj was Ustad Ahmad Lahori, an Indian of Persian descent who later on built the Red Fort Delhi. Some nineteenth century works mention Ustad Isa Afandi, a Byzantine Turk or native of Shiraz in Persia as the designer of the Taj Mahal. Some European scholars held the view that the Taj was designed by a Venetian jeweller or goldsmith, Geronimo Veronco. However, it must be emphasized that the design of the Taj Mahal can't be ascribed to any single mastermind, Ustad Isa or anybody else. The name of many of the builders who participated in the construction of the Taj in different capacities has been drawn to us through Persian sources. Amanat Khan Shirazi has unanimously been mentioned as the calligrapher and this fact is attested on the Taj gateway where his name has been inscribed at the end of the inscription. The names of the many Hindu inlayers have also been recorded.[34]

Mohd Moinuddin mentions that for the construction of this miracle of architecture, Shah Jahan invited to his court all the eminent artists of various countries, architects and masons and artists in his own territories, as well as from foreign countries; such as Persia, Arabia and Turkey. Master Isa Afandi, the designer and Amanat Khan Shirazi Tugra—writer, Mohammad Sharif from Samarqand—Draughtsman, superintendent of the masons, Mohammad Hanif of Akbarabad, were appointed each on a monthly salary of Rs. 1,000. Mohammad Khan as calligrapher from Shiraz, Kadir Zaman Khan from Arabia as general artist, Chiranjee Lal of Delhi as mosaicist, received the salary Rs. 800 a month; Baldeo Dass of Multan as *gultarash*, received Rs. 690 a month; Munnu Lal from Lahore, Jamuna Dass of Delhi, as inlayer, received Rs. 680 a month; Abdullah mason, Rs. 675 a month; Barkat Ali, inlayer, Rs. 632 a month; Bhagwan Dass of Multan, inlayer, Rs. 630 a month; Mohammad Yousuf Khan of Delhi, inlayer, Chhote Lal of Multan, inlayer, Jhumar Lal, inlayer, Abdul Ghaffar calligrapher, Wahab Khan of Persia, calligrapher, Amir Ali of Multan as *gultarash*, Ismail Khan of Turkey as dome-maker, Rs. 600 a month; Mohammad Sajjad of Balkh as a mason, Rs. 550 a month; Mohammad Khan of Baghdad as calligrapher, Mohammad Siddiq of Delhi as mason, Ata Muhammad of Bukhara for sculpture, Abu Yusuf of Delhi as inlayer, Abu Turrab Khan of Multan as a mason, received the salary of Rs. 500 a month; Shakrullah of Multan as *gultarash*, Rs. 475 a month; Shakir Mohammad of Bukhara as *gultarash*, Baushan Khan of Syria, as a calligrapher, Rs. 400 a month; Shivji Lal of Multan as inlayer, Rs. 342 a month; Mohan Dass of Multan as inlayer, Kazim Khan of Lahore as *kalash*-maker, Rs. 200 a month, etc. In short, the services of the most skilful men of the age in Asia were secured for the production of this wonder of wonders.The whole gang of labourers and workmen numbered some 20,000 men. Makramat Khan and Mir Abdul Karim were the inspectors-general of the several branches into which the establishment was divided.[35]

No doubt it is a masterpiece of the beauty and incomparable example of art and architecture. E.B. Havell remarks that what were the thoughts of the designers and Shah Jahan himself, when they resolved to raise a monument of eternal love to the Crown of the Palace—Taj Mahal? Surely not only of a mausoleum—a sepulchre fashioned after ordinary architectural canons but of an architectonic ideal, symbolical of her womanly grace and beauty. Those critics who have objected to the effeminacy of the architecture unconsciously pay the highest tribute to the genius of the builders. The Taj was meant to be feminine. The whole conception and every line and detail of it, express the intention of the designers. It is Mumtaz Mahal herself, radiant in her youthful beauty, who still lingers on the banks of the shining Jamuna, at early morning, in the glowing midday sun, or the silver moonlight. Or rather, we should say, it conveys a more abstract thought; it is India's noble tribute to the grace of Indian womanhood—the Venus de Milo of the East.[36]

During the downfall of the Mughal Empire, the Jats of Deeg and Bharatpur severely sacked the Taj building and carried away the valuable items and precious stones including two silver doors of the Taj in 1764. They retained Agra under their control for ten years. The Marathas also looted these buildings on their turn. The British under Captain Taylor also looted these buildings and auctioned the marbles jewels. They looted and plundered not only the Taj but Agra Fort also. Akbar's tomb at Sikandara was also looted and his grave unearthed and his bones were burnt by the Jat king Raja Ram. A sheet of pearls, valued at several lakhs, made to cover the sarcophagus was carried off by the Amir Husain Ali Khan, in 1720, as part of his share of the spoil of Agra. Naturally, this was the big cultural and material loss of India as if these buildings were remained intact, independent India must have culturally and materially benefitted much more.

E.B. Havell says that Lord William Bentinck in his rule in India ordered for auction of Taj Mahal. But the Taj escaped the same fate because the proceeds of this sale were unsatisfactory. It was first auctioned in 1831 in the bid of Rs. 2 lakh. Seth Lakhmichand Jain of Mathura was the highest bidder. But the locals claiming to be the descendants of workers of the Taj resisted the move. In 1832 Taj was again auctioned in addition to four other properties of Agra. Seth Lakhmichand was again the highest bidder of Rs. 7 lakh. But the deal of the Taj was not finalized because when the Magistrate asked the Seth that what he will do to such a huge monument; the Seth replied that he will dismantle the monument and sell the stones in the market. Then the magistrate cancelled the bid and saved the monument. But some related stories tell that Lord Bentinck wanted to dismantle the Taj for the sake of marbles and gems but due to the fear of disturbances among the natives, the plan could not be materialized. At the beginning of the twentieth century, Lord Curzon ordered the Taj restoration project that got completed in 1908. The buildings were repaired; the gardens were restored and even got the canals working again.[37]

Taj Mahal is a fine example of Hindu and Muslim architecture, cultural synthesis and a fine piece art, architecture, science, technology and feminine character. Some Hindutva scholars claim that the Taj was a Rajput Palace or Shiva Temple converted into the tomb is fully baseless. In view of the evidence from the Persian sources and the accounts of foreign travellers, particularly Peter Mundy, Tavernier, Munucci and Bernier, claim that the Taj was built by Emperor Shah Jahan and the claim of the Hindutva storyteller is completely absurd and without a warrant.[38]

Controversy arose over Taj Mahal when a fringe Hindu-centric self-proclaimed historian Purushottam Nagesh Oak wrote a book in 1989, *Taj Mahal: The True Story*. Oak claimed the monument was built in 1155 and not in the seventeenth century as stated by the ASI, which is responsible for archaeological research, conservation and preservation of historical sites, monuments, artefacts, etc. Oak propounded the structure was built centuries before the Mughals invaded India and claimed the name Taj Mahal was an obscure corrupted form of a Sanskrit term "Tejo Mahalaya". Oak claimed, Taj Mahal was most likely built by Hindu ruler Jai Singh I and the Taj Mahal was, actually, a Shiva Temple and Rajput royal palace named Tejo Mahalaya. It was captured by Shah Jahan and then turned into a tomb and renamed as Taj Mahal, he claimed. The Supreme Court quashed Oak's petition in 2000 to declare Taj Mahal was built by a Hindu king.[39]

P.N. Oak fabricates a story as an eye-witness that soon after Mumtaz's death she was buried in Burhanpur. Six months later when Shah Jahan visualized the possibility of ousting Jai Singh from his resplendent hereditary palace, using the death of his wife as a lever, he kept exerting his royal pressure in talking Jai Singh out of his luxurious ancestral home. Since Jai Singh could not be so easily prevailed upon, Shah Jahan had the body of Mumtaz brought from Burhanpur to serve as a sort of an ultimatum. When the body itself was there as a handy asset for the emperor and the entire Muslim nobility to browbeat Jai Singh with could he hold out any longer? He had to surrender his ancestral palace. Within a few months, its central octagonal throne chamber was dug up. Two trenches were made in the basement and Mumtaz's exhumed body was interred in one. Above the basement, in the throne chamber, two cenotaphs were raised to be directly above the graves in the basement. The other trench in the basement was for Shah Jahan. The cenotaph above his trench could have been completed even with that of Mumtaz because after Shah Jahan's death he could easily be buried in the open trench in the basement without disturbing the cenotaph above. This was necessary to ensure a grand burial for himself alongside Mumtaz when he knew that none of his sons cared for him two hoots. The cenotaphs had to be erected in the throne-chamber above the basement lest while the royal bodies lay underneath others would use the main upper chamber for temporal purposes thereby violating the sanctity of the departed souls and the dignity of royalty, albeit deceased.[40]

In his another work P. N. Oak mentions that Taj Mahal was a Hindu temple dedicated to Lord Shiva of 1155 CE. For that, he makes the reference of a stone inscription known as the Bateshwar inscription kept in the Lucknow Museum. In the inscription it is mentioned,

> "He (King Parmardi Dev ... or on his behalf his Minister Salakshana) raised a palace which had inside the idol of Lord Vishnu whose feet the King used to touch with his (bowed) head. Similarly the King also had constructed this temple (dedicated) to the God who bears the crescent on his (fore) head made of crystal-white stone. Consecrated in that (magnificent) temple the Lord (was so pleased that He) never thought of repairing to His

(Himalayan) abode in Mount Kailash (this inscription is) dated 1212 Vikram Era, Ashwin (month), Sunday, the fourth day of the bright lunar fortnight."

Oak further say,

> "In my view the two buildings referred to the Bateshwar inscription still exists in Agra in all its marble splendour. They are the so called Itemad-ud-Daulah Tomb and the Taj Mahal. What the inscription refers the Kings Palace is the present Itmad-ud-Daulah Tomb. The Chandramauleeshwar is the Taj Mahal."[41]

In this inscription mentioned by Oak, it is not mentioned that to which building it has been stated or where these buildings are situating. The language also does not prove the authenticity of the inscription. P.N. Oak very cunningly has connected this inscription with the Itmad-ud-Daulah Tomb and the Taj Mahal building. Moreover, Oak himself is confused that whether Taj Mahal is a Rajput palace or Hindu temple. Once he says that Taj was a Rajput palace and in his another work he declares the Taj as the Shiva Temple, Tejo Mahalaya. On the calligraphy, the jewels from all around Asia, he keeps shut and unable to prove his claim. He has only one point programme that Mughals were invaders and they destroyed the temples and built mosque and tombs over there. He shows his anti-Muslim tinge in his books and baselessly fabricates the stories.

In 2014, when the Narendra Modi government of BJP came into power, its leader Lakshmikant Bajpayee, to renew the theory of Oak, claimed that "Tejo Mahalaya" existed before the Taj Mahal. In April 2015, Agra district court admitted a petition by six lawyers who claimed the Taj Mahal was a Shiva Temple. They wanted Hindu devotees to be allowed inside the premises to perform *darshan* and *arti*. The court asked the centre, Culture Ministry, Home Secretary and Archaeological Survey of India to submit their replies in the case. The ASI gave a written reply to the Agra court in August saying the monument, which is widely regarded as an architectural marvel, is a only a tomb and not a temple.[42]

While replying to a question in parliament in November 2015, then Union Minister of Culture Mahesh Sharma said the government has no evidence of the Taj Mahal being a Shiva Temple. In 2017, the BJP leader Vinay Katiyar raised a fresh controversy over the Taj Mahal by repeating the theory of P.N. Oak. Vinay Katiyar claimed that the seventeenth century monument was built by Mughal emperor Shah Jahan after destroying a Hindu temple. Katiyar claimed the Hindu temple which existed there earlier was called "Tejo Mahalaya" and it housed a Shivalinga. This was, however, not the first time a member of the BJP had made similar claims.[43]

Shah Jahan loved pomp and show and considerably increased the royal retinue, the state establishments and the magnificence of the court. The Peacock Throne, the Taj Mahal, the Agra Fort and numerous other works of architecture and art testify to his wealth as well as his aesthetic sense. He was an excellent calligraphist. His patronage of men of letters and of artisans and craftsmen was in keeping with the traditions of his family. Poets, philosophers, scholars, artisans—all flocked to his court and received his favours. He recognised merit and rewarded it generously. Poetry, music, painting, dancing, astronomy, mathematics and medicine flourished under the generous and intelligent patronage of the emperor. He was fond of Hindu music and patronised Hindu poets like Sundar Das, Chintamani and Kavindra Acharya. Amongst the royal musicians were Lal Khan, son-in-law of the famous Tan Sen, Jagannath, who received the title of Maha-Kavi-Rai, Sukh Sen and Sur Sen.

Shah Jahan was a loving father, a doting husband, a loyal friend, a capable ruler and wise statesman. He was harsh and vindictive to his enemies, but kind and generous to his friends. He punished the unruly and recalcitrant with severity, amounting to cruelty, but he was affable, kind and forgiving to those who sought his friendship or forgiveness. His supreme endeavour was to eradicate lawlessness and rebellion, to guarantee security of life and property to his subjects and to promote their material and moral welfare. Orthodox as a Musalman and anxious to fortify and strengthen the Muslim *millat*, he was never unfair to, or unmindful of, the interests of his non-Muslim subjects.

Shah Jahan as an Emperor was free to maintain law and order in his country and punish the rebellious chiefs by even demolishing a few temples. It was not but common practice of the invaders and victorious armies. At the end of the nineteenth century, the Marathas, the staunch Hindus of south India attacked the capital of Tipu Sultan and looted and destructed the famous temple of Srirangapattam. At the end of the twentieth century, after the independence of India, the mob of the Hindus instigated the leaders of the political parties, attacked and demolished the Babari mosque at Ayodhya and temporary Rama Temple was built over the site. It followed the killing of many hundreds of innocent Muslims and destroying thousands of mosques by showing the bigotry. One can see that, how the Mughal royal forces could be controlled by demolishing temples of the rebellious and defeated chieftains during medieval times. The Hindutva historians must see in their collars and hundred times think the liberal policies of the medieval rulers like Shah Jahan and Aurangzeb. Even Akbar had constructed many temples in many parts of India. Akbar has gone on its height and constructed a temple by destroying a mosque at Kurukshetra.

Last Days of Shah Jahan

Shah Jahan, in his old age in 1658, was overthrown by his rebellious son Aurangzeb and remained confined in a set of apartments of the Agra Palace for seven years. None of the great Mughal emperors attained to such grandeur and success as Shah Jahan, and none was destined to greater humiliation and suffering at the end of his reign. The relation between Aurangzeb and Shah Jahan since the latter became a captive in the Agra fort on 18 June 1658, was very bitter. During the period of this captivity of the father, the son never visited Agra and his treatment of the former was a pitiable instance of open disregard for decorum and canons of morality and justice. Shah Jahan gradually realized the position into which he had been cast by the cruel hand of destiny. He was closely surrounded by the emperor's guards and his movements within the fort were watched with strict vigilance.

Shah Jahan spent his time in prayer, religious discourses, reading the Quran and performance of all other duties according to the canons of Islam. It was a great solace to him to receive till the last moment of his life the loving care of his eldest daughter, Jahan Ara, who shared with him all sorrows and miseries, consoling him with tenderness of a mother and daughter combined in one. Deprived of liberty, bereft of all powers and stricken down with bereavements, he only waited for deliverance from such a sad and gloomy existence and at last it came on 22 January 1666, at the age of seventy-four, after an illness continuing for about fifteen days. On her father's death, Jahan Ara retired to Delhi and she lived there, until 1681.

Shah Jahan is severely targeted by the Hindutva scholars and branded as intolerant ruler. They claim that Shah Jahan made many conversions and was responsible for many temple destruction. But Shah Jahan can't be branded as bigot and intolerant as he had also full sympathy with his Hindu subjects. He trusted his Hindu officers and assigned commands of the campaign and *jagirs*. Moreover, Shah Jahan was deeply influenced by the culture of Hindustan as well as the Sanskrit poetry. Under his patronage, his son Dara Shikoh, a learned Sanskrit scholar and fond of the Hindu religious literature translated many Sanskrit philosophical texts into Persian such as Upanishads and *Harivansa*. Dara Shikoh supported Sufism, Hinduism Christianity and Judaism. Prince Aurangzeb, an able administrator was not his choice of succession due to his non-secular character.

Notes

1. *The Hindus*, *op. cit.*, p. 536.
2. Elliot & Dowson, vol. VII, *op. cit.*, p. 32.
3. *Ibid.*, pp. 32-33; Majumdar, *op. cit.*, p. 201.
4. *Ibid.*, pp. 34-35; Majumdar, *op. cit.*, p. 201.
5. Sri Ram Sharma, *op. cit.*, p. 105; Majumdar, *op. cit.*, p. 211.
6. *Ibid.*, Majumdar, *op. cit.*, p. 212.
7. Majumdar, *op. cit.*, p. 212.
8. Sri Ram Sharma, *op. cit.*, p. 106.
9. Elliot & Dowson, vol. VII, *op. cit.*, p. 36; Harbans Mukhia, *op. cit.*, p. 24.
10. *The Hindus*, *op. cit.*, p. 536.
11. Sri Ram Sharma, *op. cit.*, pp. 106-07.
12. *The Hindus*, *op. cit.*, pp. 546-47; Harbans Mukhia, *op. cit.*, p. 39. (In independent India during BJP's rule, the history repeated in the form of Love Jihad, Ghar Wapasi and destruction of mosques and construction of the temples over there.)
13. Sri Ram Sharma, *op. cit.*, pp. 110-11.
14. *The Hindus*, *op. cit.*, pp. 546-47.
15. Sri Ram Sharma, *op. cit.*, p. 153.
16. *Ibid.*, pp. 107-9. Here are the names of the *mansabdars* of 1,000 and above. Commanders of (5,000)—1. Raja Jaswant Singh of Jodhpur; 2. Raja Jagat Singh of Udaipur; 3. Raja Jai Singh of Jaipur; 4. Raja Bithal Das Gaur; Commanders of (4,000); 5. Raja Rai Singh son of the late Maharaja Bhim Singh of the house of Mewar; Commanders of (3,000); 6. Raja Pahar Singh Bundela of Urchha; 7. Rao Satarsal Hada of Bundi; 8. Madho Singh Hada of Bundi (uncle of the above); 9. Udaji Ram; 10. Parsoji Bhonsla; 11. Jadu Rai; 12. Mankoji Nimbalkar; 13. Rawat Rai; 14. Dattarji, Commanders of (2,500); 15. Raja Devi Singh Bundela; Commanders of (2,000); 16. Raja Rajrup of Nurpur in the Punjab; 17. Rao Karn Bhurtiya of Bikaner; 18. Raja Jairamdas Bargojar; 19. Prithvi Raj Rathor; 20. Rup Singh Rathor; 21. Ram Singh Rathor; 22. Patoji; 23. Arirai; 24. Babaji; Commanders of (1,500); 25. Rawal Punja of Dongarpur; 26. Ratan Rathor; 27. Rao Rup Singh Chandrawat; 28. Chand Ratan Bundela; 29. Sujan Singh Sissodia; 30. Rai Todar Mal Diwan; 31. Anrodh, 12 Shivram; 33. Raiba Dakhanni; Commanders of (1,000)- 34. Rawal Samarsi of Banswara; 35. Raja Gursen of Kishtwar, Kashmir; 36. Raja Prithi Chand of Chamba; 37. Raja Badan Singh Bhadorya; 38. Kanwar Ram

Singh son of Raja Jai Singh of Jaipur; 39. Gopal Singh Kachhwaha, 40. Pratap; 41. Girdhar Das Gaur; 42. Rai Singh cousin of Jaswant Singh of Jodhpur; 43. Arjun son of Bithal Das; 44. Rai Singh Jhala; 45. Raja Amar Singh; 46. Bhojraj Dakhani; 47. Rai Kashi Das provincial Diwan; 48. Rai Dayanat Rai Accounts Department; 49. Rai Bhar Mal provincial Diwan; 50. Mahesh Das Rathor; and 51. Raja Tralok Chand Kachhwaha.

17. *Ibid.*, p. 111.
18. Elliot & Dowson, vol. VII, *op. cit.*, p. 32.
19. Sri Ram Sharma, *op. cit.*, p. 112.
20. *Ibid.*, p. 113.
21. *Ibid.*
22. *Ibid.*, p. 114. Dalpat, a Hindu of Sirhind, had converted a Muslim girl, Zinab, given her the Hindu name, Ganga and brought up their children as Hindus. He had also converted one Muslim boy and six Muslim girls (his own) to Hinduism. The emperor was now exasperated by this persistence and defiance of his orders. To put a stop to this practice and warn all future transgressors of the law, Dalpat's wife and children were taken away from him and he was sentenced to death.
23. *Ibid.*, pp.114-15.
24. *Ibid.*, p. 114.
25. *Ibid.*, p. 116.
26. *The Hindus, op. cit.*, p. 536.
27. Ebba Koch, "Diwan-i-Aam and Chihil Sutun: The Audience Halls of Shah Jahan", in idem, *Mughal Art and Imperial Ideology: Collected Essays*, New Delhi: Oxford University Press, 2001, pp. 239-49.
28. Jean-Baptiste Tavernier, tr. V. Ball, *Travels in India*, (1889; repr. Lahore: Al-Biruni, 1976), vol. I, pp. 381-84.
29. H.G. Keene (1899). *A Handbook for Visitors to Agra and its Neighbourhood*, Calcutta, pp. 1-4; *A Handbook to Agra, op. cit.*, pp. 4 & 39.
30. R. Nath (1972). *The Immortal Taj Mahal: The Evolution of Tomb in Mughal Architecture*, Bombay, pp. 53-54; *Encyclopedia Britannica* and *A Handbook for Visitors to Agra, op. cit.*, pp. 23-24. (Havell says that at the time of Mumtaz's death the emperor was overpowered with grief. For a week he refused to see any of his ministers or to transact any business of the state. He even contemplated resigning the throne and dividing the empire among his sons. For two years the court observed strict mourning. No music or festivities were allowed; the wearing of

jewels, the use of perfumes and luxuries of all kinds were forbidden. The month of *Zicad*, in which she died, was observed as a month of mourning for many years afterwards. *A Handbook to Agra, op. cit.*, pp. 72 & 74.)

31. *The Immortal Taj Mahal, op. cit.*, pp. 53-54; *A Handbook for Visitors to Agra, op. cit.*, pp. 23-24; *A Handbook to Agra, op. cit.*, pp. 75-76; Moinuddin, Mohd (1906), *The History of Taj and Buildings in its Vicinity*, Agra, pp. 11-12.
32. *The Immortal Taj Mahal, op. cit.*, pp. 53-54; *history.com*, 22 November 2019. (Taj Mahal suffered from neglect and disrepair during the two centuries after the death of Shah Jahan. However, at the beginning of the nineteenth century, Lord Curzon, the British Viceroy of India ordered the major restoration of the mausoleum complex to preserve India's artistic and cultural heritage. After the independence of India, Taj Mahal emerged as the highest revenue yielding monument in India, one of the Seven Wonders of the World and one of the most visited world heritage monuments across the globe. According to the *Times of India* report, the government of India earned 200 crore in the last three years. timesofindia.com, 6 December 2019.)
33. *The Immortal Taj Mahal, op. cit.*, pp. 53-54; *A Handbook for Visitors to Agra, op. cit.*, p. 26. (Havell mentions that the master-builders came from many different parts; the chief masons from Baghdad, Delhi and Multan; the dome builders from Asiatic Turkey and from Samarkand; the mosaic workers from Kanauj and from Baghdad; the principal calligraphist for the inscriptions from Shiraz. Every part of India and Central Asia contributed the materials; Jaipur, the marble; Fatehpur Sikri, the red sandstone; the Punjab, jasper; China, the jade and crystal; Tibet, turquoises; Ceylon, lapis lazuli and sapphires; Arabia, coral and cornelian; Panna in Bundelkhand, diamonds; Persia, onyx and amethyst. *A Handbook to Agra, op. cit.*, pp. 74-75.)
34. *The Immortal Taj Mahal, op. cit.*, pp. 54-56; *A Handbook for Visitors to Agra, op. cit.*, pp. 23-24; and *A Handbook to Agra, op. cit.*, p. 74.
35. *The History of Taj, op. cit.*, pp. 14-16.
36. *A Handbook to Agra, op. cit.*, pp. 77-78.
37. *Ibid.*, p. 54; Percival Spear, *Bentinck and the Taj, The Journal of the Royal Asiatic Society of Great Britain and Ireland*, No. 2, (October 1949), pp. 180-87. *Hindustan Times* (Lucknow), 26 October 2017, tajmahal.org.uk. and heriagewalkcalcutta.com.
38. *The Immortal Taj Mahal, op. cit.*, pp. 54-56.
39. *Indian Express*, 18 October 2017.

40. Oak, P.N. (1965). *Taj Mahal Was a Rajput Palace*, New Delhi, pp. 27-28.
41. Oak, P.N. (2003, the first edition was published in 1974). *The Taj Mahal is a Temple Palace*, New Delhi, pp. 198-200.
42. *Indian Express*, 18 October 2017.
43. *Ibid.*

Chapter
5

Religion and Society Under Aurangzeb

Abul Muzaffar Muhiuddin Mohammad Aurangzeb Alamgir (1658-1707) was born in the autumn of 1618 in Dohad, Gujarat to Emperor Shah Jahan and Mumtaz Mahal. Aurangzeb was Shah Jahan's third son, preceded by his brothers, Dara Shikoh and Shah Shuja and would be followed a year later by a fourth son, Murad. Aurangzeb studied Islamic religious texts, including the Quran, the Hadith (sayings of the Prophet Mohammad) and religious biographies. He also read Turkish literature and learnt the art of calligraphy. Mughal princely education emphasized the Persian classics, especially the great poets and scholars that are still beloved today, such as Shaikh Saadi, Nasiruddin Tusi and Hafiz. Aurangzeb also spoke fluent Hindi from childhood.

Aurangzeb was a man of small stature with olive-coloured skin and a large nose. He led a very simple, well-ordered and pious life, slept little and worked so hard even in his extreme old age that it was a wonder to his contemporaries. He held daily courts, sometimes twice a day, even personally writing orders on letters and petitions and dictating official replies. He was an expert calligraphist, had a passion for reading books and a master of Arabic and Persian and also could also speak Turki and Hindi fluently.

On 7 June 1633, Shah Jahan indulged in one of his favourite pastimes: watching two huge male elephants engage in combat. The spectacle was usually performed near the banks of the Jamuna and viewed from a balcony built into the emperor's palace in Agra. Shah Jahan and his three eldest sons Dara Shikoh, Shuja and Aurangzeb went down to the ground level, mounted horses and rode out to have a closer look. Noticing the newcomers, one of the elephants suddenly wheeled, trumpeted loudly and charged the 14-year old Aurangzeb. The lion-hearted youth with the greatest courage and intrepidity did not stir from his post; but as soon as the elephant approached, he galloped at it and rose up in his stirrups and hurled his spear with his whole strength against its forehead. The monster, smarting from the wound, again rushed furiously but Aurangzeb stood against the beast with his sword. A year later, Shah Jahan gave Aurangzeb a *mansab* of 10,000, his first position in the Mughal hierarchy. A year after that, in 1635, he was sent off on an imperial campaign to capture and punish the rebel chieftain Jujhar Singh Bundela. Aurangzeb was next sent to the campaign Deccan in Burhanpur to cover Nizam Shahi kingdom of Ahmadnagar, Adil Shahi kingdom of Bijapur and the Qutb Shahi kingdom of Golconda.[1]

In late March 1658, on hearing the serious illness of his father Shah Jahan, Aurangzeb left Burhanpur for north India. In the way to Agra, Aurangzeb gained two grand victories in the war of succession. In mid-April his army joined that of Murad south of Ujjain and several days later, at the Battle of Dharmat, their combined forces of 40,000 completely routed an imperial force of the same size fighting on behalf of Dara on 15 April 1658. Near the village of Samugarh, 35 km south-east of Agra their armies again clashed on 29 May 1658. Although Dara's forces of 60,000 far surpassed in number those of Aurangzeb and Murad, but the imperial force again met a crushing defeat. Dara Shikoh fled for Delhi for safety. Shah Jahan was still in his palace in Agra but reduced to an emperor with no empire. Aurangzeb ordered his men to take possession of all royal effects, treasures and so on and to keep the emperor confined in the palace. Until his death seven years later, Shah Jahan would never again leave the fort.

Aurangzeb ascended the throne at Delhi on 21 July 1658 at the age of 39 with the lofty title of Abul Muzaffar Muhiuddin Mohammad Aurangzeb Alamgir Padshah Ghazi.[2] However, the actual ceremony took place on 13 May 1659, during war of succession. After ascending the throne, Aurangzeb firstly imporisoned his younger brother Murad in Mughals' state prison in Gwalior. As for Shuja of Bengal, Aurangzeb and his ally Mir Jumla defeated him at the Battle of Khajwa on 5 January 1659 near Faizabad district, Uttar Pradesh. Shuja fled to Burma's Arakan coastal region, where he vanished from historical record. The next target Dara Shikoh was roaming in Afghanistan, Rajputana and Gujarat for help. In early June 1659, near the mouth of the Bolan Pass, a *zamindar* whom Dara thought he could trust betrayed him to Aurangzeb's men and in August 1659, he was taken to Delhi in chains. There he was publicly paraded through the streets and bazaars of Shahjahanabad, wearing coarse cloth and mounted on a miserable, worn-out elephant. After a council of clerics drew up a list of charges against him, he was executed on 30 August 1659 and his body was buried in the grounds of Humayun's tomb.[3]

After consolidating his power and position, Aurangzeb richly rewarded the nobles who had aided him during the two years' struggle and pardoned those who had supported any of his brothers. He confirmed to Raja Jai Singh the present made to him of the province of Sambhar; the pay of others was increased; each noble received a set of robes, to the greatest being given a scimitar covered with precious stones, having a rich and handsome hilt, an elephant and a horse. He also sent off new governors and viceroys to the provinces and kingdoms to displace the old ones. Although he did not fail to give the new governors good instructions. To maintain administrative continuity with Shah Jahan's regime, he retained his father's last finance minister, Raja Raghunath, whom he repeatedly praised for his dedication and competence. To neutralize factions within his immediate family, he arranged marriages between his own children and those of his defeated brothers: two of his daughters were married to Dara's son Sipihr Shukoh and Murad's son Izzat Bakhsh after both were released from prison and given official ranks, while his own son Mohammad Azam was married to Dara's daughter Jani Begum.

Aurangzeb's long reign of fifty years is naturally divided into two equal parts, each of about twenty-five years' duration. During the earlier of these two periods, namely, from 1658 to 1681, the Emperor himself stays either at Delhi or at Agra. In the second half of the reign the centre of political gravity is shifted from the north to the south. The Emperor with his family, his court and the bulk of the army, moved southward in 1681 and spent the rest of his life in a long and unprofitable struggle with the Muslim powers of the Deccan and with the Marathas.

Aurangzeb succeeded in destroying the ruling Muslim houses of Bijapur and Golkonda, but failed wholly to crush the nascent power of his despised Hindu opponents. The struggle was disastrous for the empire and precipitated the dissolution of the Mughal power. The great political edifice erected by the genius of Akbar and preserved morc or less intact by Jahangir and Shah Jahan now showed signs of impending disruption and actually collapsed within two decades after Aurangzeb's death. He died in the winter of 1707 at the age of 88. He was buried in a simple, open-air grave in Khuldabad, Maharashtra. Following Aurangzeb's wishes, the tomb was plain and unmarked, located within a Sufi shrine.

Aurangzeb as a Muslim

Aurangzeb was a pure Sunni Muslim but after all he was the ruler of a Hindu majority country which bound him to follow the secular policies of his forefathers. Undoubtedly on many places, events and policies he was tilted more towards his co-religionists. Actually, Aurangzeb was brought up in the religious atmosphere. While a prince, Aurangzeb came into contact with Khwaja Mohammad Masum, son of Mujaddid Ahmad Sirhindi. He held him in high esteem and sought his advice on important matters of Muslim theology. After his accession to the throne also, he maintained his contact with the Khwaja and his son Mohammad Saifuddin as well and their influence had much to do in bringing him within the fold of the orthodox school and shaping his puritanic state policy. Aurangzeb's life and activities were greatly influenced by the orthodox reform movement in Indian Islam started by Mujaddid Alf-i-Sani Shaikh Ahmad Sirhindi (1563-1624), the aims of which were regeneration and rejuvenation of Islam in strict accord with the Shariyat and the establishment of a true Islamic state conforming to Islamic ideas and practices in all its activities. In other words, he believed in the Islamic theory of kingship according to which the ruler is to enforce strictly the Quranic law in the administration of his empire.

The reason of his Muslim tinge could be traced as circumstantial measure not as personal preoccupation. At the time of succession he was bound to prove himself as orthodox Muslims as he had violated religious law by dethroning his father Emperor Shah Jahan. At that time Prince Aurangzeb was in Deccan and he left for Delhi genuinely believing that Shah Jahan was at the point of death, if not already dead. But, by the time he reached Agra and found his father in good health, what had begun as a war of succession, he had already defeated Dara's armies twice, suddenly became an act of usurpation and the usurpation of another person's land or property is prohibited in Islamic law.

For a man professing strict observance of that law, the newly-crowned emperor suddenly found himself in an untenable position, the more so when experts on canon law refused to sanction his seizure of power since the lawful sovereign, his own father, was still living. In this circumstance Aurangzeb solicited the opinion of Abdul Wahab, the former *qazi* of Patan, Gujarat, who obligingly decreed that since Shah Jahan was physically unfit to govern (despite evidence to the contrary), the throne was virtually vacant. Aurangzeb's accession as Alamgir had therefore not violated Islamic law. As a reward for this valuable hermeneutic service, Abdul Wahab was made the empire's supreme judge (Qazi-ul-quzat), a post he held until his death in 1675. This made made Aurangeb more religious or to show himself orthodox Muslim to fade the act of usurpation accompanied by the elimination of his brothers and the confinement of his father. Notwithstanding Abdul Wahab's whitewashing of the process, the emperor craved legitimacy in the eyes of the wider Islamic world, for which purpose he sought the blessings of the guardian of the holiest shrines in the Muslim world, the Sharif of Mecca.[4]

Moreover, Aurangzeb was free from the habit of drinking wine and other habitual vices of his contemporaries. The number of his wives was within the Quranic limit of four; of them Dilras Banu and Aurangabadi Mahal died in 1657 and 1685, respectively; Nawab Bai led a retired life at Delhi after 1660 and Udaipuri was his only companion after the death of Aurangabadi in 1685. He was ever faithful to his conjugal love and weakness for women never tarnished his name. He was a devout Muslim and followed all the precepts and observances of his religion with sincerity and strictness. His stern and austere mode of living according to the injunctions of Islam was highly admired by his people. But the way in which he secured the throne is hard to defend.

Bhimsen in the memoir describes an incident during the monsoon of 1697 when the Bhima flooded its banks at Aurangzeb's camp at Machnur, drowning many people and bringing its waters to within a metre of the emperor's tent. With the whole camp plunged in a state of distress, the emperor wrote a prayer on a slip of paper and cast it on the river's surface. The water immediately subsided and, records Bhimsen, "the prayer of the God-devoted Emperor was accepted by God and the world became composed again".[5]

Similarly, in 1672 a peasant uprising, the Satnami revolt, broke out in Narnaul (in modern Haryana), in the course of which a prophetess appeared proclaiming that she could use spells to raise an invisible army. When the uprising took an alarming turn, the emperor dispatched a large force with banners on which he wrote prayers and magical figures with his own hand. Fighting magic with magic, 'Alamgir was seen by his contemporary subjects as having bridged the spiritual and mundane worlds. Indeed, he was popularly known as 'Alamgir *Zinda Pir* (Alamgir, the living saint).[6]

It was even believed that he was capable of making himself invisible whenever he wished and could instantly appear in Mecca and converse with the Prophet Muhammad. "From this cause", noted Manucci, "the people revere him and hold him in the greatest respect". One hundred six Indians of this day assessed the spiritual status of their leaders by their observed actions. On one occasion, the emperor spent a week in Gulbarga paying respects to the shrine of the Deccan's most renowned Sufi Shaikh, Muhammad Gesudaraz and conversing with reclusive Sufis there. For Bhimsen, the emperor's behaviour was salutary and redemptive, as would be expected of a sovereign perceived as connecting the divine and earthly worlds. By contrast, Shivaji's plundering of the town of Jalna, home of a spiritually gifted holy man named Jan Muhammad, was in Bhimsen's view a reckless act unbefitting a proper sovereign and the probable cause of the Maratha king's untimely death.[7]

Aurangzeb possessed uncommon physical strength and unusual bravery, of which he gave proof even at the age of 15 when he faced a furious elephant alone. He braved all risks with a cheerful mind and coolness of temper and encouraged his men even in the midst of thickest dangers. As an expert strategist, he took advantage of any opportunity which he could get out of the mistakes and weaknesses of his adversaries. He was a skilful diplomat whose subtle activities were too much for his enemies to cope with. He retained the military character of his government from the beginning to the end.

Emperor Aurangzeb is branded an orthodox Muslim ruler. Although, he issued dozens of documents between 1659 and 1703 supporting a variety of religious individuals and institutions: Jaina saints, *sadhus* and monasteries (*maths*), temple Brahmans, Gosains (wandering ascetics), Jangams (Shaiva priests), Hindu preceptors and *yogis*. Aurangzeb had thoroughly imbibed the culture of institutional Sufism. Many scholars believe that as a ruler his main consideration was for the Sunni Muslims only. According to them, he was a good Musalman but not a good ruler of a state of composite races, creeds and cultures.

He lived a very simple life, unlike his predecessors. His state policies as well as the religious policies reflect his nature, character and philosophy. He was bigot and zealot to his enemies, rebels and untrustworthy rulers and chieftains. He crushed the rebels brutally and one can imagine that when didn't spare his brother Dara Shikoh, paraded in the Agra streets and cut to the pieces and even imprisoned his own father, how can be liberal to the rebellious chiefs. The royal army knowing the mentality and intentions of the ruler also committed brutality including the massacre of the rebels and destruction of their temples.

The scholars of history during the British period, such as the earliest chronicler of Aurangzeb Sir Jadunath Sarkar and many of the scholars of independent India have perhaps ignored thc fact of his nature. They have described only the acts without proper scientific and philosophical inquiry. Satish Chandra and Athar Ali, etc., have fully analysed the facts and situations during the reign of Aurangzeb and concluded that he was no doubt an orthodox or true follower of Islam but not the oppressor for his subjects. Aurangzeb never oversaw a large scale conversion programme that offered non-Muslims a choice between Islam or the sword. Aurangzeb did not destroy thousands of Hindu temples (a few dozen is a more likely number). He did not perpetrate anything resembling the genocide of Hindus. In fact, Aurangzeb appointed Hindus on top positions in his government. He protected the interests of Hindu religious groups, even ordering fellow Muslims to cease harassing Brahmans. He tried to provide safe roads and basic law and order for all his subjects. In many cases, he didn't follow all tenets of Islam and worked for the betterment of his empire. He was cruel to his enemies, whether they were Hindus or Muslims or even his father and brother. He was equally sympathetic to his friends irrespective of their religion and beliefs.

He is being branded as intolerant ruler disrespecting the Shias, Hindus and Sikhs but the reality was something different. As a Muslim ruler, Aurangzeb's religious ideals demanded that he dispense justice and protect his citizens. As the king put it in a letter to his grandson Azimusshan, "You should consider the protection of the subjects as the source of happiness in this world and the next". Aurangzeb persisted in his view that there ought to be no religious litmus test for Mughal employment.

On another occasion, a Sunni Muslim petitioned the emperor for a post as imperial paymaster on the grounds that the two existing paymasters were both Shia and that appointing him would bring sectarian balance to the office. Irritated by the request, Alamgir replied,

> "What connection have earthly affairs with religion? And what right have administrative works to meddle with bigotry? 'For you is your religion and for me is mine' (Qur'an 109:6). If this rule (suggested by you) were established, it would be my duty to extirpate all the (Hindu) Rajahs and their followers. Wise men disapprove of the removal from the office of able officers."[8]

On one occasion Aurangzeb referred to his chief *qazi* the question of whether captured Hindu rebels should be treated differently from captured Muslim rebels. The *qazi* decreed a light punishment for Muslim rebels, but release for Hindus if they converted to Islam. Alamgir, however, returned the decree, ordering that a different ruling should be found, so "that control over the kingdom may not be lost". Accordingly, the *qazi* and his learned advisers returned a new judgement, that all the prisoners should be executed regardless of their religion, a decision the emperor accepted.[9]

After all, Rajputs, Marathas, Brahmans, Jains, Kayasthas and other non-Muslims were essential for running the empire's vast administrative and military systems. This much is seen in the significant increase in the number of Hindus serving in 'Alamgir's mansabdari corps. Under Shah Jahan, Hindus comprised less than a quarter (22.4%) of all nobles holding a rank of 1,000 *zat* or higher. By the last years of 'Alamgir's reign that figure had risen to nearly a third (31.6%) of the total.[10]

Aurangzeb did not destroy thousands of Hindu temples (a few dozen is a more likely number). He did not perpetrate anything resembling genocide of Hindus. He protected the interests of Hindu religious groups, even ordering fellow Muslims to cease harassing Brahmans. He tried to provide safe roads and basic law and order for all his subjects. Aurangzeb never oversaw a large scale conversion programme that offered non-Muslims a choice between Islam or the sword. In 1700, Mughal soldiers captured nine Hindus and four Muslims during the siege of Satara Fort, a Maratha stronghold. A Mughal judge sentenced the Muslims to three years in prison and offered the Hindus a full pardon if they converted to Islam. Dissatisfied with such leniency, Aurangzeb ordered the judge to "decide the case in some other way, that control over the kingdom may not be lost". The rebels were all executed before sundown. In a 1699 letter, for example, Aurangzeb condemned two men who "boasted much of their conversion to Islam" and spoke against the emperor, labelling them "irreligious persons" (*bi-dinyan*). The king ordered both imprisoned for their insincerity.[11]

Aurangzeb was very simple in nature and character. He stopped and suppressed many practices which were more economic than religious. He stopped building the mosque where these were in abundance for the Muslim worshippers. He also stopped construction of the new temples and demolition of the newly-built temples as there were already in abundance for the worshippers. His order of destruction of one or two old temples could be seen as these temples were indulged in the rape of the lady worshippers and conversion centre from Muslim to Hinduism. Aurangzeb had also granted the land to run the many temples which were really the centre of morality and belief. He suppressed poetry and Music; dismissed dancers, musicians and artists from the royal payroll.

Like Emperor Ashoka's Dharma Mahamatta and Sushashan Mitra of Bhartiya Janata Party government in independent India, Aurangzeb appointed *muhtasib*s, censors of public morals. *Muhtasib*s were appointed in all big cities to enforce the Quranic law and put down the practices forbidden in it, like drinking of wine, gambling and illicit traffic of women. Their duties also included punishment of Muslims for heretical opinions, blasphemy, omission of obligatory prayers and Ramzan fast. In enforcing orthodoxy the emperor did not spare the Sufis and Shias, where deemed necessary. Among the important sections of the Muslim population who suffered serious persecution for heresy was the Isma'ilia or Bohra community of Gujarat. The appointment of the *muhtasib*s left a cumulative effect and surely acted as a serious wet blanket on both addiction and nightlife.[12]

Aurangzeb also discontinued some practices in his court which he seemed irrelevant. He forbade singing and dancing in the court and on the public places. Even religious music on the day of the Prophet's birth was prohibited. The ceremony of weighing the emperor on his two birthdays, according to the lunar and solar calendars, against precious articles like gold and silver was discontinued. The practice of *jharokha-darshan* on sunrise, a custom according to which the Mughal emperors used to appear every morning at the outer balcony of their palace to receive the salute of the subjects, was discontinued, as these were un-Islamic.[13] The emperor also forbade the customary rejoicings on his birthdays and on the anniversary of his coronation. Even when Aurangzeb lay dying he preferred giving charity without the formality of following this custom.

Morality Orders and Prohibition of Social Evils

Aurangzeb ruled the country according to Islamic Sharia and which was beneficial to his subjects. His religious policy was based on justice and equality which was undoubtedly more beneficial to the Muslim community as the Emperor wanted to make equal both the communities of Hindus and Muslims. Like the abolition of eighty taxes, he banned and discontinued many practices which were not suited to his puritan mind. Naturally, some of his policies annoyed to the Muslim *ulema* as well as the Hindu religious *pandits*.

He abolished the many of the practices followed by previous Mughal Emperors. Aurangzeb also forbade stamping the *kalima* on the coins in 1959 due to its religious significance. Aurangzeb ceased participating in courtly functions that conflicted with his understanding of Islam. The celebration of the Persian New Year's Day, Nauroz, was also forbidden since Aurangzeb believed that it was an innovation on the orthodox practice of Islam. Similarly ordinances were issued against the astrologers, forbidding them to draw up almanacs or forecasts of events since they were inconsistent with the practice of Islam. Aurangzeb forbade in applying *tika* on the foreheads of subordinate kings, or having himself weighed against gold or silver on his birthday.[14]

Aurangzeb took steps against the excessive number of musicians. In Hindustan both Mughals and Hindus are very fond of listening to songs and instrumental music. He therefore ordered the same official to stop music. In the eleventh year of his reign Aurangzeb even forbade the playing of music at court and the state musicians and singers, who had hitherto enjoyed honour and rank, were pensioned off. If in any house or elsewhere he heard the sound of singing and instruments, he should forthwith hasten there and arrest as many as he could, breaking the instruments. Thus was caused a great destruction of musical instruments.[15]

Other measures, such as prohibiting gambling or consuming alcohol, were intended to extend beyond the court, but they were blatantly ignored even by his closest courtiers. Aurangzeb's standard of personal and private life was very high. He abstained scrupulously trom the slightest indulgence in prohibited food, drink, or dress. He strove to live up to the ideal of a strict orthodox Muslim.

Aurangzeb continued participating in the celebration of the Hindu festival *Dussehra* as long as Maharaja Jaswant Singh and Raja Jai Singh were alive. During the celebrations Aurangzeb gave gifts to the Hindu *rajas* who were present at the court. The royal astronomers and astrologers were also dismissed. The accession of the Hindu *rajas* was solemnized by the emperor's making the sacred sign, *tika* on the forehead of the new *raja* if he was present at the court but this practice was discontinued in 1679. Aurangzeb also passed the order to remove scent-burners of gold and silver from the court. The use of silver inkstands which was conferred on some public servants as the badge of their office was discontinued. Garments of cloth of gold were forbidden. The manufacture of the cloth of gold in the royal workshops was stopped and so was its use.[16]

Besides discontinuing the above irrelevant practices at his court Aurangzeb also tried to impose some moral regulations and banning social evils. Further Aurangzeb ordered that prostitutes and dancing girls should marry or else leave the empire but this order does not seem to have been much enforced. Aurangzeb continued the practice of his predecessors of prohibiting the burning of unwilling *satis*. In 1688 he prohibited the castration of young children throughout his empire.

He prohibited the preparation and public sale of wine. Aurangzeb observed that in Hindustan, chiefly in Delhi, there was great licence among Muslims and Hindus in the consumption of wine. This licence began in the time of Jahangir, although Akbar was the first to give leave to the Christians to prepare and drink wine; but in his time the Muslims did not drink. The evil example of Jahangir established this custom among the Muslims. In the days of Shahjahan they drank with full liberty, just as if drinking water, encouraged by Dara's example. Nor did Shahjahan, although not a drinker himself, care to remedy this disorder, but left everyone to live as he pleased.[17]

Aurangzeb ordered that all Christians, excepting physicians and surgeons, should leave the city and remove to near the park of artillery, which was beyond the suburbs at one league's distance from the city. There they had leave to prepare and drink spirits on condition they did not sell them. Sentinels were kept over them to watch that they did not sell. When a Hindu or Muslim wine-seller was apprehended in the city, he was only whipped if he was a first offender. On repeating his offence, however, he was imprisoned till he repented of his evil ways. He also penalised the nobles and *mansabdars* for drinking wine. But it was not found possible to enforce complete prohibition; the disease had already advanced too far to be capable of an easy remedy.[18]

The Muslims were so accustomed to intoxication that the poor people, who have not enough funds to procure spirits, invented another beverage, called in the language of the country *bhang*. It was leaves of dried hemp ground down, which intoxicate as soon as taken. Aurangzeb also wanted to suppress this disorder. An order was issued by the imperial finance minister Raja Raghu Nath to the provincial *diwans* all over the empire asking them to see that *bhang* was not cultivated. He also appointed an official under the title of *muhtasib*, whose business it was to prevent the use of this beverage or of others similar to it. The cultivation, sale and public use of *bhang* were also prohibited.[19]

Aurangzeb further tried to rule the fashions of the day by various measures. For the Muslims, the allowable length of the beard was fixed at four fingers and orders were given to cut down any extra length wherever found. An official was appointed whose business it was, in company with his attendants and soldiers, to measure beards in the middle of the street and, if necessary, dock them. It was however amusing to see the official in charge of beards rushing hither and thither, laying hold of wretched men by the beard, in order to measure and cut-off the excess and clipping their moustaches to uncover the lips.[20]

The length of the trousers to be worn without socks was prescribed for the Muslims. On Hindu and Muslim festivals, clay figures of birds, animals and men and women were made to delight the children. This representation of living beings was considered unlawful and orders were given for its suppression in November 1665. In 1669 Aurangzeb stopped the celebration of the Muharram. Aurangzeb hated the Shias' due to their abuse to the first three Caliphs. Aurangzeb ordered to kill Sufi saint Mulla Sarmad for his independent and rational thoughts.[21]

Abolition of Cesses

After his second coronation, Emperor Aurangzeb gave his attention to alleviate the economic distress of the people. The prolonged war of succession and consequent disorder and confusion in the civil administration threatened the economic ruin of almost the whole of northern India and grain was selling at exorbitant prices, beyond the reach of the ordinary people. Mughal Empire Aurangzeb gave orders for the remission of almost eighty legal and illegal taxes which were burdensome to the people of his empire.

The *rahdari* (toll or road-police tax) which was collected on every highway (*guzar*), frontier and ferry was remitted although this tax brought in a large sum to the revenue.In the Crownlands alone the *rahdari* tax yielded 25 lakhs of rupees a year and if we add to this the collection made in the tracts under the *jagirdar*s and *zamindar*s and the perquisites of the office underlings, we shall not be far wrong in putting the total loss of the merchants on this head at a crore of rupees.[22]

Emperor Aurangzeb also remitted the *pandari* (a ground or house cess), which was paid throughout the Imperial dominions, by every tradesman and dealer, from the butcher, the potter and the greengrocer, to the draper, jeweller and banker. Something was paid to the government according to rule under this name for every bit of ground in the market and for every stall and shop and the total revenue thus derived exceeded (lakhs) of rupees.[23]

Emperor also had withdrawn the tobacco tax, which was undoubtedly a great source of income for the royal treasury. The Muslims consume a great deal of this article in smoking. This is why the chief tax-farmer paid five thousand rupees a day at this city (Delhi) only. From this the reader can understand what would be the revenue from tobacco paid to the King of Hindustan throughout such a great empire. It is well known that the tax-contractors who engage for the taxes and duties are most shameless and mannerless. They spare no respectable persons, except those of the highest position and that chiefly when Muslims, such persons being, as they know, very easily roused. Aurangzeb withdrew this tobacco tax as it was an unnecessary burden upon his subject and more particularly population of the lower strata.[24]

Other cesses, lawful and unlawful, as the *sar-shumari, buz-shumari* (tax on goats), the *charat* (grazing tax) of the Banjaras, the *tutva'ana*, the collections from the fairs held at the festivals of Mohammadan saints and at the *jatra*s or fairs of the non-Muslims, held near Hindu temples, throughout the country far and wide, where lacs of people assemble once a year and where buying and selling of all kinds goes on. The tax on spirits, on gambling-houses, on brothels, the fines, thank-offerings and the fourth part of debts recovered by the help of magistrates from creditors. These and other imposts, nearly eighty in number, which brought in crors of rupees to the public treasury, were all abolished throughout Hindustan. Besides these, the tithe of corn, which lawfully brought in 25 lakhs of rupees, was remitted in order to alleviate the heavy cost of grain.[25]

Many oppressive and burdensome *abwab*s (cesses) over and above the regular land revenue and customs duty were also abolished. The important abwabs or cesses were perquisites, gifts and subscriptions exacted by the officials in their own interest, fees and commissions realized for the state on various occasions, licence-tax for certain trades, duties on local sale of commodities and some special imposts on the Hindus, viz., the pilgrim's tax, a tax on the occasion of the birth of a male child and a tax for throwing the bones of the dead into the Ganges. Although they were abolished by Aurangzeb and his actions showed his pious intention to do good to the people, his edicts could not be duly enforced in all regions, especially in far off places where the people suffered almost as before.

Ban on Music

In India both Mughals and Hindus were very fond of listening to songs and instrumental music. Almost all the Mughal emperors promoted and patronized the music in the empire. This practice was so costly and musicians were very highly paid and their gifts were even more burdensome. Moreover it was also against the Islamic law. Emperor Aurangzeb took steps against the excessive number of musicians. He therefore ordered the officials and *muhtasibs* to stop music. Munucci says that if in any house or elsewhere he heard the sound of singing and instruments, he should forthwith hasten there and arrest as many as he could, breaking the instruments. Thus was caused a great destruction of musical instruments. Finding themselves in this difficulty, their large earnings likely to cease, without there being any other mode of seeking a livelihood, the musicians took counsel together and tried to appease the emperor Aurangzeb in the following way:[26]

> "About one thousand of them assembled on Friday when Aurangzeb was going to the mosque. They came out with over twenty highly-ornamented biers, as is the custom of the country, crying aloud with great grief and many signs of feeling, as if they were escorting to the grave some distinguished defunct. From afar Aurangzeb saw this multitude and heard their great weeping and lamentation and, wondering, sent to know the cause of

> so much sorrow. The musicians redoubled their outcry and their tears, fancyingthe king would take compassion upon them. Lamenting, they replied with sobs that the king's orders had killed music; therefore they were bearing her to the grave. Report was made to the king, who quite calmly remarked that they should pray for the soul of music and see that she was thoroughly well buried." In spite of this, the nobles did not cease to listen to songs in secret. This strictness was enforced in the principal cities.[27]

Emperor Aurangzeb also ordered that the dancing women be forced to marry. Before the reign of Aurangzeb and even in the reign of Shah Jahan the female dancers and public women enjoyed the great liberty and they were found in great numbers in the cities. For a time, at the beginning of his reign, Aurangzeb said nothing, but afterwards he ordered that they must either marry or clear out of the realm. This was the cause that the palaces and great enclosures where they dwelt went to ruin little by little; for some of them married and others went away, or, at least, concealed themselves.[28]

Aurangzeb and Muslim Mendicants

The greatest abuse in the Mughal Empire was due to the cheating and hypocrisy of the holy mendicants. These men call themselves Sayyed, descendants of Prophet Mohammad (PBUH) and deceive the people with hypocrisy and pretended miracles, so that many resort to them as saints, either to ask for sons, or to obtain wives or husbands. The people used to visit them to secure employment or places at court, to win victory over their enemies or to gain success in business. Each man visited their abode for blessings according to his need. Each man went to them having something as an offering. Thus these holy men lived a very luxurious life. They knew how to cover their impostures by deception and with the aid of the devil hold the people under their spells by written incantations and bonds. Above all, they had control of the women, who resort to them in large numbers.[29]

Munucci says that these Holy Mendicants were aware that how to make use of their opportunities, sparing neither Muslims, Hindus and Christian women, if they are good-looking. In addition, they had numerous wives and slave girls in their houses, whom they send out at night in all directions as pretended devotees to earn an illicit livelihood. These women also serve to find out about those who come to ask for any favour and whether or not they have obtained what they desired. This is done to obtain information beforehand. These women also serve to persuade people that the holy man's supplications are especially effective; also to find out what is going on and thus give their master occasion to reveal secrets, as is fitting to holy men who know hidden things. All the same, the populace in the Mughal realm and also the nobles, retain great esteem for these people, sending them valuable presents; even gardeners carry to them the best of their fruit and vegetables and goat-herds their kids and milk. Thus these mendicants lead a more luxurious life than any grandee, being at the same time obeyed by princes and governors. Moreover all these stupidity was done under a covering of religion.[30]

To these abuses Aurangzeb resolved to take revenge upon twelve of them who lived in Delhi. They had prophesied to Dara that he would be emperor of the whole Mughal Empire. Emperor called them and begged them to perform some miracle in his presence, so that he, too, might acquire reasons for becoming their disciple. For this purpose he granted them three days in which to comply with the royal pleasure. Over this request of the emperor two of them said at once to Aurangzeb that they were descendants of Sultan-ul-Mushaikh, a famous saint of Balkh and were thus venerated by the people as saints, although they knew themselves to be the greatest sinners in the world and it was useless to look for miracles from them. Aurangzeb ignored this reply and told them all that it was necessary for them within three days to perform some miracle in his presence and thus sent them away. On the third day Aurangzeb asked them to produce a miracle. Being neither able to say anything nor perform a miracle, some were ordered to be banished and others were sent prisoners to fortresses. Emperor told them that when they showed him a miracle he would order their release.[31]

The corruption over the name *mazars* and saints was once more exposed by the emperor. Aurangzeb once passed close to a tomb and seeing so much adornment, asked what saint was buried there. The *faqir* of the shrine replied that it was the tomb of Malik Dinar. Aurangzeb began to think over this answer and said he had never heard of such a saint. He ordered the tomb to be opened and in it was the skeleton of a horse. The king directed that everything round it should be destroyed and after the faqir had been flogged he was banished.[32]

Jazia

Aurangzeb is generally blamed for re-imposition of *jazia* and his policy was described as his rage against the Hindus. It was a protection tax for the non-Muslims not serving state in any position and had to be paid by an assessee in person. On 2 April 1679 Alamgir issued an order reinstating the discriminatory *jazia* tax levied on all non-Muslim males. This tax was levied on Hindus except for Rajput and Maratha state officials and Brahman religious leaders, but the Jainas, Sikhs and other non-Muslims were obliged to pay. Most of the middle and upper class non-Muslims were generally government officials and were exempted from the tax *jazia*. Women, children below fourteen, slaves, beggars and paupers were also exempted from this tax.

Considering the timing of the decree, it has been suggested that the emperor felt the need to make some dramatic move to rally the empire's Muslims around major political and military initiatives then being contemplated for dealing with deteriorating affairs in the Deccan. Ever since 1663 Shivaji had flagrantly defied Mughal authority and by the late 1670s, with both Bijapur and Golconda often colluding with the new Maratha kingdom, the emperor's Deccan policy lay in shambles. The non-Muslims living under

Mughal rule were, in a narrowly legal sense, a protected population (*dhimmi*) who were obliged to pay this tax to compensate for not serving in the state's armed forces. Curiously, though, to the contemporary Hindu writer Bhimsen, it was not the tax itself that was offensive; rather, it was the corruption of the venal officials who had been recruited from the lower ranks of the Muslim clergy to collect it.[33]

For its assessment and collection the non-Muslim population was roughly divided into three grades; the first grade having an income above 10,000 dirhams had to pay 48 *dirhams*, the second, whose income was from 200 to 10,000 *dirhams* paid 24 *dirhams* and the third, i.e., those whose income fell below 200 *dirhams* paid 12 *dirhams* a year, the value of a dirham being a little more than a quarter of a rupee.[34] The poor non-Muslim population which was engaged in agriculture and prtty trades suffered a lot. Of the monks, the heads of wealthy monasteries only had to pay *jazia* tax. The peasants and petty traders protested the re-imposition of *jazia* but Aurangzeb ignored all protests and remained adamant in realizing the tax. When a large crowd rioted in protest against the *jazia*, Aurangzeb brutally crushed them.

For re-imposing of *jazia* and pilgrim tax, Aurangzeb is being still criticized and branded as anti-Hindu. The Hindutva historians generally avoid answering why he imposed these taxes so late after completing twenty years of his reign, if he was an anti-Hindu? Actually, Aurangzeb was most of his time busy in military campaigns which exhausted the royal treasury. He saw that Hindu traders, businessmen and landlords could easily meet out the financial constraints of the state. So, he imposed the *jazia* tax to recover the loss and moreover, these taxes were not new to the public. He didn't spare the Brahmans because they had enough income from the temples and other religious sources. The landless and poor, which were unable to pay, were exempted or rather not forced to pay. By imposing the *jazia* he had not purely religious motifs but the interest of the state was foremost. Moreover, the Muslims were also taxed the same type tax *zakat* by the government.

Jats

The Jats are a hardy tribe, pre-eminently agricultural and well known for their valour, indefatigable energy, martial spirit and untiring perseverance. The region mainly occupied by them may be roughly defined as the whole Pakistan and in India western Uttar Pradesh, Punjab, Haryana, Rajasthan and some areas of Madhya Pradesh. All of them do not belong to the same religious fraternity but prefer different religions, viz., Hinduism, Sikhism and Islam and they take their tribal name as a proud heritage. The origin of the Jats, like that of the Rajputs, has been a subject of keen controversy. Some regard them as descendants of the nomadic Scythian hordes of Central Asia who invaded India through the north-western passes like the Shakas and the Hunas and settled in India. Now the theory or Aryan origin is more acceptable as of the Meos and Rajputs. The Jats claim that they are descendants of the ancient Yadavas.

In 1669, the Jat peasants rose under their leader Gokla, the *zamindar* of Tilpat. Seizing the occasion of Aurangzeb being in the Deccan near to Bijapur, they proved that they cared neither for his power, his policy, nor his governors. They planned and succeeded in, a very bold undertaking. The *faujdar* of Mathura Abdun Nabi, who opposed them, was slain in the action. The rebels then sacked the pargana of Sadabad and disorder and confusion followed in the neighbouring district of Agra also. Gokla assembled 20,000 men, met the Mughal army under Hasan Ali Khan, *faujdar* of Mathura, at a place twenty miles off from Tilpat. Gokla was defeated with the loss of 5,000 men and 7,000 Jats with Gokla and his family were made prisoner. Mughals also met a heavy loss of 4,000 men. Gokla was eventually slain at Agra.[35]

But the spirit which Gokla had infused into his men did not die with him and after several years, other capable leader Rajaram, son of Bhajja Singh, Chief of Sinsini, took his place against the Mughals. He gave military training to the Jat peasants, equipped them with fire-arms and gave them the semblance of an organized and regular army. They carried on plundering raids on this highway and the suburbs of Agra. The emperor's long stay in the Deccan and consequent military weakness in northern India had encouraged them to plunder the ill-guarded rich convoys passing through their region.

Under Rajaram, a great number of Jats assembled and marched to the mausoleum of Akbar at Sikandara. They began their pillage by breaking in the great gates of bronze which it had, robbing the valuable precious stones and plates of gold and silver and destroying what they were not able to carry away. The Jat leader Rajaram even tried to ransack Akbar's tomb, which was foiled by *faujdar* Mir Abul Fazl. A fierce fight followed and Rajaram was driven back after losing about 400 of his men.[36]

In 1688, Mahabat Khan, on his way from Gujarat to his new Government of Lahore, was encamped at Sikandara and, taking the field against the Jats, killed 400 of them. At this time Shaistah Khan, the Emperor's uncle, was appointed governor; but, before he took charge, the Jats renewed their attack on Sikandara and plundered the tomb, taking the carpets, with the silver and gold vessels and damaging most of the tombs and the mausoleum. However, Rajaram sacked the tomb of Akbar and damaging the building, carried away carpets, lamps, precious stones and gold and silver vessels, etc.[37]

Their actions grew more shocking that they even desecrated the Emperor Akbar's remains from his grave. Attacking the dead emperor's remains was an act of deep disrespect to the departed soul. Throwing relics, as has been written of earlier, reportedly into a fire was a clear sign of Hindu rebellion against Mughal. During a fierce fight sometime later, Rajaram was killed by a Mughal musketeer who was hiding in a tree.[38]

Highly perturbed at the atrocious deeds of the Jats, Aurangzeb sent his seventeen year's grandson Bedar Bakht to take charge of the military operations against them. In July 1688, a severe battle was fought between them and the Jat leader Rajaram was killed by a Mughal musketeer. Bedar Bakht then besieged the fort of Sinsani in 1690. Meanwhile, Bishan Singh Kachhwaha, Raja of Ambar (Jaipur), who had been appointed faujdar of Mathura with special duty of suppressing the Jats besieged the fort of Sogor on 21 May 1691.[39] Thus fell the two important strongholds of the Jats and their power was humbled for the time being but not crushed permanently.

Satnamis

The Satnamis, a set of low-caste men, were a peaceful sect, believing in the unity of God, mostly employed in agriculture. They were honest, industrious and formed a brotherhood, calling themselves Satnamis, Satnam meaning true name. As they used to shave their head and face including eyebrows, they were popularly called Mundiyas or Mundas. According to their belief they used to take bath on every full moon in Pohkar Lake west of Ajmer which was their place of pilgrimage. They collect from all directions at that place of pilgrimage, adjoining the country of Kirat Singh, younger son of Raja Jai Singh. A formidable rising of the Satnamis took place in the districts of Narnaul and Mewat which were their native place. In 1672, a petty quarrel near Narnaul between a Satnami cultivator and a Mughul foot-soldier of the local revenue collector led to the outbreak.

The petty quarrel soon developed into a religious war against the Mughals. The Satnamis defeated the imperialists on several occasions and took possession of the town and district of Narnaul. In these circumstances on the occasion of full moon the Satnamis collect from all directions at a place of pilgrimage, the assembly amounted to some 25,000 upon the bathing-day. After the bathing ceremonies were completed, an old sorceress told them that if they would follow her orders she would make them masters of the city of Delhi, the king not having more than ten thousand horsemen, because all his other troops had gone with Shah Alam on the expedition against Shivaji.[40]

The Satnamis agreed to the proposal of the old sorceress and marched towards their homeland Narnaul with such vigour that when the news reached the court Aurangzeb was particularly disturbed in mind and sent out against them his 10,000 horsemen. The Mundas fought with such vigour, upheld by the sorceries of the old woman, that they routed Aurangzeb's army. At this result he was more disturbed than ever. They had already arrived within fifteen leagues (45 miles) of Delhi, when he ordered out all the troops he had been able to raise. But Aurangzeb felt that these men would never have undertaken such a great attempt without the help of sorcery. He therefore wrote out himself several papers and sent them to be hung on the heads of the elephants and horses and on the standards, fatiguing himself greatly with the preparation of all those papers.[41]

Aurangzeb found himself at this moment in greater danger than at any time in the rest of his life, because, he had very few troops. But the strength of these magical writings overcame the Murids, since, elated at having gained one battle. The spells of Aurangzeb prevailed over those of the old woman and the 2,000 Mundas of this sect fell fighting on the field and many of them were killed during the pursuit including the old woman herself. The rebellion was thus crushed and the affected areas brought under control. Aurangzeb came out of this affair with the reputation of a saint.[42]

Sikhs

Aurangzeb is a severely misunderstood historical figure who has suffered perhaps more than any of the other Mughal ruler in the present-day biases. He is being branded as the religious intolerant because he dealt harshly against the rebellious chiefs such as Hindus and Sikhs, although Muslims were also among them. As for the Sikhs, Aurangzeb had animosity as they supported the cause of Dara Shikoh in 1658 succession crisis. They were also charged for preaching and proselytizing Sikhism among the Muslims and Hindus under the ninth Sikh Guru Tegh Bahadur. Under his influence many Muslims were converted into Sikhism. Aurangzeb condemned Guru Tegh Bahadur for blasphemy and executed him in 1675. However, according to some Sikh and Persian sources, Guru Tegh Bahadur militarily opposed Mughal state interests and so was a legitimate target for a death sentence. His religious stature did nothing to mitigate the overarching commitment of Aurangzeb's administration to meting out punishment, including capital punishment, to enemies of the state.[43]

Bakhtmal writing early in the eighteenth century actually gives this reason for his execution. It is possible that the arrest and subsequient execution, of the Guru was the result of Aurangzeb's fanatic campaign against active leaders of anti-Islamic thought in his dominions. It is possible that somebody might even have brought up the proselytizing activities of Guru Hargovind whom Muhsin Fani credits with converting many Muslims. The Guru's execution may have inspired a Sikh at Agra to throw a stone at the emperor while he was returning fiom Friday prayers in the Jama Masjid. The culprit was arrested and must have been executed.[44]

Guru Tegh Bahadur's successor and only son Govinda Singh was determined to avenge his father's murder. These days Emperor Aurangzeb was busy in Deccan fighting with his co-religionists. Guru Gobind Singh had taken advantage of the respite granted to him and put his Sikhs together as a devoted band of the faithful and transforming the Sikhs into a military community and instituted the custom of baptism with a new oath. Those who accepted this baptism were known as the *khalsa* (pure) and the members were required to put on a distinctive dress, keeping five things on their person, viz., *kesh* (hair), *kangha* (comb), *kripan* (sword), *kachha* (underwear) and *Kara* (iron bangle). Guru Gobind Singh insisted that Sikhs use epithet Singh (lion). In 1693 it was reported to the emperor in the south that Guru Gobind Singh had proclaimed himself an incarnation of Guru Nanak.[45]

While realizing the rising power of the Sikhs under Guru Gobind Singh, Emperor Aurangzeb ordered to quell them. In the hilly regions of the northern Punjab, Guru Gobind fought against the local Muslim chiefs and Hindu *rajas* who had been asked to cooperate with the imperial forces in suppressing him and won some victories over them. His stronghold at Anandapur was besieged five times and at last he had to leave it to take refuge in the plains, hotly pursued by the imperialists on 21 December 1704. His four sons were slain and he had no alternative but to proceed to the Deccan through Bikaner. He came back to northern India after the death of Aurangzeb and joined Bahadur Shah in the war of succession with his brothers. He also accompanied Bahadur Shah to the Deccan and, while encamped at Nander on the Godavari, he was murdered by an Afghan follower in 1708.[46]

Guru Gobind Singh made the Sikhism not only the movement for religious and social reform but a political and military force to be reckoned with. He was the tenth and last Guru of the Sikhs. Before his death, his instruction to his followers was to get themselves organized into a military democracy, without having any more need of a Guru.

Rajputs

Aurangzeb was having good relations with Rajput chiefs and granted *mansabs* and honour to them more especially to Raja Jai Singh of Amber, Raja Jaswant Singh of Marwar and Raja Raj Singh of Mewar. Raja Jaswant Singh, who had fought against Aurangzeb in the battle of Dharmat was afterwards appointed by the emperor in responsible positions. Since the death of Raja Jai Singh of Amber in 1667, he occupied the foremost place among the Hindu peers in the Mughal court. While commanding the Mughal frontier posts in the Khyber Pass and the Peshawar district, he died at Jamrud on 10 December 1678, without an heir.

After death of Raja Jaswant Singh without any hier in late 1678, a crisis arose in his kingdom. Indra Singh Rathor, the chieftain of Nagaur and grand-nephew of Jaswant Singh was recognized as the Maharaja of Marwar on payment of a succession fee of Rs. 36 lakhs, although his candidacy was widely opposed by Rathor clansmen. Meanwhile, in February 1679, a male child named Ajit Singh was born to one of Jaswant Singh's wives. Not wishing to put Marwar under a regency until the boy had attained majority, 'Alamgir ordered the child placed under imperial custody while naming Indra Singh the state's new *raja*. The family of Jaswant Singh, including the surviving son Ajit Singh, reached Delhi. The rights of Ajit Singh had been urged before the emperor more than once. They rejected the emperor's compromise proposal to partition the state between the infant Ajit Singh and Indra Singh. In July 1679, Durga Das, a leading Rathor chieftain, kidnapped Ajit Singh from imperial custody in Delhi and dashed off to Jodhpur, Marwar's capital, where the child was acclaimed the next Rathor *raja*. Since such defiance of imperial authority amounted to rebellion, in September 1679, Alamgir despatched his son, Prince Akbar, with a large army against the Rathors. Success attended Mughal arms and all the great towns including Jodhpur were plundered. The entire kingdom was placed under direct Mughal administration, pending resolution of the succession issue. The emperor also sent in imperial agents to prepare inventories of Jaswant Singh's estate, since the property of any Mughal noble automatically reverted to the state upon his death.[47]

With the Mughals occupying the Rathor capital of Jodhpur, Durga Das with the infant Ajit Singh took refuge in neighbouring Mewar, then ruled by Rana Raj Singh. Raj Singh of Mewar favoured the Marwar as the mother of Ajit was a Mewar princess. In response, in November 1679 'Alamgir personally invaded Mewar only to find the Sisodiya capital of Udaipur vacated, as Rana Raj Singh and his entire cavalry had abandoned the plains for the hills. After nearly a year of Mughal–Sisodiya military stalemate, Raj Singh died and was succeeded by Jai Singh, who opposed his clan's continued involvement in the Rathor succession struggle and negotiated a separate peace with 'Alamgir. The emperor, in turn, confirmed Jai Singh in his position as Mewar's *raja* and made him an imperial *mansabdar* with the rank of 5,000. For the rest of 'Alamgir's reign Mughal relations with Mewar remained cordial, with Sisodiya commanders and troops once again taking up imperial service throughout the empire.[48]

At the height of the Rajput rebellion, in mid 1680, the emperor had given the command of military campaigns in southern Marwar to his favourite son, Prince Akbar. But the prince, flushed with several battlefield victories and knowing how his father had usurped power from Shah Jahan, made the rash decision to confront Alamgir for the Mughal throne. In this he was urged on by 'Alamgir's erstwhile enemies, Durga Das and Rana Raj Singh, who assured him that all Rajputs would certainly rally to his cause. So in early 1681 Akbar, accompanied by his newfound Rajput allies and addled by visions of the gem-studded Peacock Throne, declared himself emperor and marched the 200 km to his father's camp in Ajmer. On the eve of the battle, however, 'Alamgir tricked the Rajputs into believing that Akbar was actually leading them into a trap. As a result, the prince awoke at dawn to find that all his Rajput allies had vanished, leaving him with just a few hundred men to face his furious father. Hastily backtracking, the prince caught up with Durga Das, who was dismayed to learn that 'Alamgir had wiped an entire army off the field without shooting a single arrow. Finding that the Rajputs had no appetite for battling Alamgir, Durga Das, together with Prince Akbar, marched south seeking asylum with any anti-Mughal community they could find.[49]

Meanwhile the Rathors of Marwar wearily came to accept rule by Mughal governors. But their relations remained strained, as Durga Das kept up a guerrilla resistance for another two decades, albeit with only desultory support from his kinsmen. Ultimately, by 1699 both Durga Das and Ajit Singh, by then an adult, had submitted to Mughal rule and become imperial *mansabdars*, formally ending Marwar's rebellion against 'Alamgir. The Rajput rebellion also led to 'Alamgir's fateful decision not to return to Delhi, but to continue south and conduct military operations in the Deccan. These operations would occupy his remaining twenty-five years of life and permanently alter the course of Mughal history.

Marathas

The founder of Maratha power Shivaji Bhonsale belonged to House of Bhonsle which was initially founded in 1577 by Maloji Bhonsle, a predominant general of Malik Amber of Ahmadnagar Sultanate. He was given the title of *raja* and some *jagir* including Pune by the ruler of Ahmadnagar. These positions were inherited by his sons. The house of Bhonsle is claimed to descent from the Rajput Sisodia dynasty but was likely Kunbi Marathas. Jandunath Sarkar claims that Bhonsles were predominantly Deccani tiller-plainsmen from the Shudra caste. However some scholars disagree with Sarkar and called the Bhonsles were Kshatriyas, who enjoyed reasonably high social status as landholders and warlords, being in the service of Deccan Sultanate or Mughals.

Shivaji Bhonsale was born on 10 April 1627 at the fort of Shivneri in Maharashtra. Shivaji was named after a local deity, the goddess Shivai Devi. He was the son of Shahaji Bonsale, a military leader who served the Ahmadnagar Sultanate, Bijapur Sultanate and Mughal Empire at various points in his career. His mother, Jijabai, was an extremely religious woman. Shivaji grew up at Pune under the strict supervision of his mother and his teacher, Dadaji Kondadev. The fall of the Bijapur and Ahmednagar sultanates intensified his territorial ambitions. At the age of 16, in 1646, he captured the Torna Fort of Bijapur Sultanate. Shivaji constructed a strategic fort at Purandhar, Kondana Pratapgarh and Chakan and his strength increased in Maharashtra. From 1656. Shivaji accelerated his conquest which created fear in the Sultan of Bijapur and he began to look for ways to capture Shivaji. He appointed Afzal Khan for this task. When Afzal Khan arrived at Pratapgarh,

Shivaji sued for peace and pardon and came down from the fort with five guards. During the hugging Shivaji killed Afzal Khan with a weapon known as a Baghnakh on 10 November 1659. From this time Shivaji began to plunder the territories of the Mughal in addition to those of Bijapur. He took various strongholds, more frequently by deceit than by force of arms. He ravaged towns and cities, above all Surat, one of the busiest ports on the western coast with a population of 2,00,000, gathering all that there was of gold and silver in that famous port.[50]

Mughal Emperor Aurangzeb decided to chastise Shivaji and at the request of Badi Begum of Bijapur, Mughal EmperorAurangzeb sent his maternal uncle Shaista Khan with a large army in 1660 to attack Shivaji in conjunction with Bijapur's army led by Siddi Jauhar. As soon as Shaista Khan reached south, he seized Pune from Shivaji. Outside it he lived in a mud house that he had caused to be built near a tank. There he meant to pass the rainy season. On the night of 5 April 1663, Shivaji led a daring night attack on Shaista Khan's camp and wounded him with the loss of index finger and his son. When Aurangzeb, being then in Kashmir, received a report of this treachery of Shivaji, he wrote to Shaista Khan directing him to proceed as governor to Bengal. When Shaistah Khan left the Deccan, Aurangzeb recalled Jaswant Singh to court, who, instead of obeying, retired to his own territory. Aurangzeb ordered Mahabat Khan to march with all rapidity possible to take up the office of Shaista Khan and continue the campaign against Shivaji, sending also his own son, Shah Alam, not as commander, but as representative of the royal person in matters of parade. Mahabat Khan, in spite of having a large army, could not restrain the fury of this rebel. While Mahabat Khan was investing a fortress, Shivaji went off once more and plundered Surat city for many days in January 1664. Mahabat Khan was called back to take charge of Gujarat.[51]

In 1665, Aurangzeb ordered Kachhwaha Rajput chief Mirza Raja Jai Singh along with Diler Khan, Daud Khan and even Munucci with astrong force to defeat Shivaji. Raja Jai Singh attacked the places like Pune, Purandhar, Singarh and Raigarh. Munucci says, that during the time that he was carrying out his deputation, which lasted nearly seven months, Raja Jai Singh by his valorous enterprise gave Shivaji as much to do as he could manage, never letting him rest. In the end, when Shivaji's fortress of Banagar was invested, Jai Singh, in his foreseeing way, began to write to Shivaji, pointing out to him that if he would only listen to his words, things should be so arranged with Aurangzeb that he (Shivaji) should be propitiated and appointed by the king as governor of the Deccan.[52]

A treaty was prepared between Jai Singh and Shivaji and signed in the Purandar hill fort. In a treaty known as "Treaty of Purandar", Shivaji agreed to surrender twenty-three of his thirty-five forts; join Mughal campaigns against Bijapur; give the Mughals a portion of plundered wealth from future conquests of Bijapuri assets; and agree to his son Sambhaji enrolling in Mughal service. Suspecting that the Maratha leader might renege on these provisions, Jai Singh proposed and 'Alamgir agreed, that Shivaji and Sambhaji should personally appear at the imperial court in Agra.[53]

Shivaji visited Aurangzeb's court at Agra on 12 May 1666, offended at having to stand in court among officers he considered beneath his stature. Shivaji said resolutely to Aurangzeb that the position allotted was not according to that promised to him under oath, nor to the agreement made with Raja Jai Singh and in anger he came out. Some of the courtiers managed to console him, saying it was the habit of the King of Hindustan not to give forthwith the first place to those who had newly come to court. But he was certain to do so afterwards and he must wait with patience for a few days. Shivaji was ordered to stay in the tent and after poassing some months he sent to ask permission for his soldiers and captains to leave for their own country. Shivaji, on the advice of Ram Singh, son of Raja Jai Singh, who was one of the captains on guard over him, sent several times each week large covered baskets of sweetmeats to be shared among the officers and others. Aurangzeb took no precautions about this and he supposed such presents were sent by Shivaji by reason of his desire to give alms in thanks to God for his freedom. Munucci says that in connivance of Jai Singh and his son Ram Singh, Shivaji concealing himself within one covered sweetmeat baskets, he arranged to be carried away, he and his son, to a place of security, whence with good riding-horses he could take flight for his own country. In 1669, Shivaji renewed his flagrant denial of Mughal authority by launching fresh attacks to regain the forts he had surrendered a few years earlier.[54]

In 1670, Shivaji plundered Surat and other places repeatedly. For the next four years, he raided Mughal strongholds in the north of Maharashtra, such as Khandesh, Berar and Baglan and met with opposition from Imperial and Bijapuri troops alike. In 1672 Shivaji fashioned himself as an explicitly Hindu monarch, one of his titles being *Haindava Dharmoddharakla* (Protector of the Hindu faith). Shivaji arranged for a celebrated Brahman from Benares, Gagabhat, to come to Maharashtra and in June 1674 he sponsored a lavish and carefully choreographed coronation ceremony at Raigarh, in which he had himself invested with the sacred thread of the twice-born castes, accompanied by elaborate purification rituals, Vedic verses and Brahmanical chants. While Shivaji sat on a golden throne covered with lion and tiger skins, Gagabhat raised the royal umbrella over his head, hailing him Shiva Chhatrapati. The extravagant ceremony, in which thousands of Brahmans were fed and given gifts, cost an estimated five million rupees. Aurangzeb fought the Marathas, with limited success, for the rest of his life. Shivaji died of dysentery in 1680. After the death of Shivaji, brief succession struggle ensued between Rajaram and Sambhaji. Sambhaji won and succeeded his father in continuing destruction to Mughal interests in the Deccan.[55]

The Maratha state, ruled since 1680 by Shivaji's first son Sambhaji, now felt the full brunt of Mughal arms. In early 1689 Sambhaji was captured, taken to 'Alamgir's camp and brutally executed. In the Maratha capital of Raigarh Shivaji's second son, Rajaram, was hastily crowned, but the kingdom's leaders, fearful for the young king's security with Mughal armies nearby, arranged for his escape to distant Jinji in the Tamil country. Just months later, Raigarh too fell to Alamgir. At this point it seemed that the Maratha state had been crushed. Alamgir had captured all Shivaji's remaining treasure, his resplendent golden coronation throne, all the government's records and the royal horses and elephants. Although Rajaram had eluded their grasp, the Mughals did capture Sambhaji's 9-year-old son Shahu, whom 'Alamgir confined in his mobile court, where he was well treated. He would be raised in Persianate Mughal culture but not converted to Islam.

In late 1697, the Maratha cause revived when Maratha fugitive Rajaram went tords Maharashtra from Jinji. Reaching Maharashtra in early 1698, Rajaram began rebuilding his father's state, establishing a new capital at Satara and mounting counter-attacks against the Mughals in the northern Deccan. But Rajaram's efforts would be cut-off by his early death, in 1700. His two wives were hoping that their infant son might succeed Rajaram as king. One of these wives was Tarabai, the proud and strongwilled daughter of Shivaji's former commander-in-chief, Hambir Rao Mohite. Now, following Rajaram's death, Tarabai boldly had the sacred thread ceremony performed for her 4-year-old son, confirming his ritual status as a Kshatriya warrior and revealing her intention to crown him king, with herself as regent. Prominent Maratha Deshmukhs now rallied around the 25-year-old Tarabai, recognizing her as the most likely remnant of Shivaji's family to salvage the kingdom's sagging fortunes, despite her gender. She boldly sent Maratha armies on military expeditions deep into Mughal domains to the north. In 1700, she dispatched 50,000 troops as far north as the Chanderi region in north-western Madhya Pradesh, nearly 1,000 km from the Maratha headquarters in Satara. In 1702 she sent armies into Mughal Khandesh, Berar and Telangana. The next year she attacked cities in Khandesh and Malwa and in 1706 her generals struck cities in Gujarat.[56]

The conflict between Mughal and Maratha was only a political conflict and not related to the religion or race, as modern chroniclers or Hindutva historians claim. When Shivaji captured Muslim kingdom Bijapur, his men took the treasure, horses and elephants and enlisted to their side most of the Bijapuri troops, some of whom were Maharashtrians, while some of Shivaji's men were Muslims. Shivaji allied with numerous Islamic states, including Bijapur, Golconda and even the Mughals when it suited him (sometimes against Hindu powers in south India). Shivaji welcomed Muslims within his army; he had *qazis* (Muslim judges) on his payroll and Muslims ranked among some of his top commanders. In this, as in so much of medieval Indian history, allies and enemies were formed on political and military grounds than on religious ones. However, in later centuries the Hindutva historiographer continues in posing Shivaji as Hindu Hero and godfather of Hindu militantism against Muslims.[57]

Aurangzeb's relation with Guru Gobind Singh and Shivaji and other like-minded rebel leaders could not be seen on the religious ground but more compatible with the political affairs. Aurangzeb had a national interest and wanted to unify the whole region of Indian subcontinent. However, Guru Gobind Singh and Shivaji had the regional interest and wanted to establish their own kingdom on the cost of the Mughal Empire. It was utterly not acceptable to the Mughal ruler Aurangzeb. For the unity of India and expansion of the Mughal Empire, he even snatched the Himalayan Mansarovar region from China and facilitated the pilgrimage of the Indian Hindus. The Hindutva historians' claim that Aurangzeb was anti-Hindu and wanted to destroy the Hindu worship places is baseless and shows their hatred for the followers of Islam.

Religious Policy

Throughout his reign, Aurangzeb's policy was to ensure the well-being of Hindu religious institutions and their leaders. He issued dozens of orders that directed officials to shield temples from unwanted interference, granted land to Hindu communities and provided stipends to Hindu spiritual figures. Hindus fared well in Aurangzeb's massive bureaucracy, finding employment and advanced opportunities. The Rajputs and other Hindus had served as full members of the Mughal administration.

Under Aurangzeb, like the Muslims, the Hindus received formal ranks known as *mansabs* that marked their status in the imperial hierarchy and fought to expand the empire. Hindus occupied elevated positions and were entrusted with critical state business. In 1657, under Shah Jahan there were 8,000 *mansabdars* in all, whereas in 1690, the number of *mansabdars* had risen to 14556. During the later seventeen years of Aurangzeb's reign the number must have increased still further. This doubling of the number of mansabdars of all classes does not show a proportional increase in the number of the Hindus who held mansabs of 1,000 and above. When Aurangzeb became the emperor, we find that the two premier nobles of the empire Raja Jai Singh and Raja Jaswant Singh were Hindus and the finance minister Raja Raghu Nath Das also was a Hindu. Maharaja Jaswant Singh served as the Governor of Gujarat, as the leader of the first Mughal expedition against the Marathas and then as a regent of a royal prince in the Government of Kabul. He was deputed wherever hard work was expected. When he was sent against Shivaji to the Deccan, Raja Jai Singh controlled all the civil and military authorities in the Deccan and became the highest ruling authority in the area. The Maratha prince Sahu was a minor had drew a salary without filling any office. Among the thirteen Hindu commanders of 5,000, nine were Marathas who were really raised to their high status on their submission; most of them had been directly appointed to their high commands.[58]

These religious institutions were entitled to Mughal state protection and Aurangzeb generally endeavoured to ensure their well-being. Aurangzeb allowed the Sahasraing Tank in Gujarat to be kept filled with water at the expense of the state. He is said to have made a grant of land to a temple at Gaya. Another grant to the priests of a temple on the Brahmaputra has been traced in Assam. Many of the Hindu temples were built in the reign of Aurangzeb are known to exist in the town of Bishalpur in Bengal. These temples date back to his reign according to the inscriptions to be found on them. Two were built in 1681 and one was built in 1690. In the south whore he spent the last twenty-seven years of his reign, Aurangzeb was usually content with leaving many Hindu temples standing.

He was tolerant and he loved the Hindus offering *pujas* (prayers) in their temples but was severely against the religious corruption and misuse of the temples. He thought that there are sufficient numbers of temples all over India and there is no need for further new temple construction. In his rule, the people of all caste, creed and religion were living peacefully and enjoyed the benefit of the state policies. The priests and temples were given generous grants and many temples were repaired and constructed out of the state purse.

If we go through the contemporary sources and documents, they will reveal that Aurangzeb protected more temples than he destroyed in some crucial circumstances. In the military philosophy of the ancient and medieval period, every victorious army shattered the defeated kingdom at its level best. They generally destroyed and dismantled the temples of the highest order or attached to the defeated king and his palaces. Hindu kings targeted one another's temples beginning in the seventh century, regularly looting and defiling images of Durga, Ganesha, Vishnu and so forth. They also periodically destroyed each other's temples.

Muslim sovereigns since the late twelfth century and Hindu *rajas* since at least the seventh, had looted, redefined or destroyed royal temples of enemy kings as the normal means of detaching defeated rulers from the most prominent manifestations of their former sovereign authority, thereby rendering such rulers politically impotent. Under Akbar, Raja Birbal's Mughal army destroyed a temple in Kangra, although it was rebuilt by Akbar. This war strategy was followed by the Hindu Marathas and destroyed many temples including the temple of Shrirangapattam under Tipu Sultan. The Badshahi mosque of Lahore built by Aurangzeb, the largest mosque at that time, was suffered some damage and repurposed for artillery storage in the early nineteenth century by

Ranjit Singh, founder of the Sikh empire. The Royal army under Aurangzeb also did the same for the rebellious chiefs of his kingdom and other defeated chiefs in other parts of India.

In his own empire, Aurangzeb touched only those buildings which were the source of conversion, misconduct, corruption and under rebels' protrction. As for the policy regarding temples under Aurangzeb, Hindu and Jaina temples dotted the landscape of Aurangzeb's kingdom. 'Alamgir supported temples with cash or land grants. He once ordered officials in Benares to punish miscreants who had been harassing Brahmans in charge of that city's Hindu temples. Aurangzeb described the temple complex of Ellora, which he visited in the 1650s, as "one of the marvels of the work of the true transcendent Artisan (God)". But his treatment of temples patronized by, or associated with, state enemies was another matter.

For the Mughals, temples formerly patronized by enemy kings became state property once that king had been defeated and his former territory annexed to the empire. However, if a Hindu patron of such a temple rebelled against the state, both he and the temple were liable for punishment. Such a principle would explain 'Alamgir's destruction of temples in Cooch Behar (north of Bengal) after local *raja*s there defied Mughal authority in 1661. The same principle accounted for his destruction of the Vishvanath Temple in Benares in 1669, people related to that temple's patron were believed to have facilitated Shivaji's escape from Agra and hence were state enemies. Similarly, the Kesavadeva Temple in Mathura, which had been supported by imperial grants and was therefore considered state property, was destroyed in 1670 in the wake of a serious Jat rebellion in the region that claimed the life of the city's commandant and patron of its congregational mosque. Moreover, three Brahmans in Mathura had harboured the son of Shivaji shortly after the latter had escaped detention in Agra. In 1679-80 'Alamgir ordered the destruction of prominent temples in Rajasthan, including Khandela, Udaipur and Jodhpur, once it was established that they, too, had been associated with anti-state rebels.[59]

Munucci mentions that after the death Raja Jai Singh of Amber the anti-Hindu policy Aurangzeb was unveiled, although he was not in favour of even Muslims or his kinsmen. Perhaps the anti-Hindu or anti-temple feelings developed in Aurangzeb's mind right from the Shivaji's escape from Agra. Aurangzeb was aware of the role of Ram Singh and his father Jai Singh in the escape of Shivaji who was under the charge of Ram Singh in Agra. Although Aurangzeb punished the lower officers but his wrath exposed against the Jaipur royal family and the Rajput *raja*s. Munucci says that Aurangzeb send orders at once for the destruction of the fine temple called Lalta, in the neighbourhood of Delhi. Among others was destroyed the great temple of Mathura, which was of such a height that its gilded pinnacle could be seen from Agra, eighteen leagues away.[60]

In the early thirteenth century, after 1540 and again during the reigns of Akbar, Shah Jahan and even Aurangzeb, many incidents of the demolition of mosques and their conversion into temples happened in several parts of India. The *jazia* and other discriminatory measures affected Hindu community and they demolished the mosques or stopped to call the prayer (*azan*).[61] Over these issues of mosque demolition, schools and temples becoming the source of conversion, misconduct and corruption greatly pained Aurangzeb and in utter disgust. Aurangzeb was very much annoyed over that and his forces also demolished the temple in revenge during the aggression or subjugation of the rebellion.

One or two cases of temple demolition took place where adultery and conversion were going on. In a *farman* granted to a priest of Benares in 1659, Aurangzeb "avowed that his religion forbade him to allow the building of new temples, but did not enjoin the destruction of old ones". In 1664, he forbade old temples to be repaired and on 9 April 1669, an order was issued to the governors of the provinces "to demolish the schools and temples of the infidels and put down their teaching and religious practices strongly. Besides innumerable temples throughout the empire, even the famous Hindu temples of Visvanath at Benares, of Keshavdeva at Mathura and Somnath at Patan were destroyed.

Even the loyal State of Jaipur was not spared and sixty-six temples were razed to the ground at Amber.[62]

Actually, the data of temple destruction was recorded with biased intentions and had no match with the reality. These records were prompted by Hindutva historians with the further multiplied figure. If we consider the Hindutva data true, then there was not a single temple would have been left after the reign of Aurangzeb. In Richard Eaton's careful tabulation, some eighty temples were demolished between 1192 and 1760 and out of these fifteen were demolished in Aurangzeb's reign. The foreign travellers testify the existence of a large number of temples in different cities during the reign of Aurangzeb. The French traveller Thevenot, too, attests to the existence of a large number of temples in Ahmedabad during the reign of Aurangzeb. Aurangzeb, who was exhibited for his religious bigotry by going on a temple demolition spree, was also recorded for financing the maintenance of several other Hindu temples and hermitages (*mathas*). This figure condemns the Hindutva propaganda of thousands of demolitions of Hindu temples.[63]

During the early Mughal rule, more particularly in the reign of Akbar and Jahangir, the Hinduism was more promoted. The Brahmans of Varanasi and Mathura re-emerged as the religious centre and hundreds of new temples were built to pose the religious greatness of these cities. The Brahmans of these cities in the association of other holy cities began to re-convert the Muslims into Hindu fold. The rape and corruption in these Hindu temples and schools also attracted royal attention. There was also doubt that the Brahmans and aristocrats of such cities were involved in intriguing against the state. How could Aurangzeb like ruler tolerate these activities? He became harsh to them and dealt severely at the time of action.

During his rule, the non-Muslim religious divines were not molested or persecuted and they were supported financially by the emperor. This reveals that he was not a fanatic or bigoted emperor but inclined towards religious toleration. However, many modern people view Aurangzeb's orders to harm specific temples as symptomatic of a larger vendetta against Hindus. Such views have roots in colonial-era scholarship, where positing timeless Hindu-Muslim animosity embodied the British strategy of divide and conquer. Aurangzeb maintained personal contacts with Hindu religious figures. For instance, he penned a letter to Mahant Anand Nath in 1661, requesting a medicinal preparation from the *yogi*. In the 1660s, he increased Anand Nath's landholdings in a village in the Punjab.[64]

According to the Royal documents of Aurangzeb (*farman*) preserved in the Bharat Kala Bhawan in Benares Hindu University, Aurangzeb was the most lenient ruler and preserver of the ancient holy temples. The *farman*, issued to the military general posted in Varanasi, reads as:[65]

> "Abul Fazl should know that—It has been decided by our religious law that neither the old temples should be dismantled nor the new temples should be built. These days the news reached to our ideal and holy court that some people due to the animosity and jealousy teasing the Brahmans of Varanasi and neighbouring areas. They also wanted to terminate temple priests Brahmans from their posts; this would certainly lead to dissatisfaction in that particular religious sect. So this is our Royal Order and I warn you that on reaching the Farman you should manage that in future the Brahmans and other Hindus should not face any injustice. In this way, they all should peacefully engage themselves in their businesses and continue their prayer and worship in our Empire granted by Allah (that will remain always). The action should be taken immediately". (5 Jamad-us-Sani 1069 H (1658-59 CE).

The incharge of Bharat Kala Bhawan Dr Rajendra Singh told that Aurangzeb had issued grants for the maintenance of the temples and salary of the temple caretakers (pujari). He told that Aurangzeb used to write the Qura'nic verses and spun skull cap and from its earnings, he spent for his livelihood and personal needs. The Head of the Kashi Vidyapith History Department, Professor Permanand Singh also told the same and opined that there are a lot of misunderstandings about Aurangzeb, he was actually not so but a little stubborn.[66]

The religious tolerance of Aurangzeb is expressed by Jagat Rai, in the colophon of an author of Digambara sect, his work *Padmanandi Panchvisika* dated Samvat 1722, writes:[67]

> "*Raja karai sri aurangasahi, jake nahi kisi parvahi,*
> *Na bhai bhita kachhu take raja, dharmi bhavijana Padhana ke kaja*".
>
> (Here rules the king Aurangzeb, who cares none. In his reign there is nothing for any religious-minded people to fear about their studies).

On another place, there is the testimony of Aurangzeb's religious tolerance that everyone during Aurangzeb's reign was free to practice his own religion. The translator of *Mahabharata* in Hindi, Sabal Singh Chauhan writes in the Shalya-Parva of *Mahabharata* that:[68]

> "*Aurangshah dilli sultana*
> *Prabal pratap jagat sat jana*".
>
> (Aurangzeb the Sultan at Delhi. His glory is known throughout the world).

Aurangzeb continued to patronize the Goswamis of Jangambari Math of Benares as his predecessors. By an order bearing the date 1071 H (27 August 1660 CE) on the reverse side, with the seal of an officer Inayatullah, Aurangzeb confirmed about 200 *bighas* of land as *madad-i-maash* to Jangams, which was previously granted by the *farman* of Akbar and Jahangir. During 1670, Arjun Mal Jangam of Benares with his followers represented himself before Emperor Aurangzeb and petitioned that a person named Nazir Beg resident of the same place, forcibly took position of the *hawelis* belonged to the Jangams. According to an order (*hasbul-hukm*) was issued to the *mutasaddis* of the *pargana* Haweli-i-Mohammadabad *urf* (alias) Benares, a dependency of Suba Allahabad, that the property of Jangams should be freed (i.e., restored) according to *Sharia* (Islamic law) and to dispossess Nazir Beg.[69]

Aurangzeb also paid much respect to *jogis* of Jakhbar and addressed their Mahant Anand Nath as Shiv Murat in a letter of early 1660. In the letter bearing the seal of Aurangzeb, it states that in the village Thar, Anand Nath hold fifteen *ghumaos* of land by way of revenue-free (*madad-i-maash*) and Aurangzeb increased that grant to twenty *ghumaos*. Aurangzeb also passed general order in 1672-73 that *madad-i-maash* grants given earlier to the no-Muslims should be resumed.[70] So, the letter of Aurangzeb and his land grant to the *mahant* of Jakhbar suggests that he paid much regard to the religions divines.

Emperor Aurangzeb also showed his sympathy with the Bairagi saints. While marching towards the Deccan, Aurangzeb encamped at the fort of Mandsaur in Malwa. During his stay, the leader of Khaki Bairagi saints, Mahant Shri Mangal Das had along with religious discourse on truth and devotion with the emperor. Aurangzeb was very much impressed and pleased with the saint and he issued a *farman* in his name to fix an annuity of Rs. 5 from each *qasba* and *mauza* and gave him a royal *farman* and the same has been engraved on copper plate handed over respectfully to the honoured Mahant with a *khila't* (robe of honour), a horse, a drum, a mace, a silver umbrella together with 200 *dirhams*.[71]

Aurangzeb brought the bulk of Benares's Vishvanath Temple down in 1669. It was re-built by Aurangzeb adjoining the destructed temple and placed *linga* under this. He also built a mosque attached to the old Vishvanath Temple. The Gyanvapi Masjid still stands today in Benares with part of the ruined temple's wall incorporated into the building. The Kashi Vishvanath Temple is also standing with full velour after certain reconstruction. The reason for destruction of this temple bears many stories but the main reason could be seen the treason. Actually, Vishvanath Temple had been built during Akbar's reign by Raja Man Singh, whose great-grandson, Jai Singh, many believed had helped Shivaji and his son Sambhaji flee from the Mughal court in 1666. Additionally, in 1669 a rebellion broke out among Benares landlords connected to the Vishvanath Temple, many of whom were also implicated in Shivaji's escape.[72]

In 1670, Aurangzeb directed the obliteration of the Keshavadeva Temple in Mathura, built in 1618 by Bir Singh Bundela, for similarly layered political reasons. Mathura Brahmans may have assisted with Shivaji's 1666 flight from Agra. Moreover, the Keshavadeva Temple had been patronized by Dara Shikoh, Aurangzeb's major rival for the throne. More immediately, Jat uprisings in the region in 1669 and 1670 dealt the Mughals heavy casualties. During the Jat rebellion, Abdul Nabi Khan, a Mughal commander and a patron of the major mosque in Mathura died. A mere eight months after Abdul Nabi's death, which undercut the patronage of Mathura mosques, the Keshavadeva Temple lay in ruins. It is also said that Hindus and Muslims alike travelled great distances to gain knowledge from this temple as early as Jahangir's reign. On hearing this practice, Aurangzeb ordered Mughal officials to investigate alleged dubious practices and finally ordered to dismantle the temple.[73]

An inscription bearing the testimony of Aurangzeb's grant for Dauji Maharaj Temple in Mahavan is as follows:[74]

> "This Royal *Nakkar-Khana* (the place of beating the drum attached to the temple) was built by Aurangzeb in Samvat 1729, 1672 CE and granted a Jagir (Estate) of five *Maafi* (revenue-free) villages for the maintenance of the temple and operation of *Nakkar-Khana*. The Mughal Emperor Shah Alam continued the *Maafi* Estate and for the arrangement of *Bhograag* (fooding) for *Nakkar-Khana* and temple, added two and a half *Maafi* villages, total Estate of seven and a half villages gifted to Goswami Hansraj Ji and Goswami Jagannath Ji, the descendant of Shri Saurabhi Vanshavtansh Aadigaur Vipravansh Martand Goswami Shri Kalyandev. And gifted two rupees revenue of each village of entire Pargana Mahavan, ownership right of Balbhadra Kund and the operation of arrangements of temple to Lord Dauji Maharaj. The *Farman* (order) was issued on 1840 *Vikram* 3 *Chaitra Shukl*."

Aurangzeb granted lands and money to another temple in Allahabad. It is also said that Aurangzeb had made grants to the Someshwar Mahadev Temple in Allahabad. A local historian Pradeep Kesharwani of Saraswati College claimed on the basis of certain historical facts that during one of his military campaign, Aurangzeb and his army had spent time near the temple. During the stay, he not only visited the temple but also offered grant and land for its maintenance. This fact is mentioned on the *dharma danda* (Religious Pillar) situated on the temple premises. The pillar has 15 sentences in Sanskrit inscribed on it, mentioning, "The ruler of the country visited the temple in 1674 and gave heavy grants to the temple, both in form of land and money".[75]

Mughal Emperor Aurangzeb issued a *Farman* on 6 June 1691, in favour of Balaji Temple of Chitrakoot and its priest Mahant Balak Das Nirvani. This royal *farman* still exists in this temple in which it is written:[76]

> "Royal order of the King is that eight villages namely Hanota, Chitrakoot.... Manak Poora are gifted to Sant Balak Dasji of Chitrakoot under Allahabad province's Kalinger Pargana in honour of Shri Thakur Balaji for his *Pooja* and *Raj Bhog*."

Further, it has been enjoined that a daily allowance of one rupee (Re. 1) be awarded to the grantee from the income of the other villages and a further grant of 330 *bigha*s of cultivable land has been conferred upon him, harvest after harvest, year after year. This *farman* was implemented literally by the then local ruler Panna Naresh Maharaj Hindupat. In this connection, Kamlesh Thapak of ancient history in Chitrakoot Gramodaya University said that for building this temple, Aurangzeb had entrusted the responsibility of staying in Chikrakoot and looking after the building and construction of the temple to his most trusted commander Ghairat Khan. He said that Aurangzeb had got this temple built as a symbol of Hindu Muslim-unity.[77]

Emperor Aurangzeb issued a *farman* in favour of Umanand Temple of Gauhati (Assam) and its priest Sudaman Brahman in ninth regnal year. The *farman*, addressed to the officials of Patta

Bangesar in the *pargana* of Pandu in the *sarkar* of Dakhinkul, that 2½ *bighas* of land out of village Sakara, the *jama* of which was Rs. 30, settled on Sudaman and his son, the *Pujari* of Umanand, according to the orders of the previous rulers. On that, they (grantees) may utilize them for their maintenance and *bhog* and engage themselves in prayers for the continuance of the kingdom to eternity.[78]

There are a large number of *parwanas* and *sanads* issued by *subahdars* of Malwa, between the 7th and 48th years of Aurangzeb's reign, granting daily allowances and charities to a certain Brahman family of Ujjain which was attached to the Mahakaleshwar Temple, which is one of the most important Shaivite temples of India. In the 7th regnal year of Emperor Aurangzeb, Kuka Brahman petitioned to Najabat Khan, the *subahdar* of Malwa that he has a big family has no means of livelihood. Therefore, a daily allowance of 3 *muradi tankas* was fixed for him. This shall be paid to him out of the income of the said *Chabutara*, so that he may utilize it for his livelihood and may pray for the perpetuity of this eternal state.[79]

Emperor Aurangzeb also fixed the grant for Mahakaleshwar Temple in Ujjain. This was the most important Shiva Temple where a lamp is continuously kept burning—day and night. Emperor Aurangzeb continued the grant of four *seers* of *ghee* daily for the illumination of the lamp in Mahakaleshwar Temple. At the request of Mahakaleshwar Temple priest Dev Narain, Prince Murad Baksh on behalf of Emperor Aurangzeb issued an order dated 5 *shawwal* 1061 H. It was ordered that for the lamp of the temple the *tehsildar* of the Chabutara Kotwal should supply four *seers* of *ghee* par day constantly.[80]

His relations with the saints of Jaina religion were also very cordial. Aurangzeb enacted similarly favourable policies towards Jaina religious institutions. Again following Akbar's example, Aurangzeb granted land at Shatrunjaya, Girnar and Mount Abu—all Jaina pilgrimage destinations in Gujarat—to specific Jaina communities in the late 1650s. He gave Lal Vijay, a Jaina monk, a monastery (*poshala*), probably sometime before 1681 and granted relief for a resting house (*upashraya*) in 1679.[81]

It was during the 27th regnal year of Aurangzeb in 1686, a Jaina saint Jinchandra Suri, petitioned before the emperor, that some people were interfering in their religions activities on account of escheat. Ultimately a *farman* was issued in the name of Jinchandra. It was ordered in the *farman* to the *jagirdars*, *faujdars*, *karoris* and *zamindars* of the empire, that no one should cause hindrance in their activities on that account, because throughout the empire, the residential houses of the people are exempt from escheat and its collection is prohibited, an order is being issued that in case of the arising of such situation it must be regarded as a rule, that no one should on this account interfere in the activities of the said people from this date onwards. So that they may live in peace and tranquillity in those houses and may pray for the perpetuation of this eternal empire and may not (be obliged to) come again to the court to ask for justice in this connection. This order should be treated as their strict responsibility.[82]

Shatrunjay Hill in Gujarat was one of the Jaina Holy places which attracted the attention of Emperor Aurangzeb and received the Royal grant. Shantidas, the Jaina merchant received the Royal order re-indorsing his community and the grant for Parshvanath temple at Shatrunjay Hill. Given such actions, it is unsurprising that we find laudatory descriptions of the emperor in vernacular Jaina works of this period, such as, "Aurangzeb Shah is a brave and powerful king" (*mardano aur mahabali aurangasahi naranda*).[83]

Aurangzeb wrote to a Rajput leader during the war of succession that, "men belonging to various communities and different religions should live in the vale of peace and pass their days in prosperity and no one should interfere in the affairs of another". Referring to nonMuslim religious practices performed in public, the French physician Francois Bernier, who visited India during 'Alamgir's first decade of rule, noted that, once in power, the Great Mogol, though a Mahometan, permits these ancient and superstitious practices; not wishing, or not daring, to disturb the Gentiles (Hindus) in the free exercises of their religion. Around 1688 an Englishman travelling through India contrasted what he perceived as the official tolerance during 'Alamgir's reign with the intolerance then prevailing in his own country. The writer was contrasting India under 'Alamgir with the religious turmoil in England between the Civil War (1642-51), the Protectorate of Oliver Cromwell (1653-58) and the Revolution of 1688.[84]

He was not exactly anti-Hindu as posed by Hindutva historians. During his time many mosques were also dismantled and temples constructed over there. Aurangzeb himself, in a letter, refers to one of his most eminent Rajput nobles, Jaswant Singh of Jodhpur, with whom he always had an ambivalent relationship, as the infidel who has destroyed mosques and built idol-temples in their stead. The letter is dated a good two decades before the *raja*'s death in 1679 when the emperor's dispute with his successors began.[85] This incident shows that Aurangzeb was lenient to his subjects and not intolerant at all for his subjects. Hindutva historians blame of intolerance was actually the reaction of the states over the injustices happened in his empire.

Death of Aurangzeb

It was while conducting one of his siege operations, fruitlessly "panting for some heaps of stone", that the emperor, a lifelong workaholic, was finally forced to abandon active military campaigning. In early 1706, in the grip of a severe illness, he was loaded on to a palanquin and carried to the ancient fort of Ahmadnagar, which he declared his "journey's end". He died there the following year in 1707. Characteristically, he rejected the idea of a grand, ostentatious tomb of the sort that towered over the graves of all his Mughal ancestors save Babur. Instead, he arranged to be buried in a simple grave open to the sky in Khuldabad, a saintly graveyard near Daulatabad.[86] In this final statement, spoken through the medium of architecture, the austere monarch asserted both his personal piety and his lifelong resolve to fashion a legitimacy and now a legacy, firmly opposed to that of his father. If Shah Jahan had cultivated the aura of a resplendent king, notes one historian, 'Alamgir cultivated one of a renunciate king, a contrast captured for ever in his father's Taj Mahal and in his own humble grave site.

Hindutva historian claims that Aurangzeb wanted to convert India into Muslim State (Darul Islam). If we believe this thesis then in Muslim state it becomes the responsibility of the state to safeguard the life, property and religion of the non-Muslims. On the other hand, Hindutva historian also says that Aurangzeb was not fair towards his non-Muslim subjects. How could both statements be correct? Both statements contradict to each other and show the mentality of the claimant that they dislike the ruler and had jealousy because the ruler was the true follower of Islam, performing five times prayer and regular fasting. Moreover, in the twenty-first century, in the age of democracy, science and technology, when the Hindutva government claims India as the Hindu Rashtra, then how they have right to criticize Aurangzeb of the seventeenth century when there was no democracy at all. Actually, Hindutva thinkers compare Aurangzeb with Akbar and Jahangir and find him more religious than his predecessors.

Hindutva historian also claims that Aurangzeb was an orthodox Muslim. But being an orthodox Muslim, he assigned villages for the expenses of the temples, appointed Hindus on the highest ranks in the administration, appointed more Hindu *mansabdars* than his predecessors, then what is wrong in following Islam in his personal life. Hindutva historians usually avoid mentioning the war between the Aurangzeb and Muslim states of south India or Deccan. He spent twenty-five years of his precious life in fighting with their co-religionists. Was it the religious war? No not at all, it was the process of expansion of the Mughal Empire and the unification of India. If we collect the information of his full reign of fifty years then we find that the affairs of Shivaji and Guru Gobind Singh were the petty affairs and being boosted by Hindutva historians for the divisive and communal purposes. In fact, the petty chieftains of his period were not subdued at all and had the courage to invade his capital in his absence. The Jats invaded the tomb of Akbar at Sikandara and unearthed the bones of Akbar and burnt in public. Nobody could think such an act during the rule of a dictator. These facts show that Aurangzeb was not a dictator, oppressor or intolerant as Hindutva historians claim.

No doubt, he was pious man and a true follower of Islam but truly following any religion by a ruler is not a negative effect to the rule of the country. Bakhtawar Khan in his *Mirat-i-Alam* says that Aurangzeb performed usual prayers, first in the mosque and then at home, both in the congregation and in private, with the most heartfelt devotion. He kept the appointed fasts on Fridays and other sacred days and he read the Friday prayers in the Grand Mosque at Delhi. During the whole month of Ramazan, he kept fast, said the prayers appointed for that month and reads the holy Quran in the assembly of religious and learned men, with whom he used to sit for that purpose during six and sometimes nine hours of the night. During the last ten days of the month, he performed worship in the mosque.[87]

Bakhtawar Khan says that if any person talked too much, or acted in an improper manner, he was never displeased and he never knitted his brows. His courtiers had often desired to prohibit people from showing so much boldness, but he remarked that by hearing their very words and seeing their gestures, he acquires a habit of forbearance and tolerance. Under the dictates of anger and passion, he never issued orders of death. In consideration of their rank and merit, he showed much honour and respect to the Saiyyads, Saints and learned men.[88]

Notwithstanding his popular reputation as a "living saint", Aurangzeb came to formulate a very different model of sovereignty for himself and for the empire he ruled. In this new dispensation, the kingdom would be governed not by a charismatic, semi-divine king, but by impersonal law namely, the sharia of Hanafi Sunnis, administered by a reconstituted and vastly empowered judiciary guided by a reformed, thoroughly codified legal system. At the same time, the emperor took dramatic and very public steps to place himself beneath that law. In 1675 he proclaimed that anybody in the empire with a legal claim against him could appeal to specially appointed judicial officials who were sent to every city, province and neighbouring territory of the empire precisely to hear such claims.[89]

In the end, the overall conclusion of Aurangzeb's reign, he may not be deemed as a very successful emperor as of his forefathers. In the last twenty-five years Aurangzeb fruitlessly spent in the Deccan fightiong with two Deccan sultanates and the Marathas. In between north India became out of control. The Jats raised themselves as powerful state, Sikhs, Satnamis, Rajputs and even Princes became rebellious and powerful. His Deccan campaign couldn't fully subjugate even Marathas. So his south campaign was futile enterprise and may not be considered much successful. Even his contemporaries such as Bhimsen knew that he was running the empire into the ground. By all conclusions, the reason of his Deccan's futile campaign was his stubbornness and industrious character. Aurangzeb worked the whole life as a clerk or middle-level functionary in the Mughals' vast bureaucracy. He lacked good political leadership, vision, imagination and flexibility. For twenty-five ruinous years he remained trapped in a quagmire of his own making, constitutionally unable to imagine a way forwards beyond his Sisyphean task of doggedly pursuing the Marathas, fort by fort.

Another possible answer to the enigma of 'Alamgir's long and fruitless Deccan campaign was his fear of his dethronement by his sons. Haunted by the fear that his sons might do to him what he had done to his own father, 'Alamgir felt compelled constantly to remain in the field, ever at the helm of the army, warily watching them and his grandsons and after defeating his rebellious son Prince Akbar his fear was confirmed. He might have learnt by many years' experience, that the kings of Hindustan when they grow old, must keep at the head of powerful armies, to defend themselves against their sons.

On the religious policy of Aurangzeb, many Hindutva scholars believe that he was communal and intolerant towards the Hindus. They have definitally the biased attitude and ideology for Aurangzeb. Aurangzeb's policicies were circumstantial and in benefit of his empire. However, in comparison of the current intolerances in independent India under democratic and secular governments, such as communal riots, destruction of the Babari Mosque, the pogrom of 2002, mob lynching, Ghar Wapasi, Love Jihad, etc. Emperor Aurangzeb or other ancient or medieval rulers are far behind. These governments, more particularly the Hindutva government of BJP, although elected by the people, is more a dictator, more intolerant and more oppressive towards the Muslim population in India. They left far behind even to the British government in India in matters of intolerance and insecurity.

Notes

1. The Chief Qazi of the Mughal Empire felt so strongly on the matter that he risked imperial wrath and refused to endorse Aurangzeb's ascension while Shah Jahan lived. Aurangzeb dismissed him and hired a more pliable man for the job, Abdul Wahab. Far beyond India, too, many censured Aurangzeb for his brutality against Shah Jahan. The Sharif of Mecca declined to recognize Aurangzeb as the proper ruler of Hindustan and even refused his financial gifts for several years over Shah Jahan's mistreatment. Playing on Aurangzeb's regnal title of 'Alamgir (World Seizer), the Safavid king Shah Sulaiman wrote a caustic letter accusing Aurangzeb of mistakenly announcing his seizure of the world (*alam-gir*) when he had merely seized his father (*pidar-gir*). (A.R. Fuller (tr.), W.E. Begley and Z.A. Desai (ed.), *The Shah Jahan Nama of Inayat Khan,* Delhi, Oxford University Press, 1990, p. 96.)
2. Francois Bernier, tr. Archibald Constable, *Travels in the Mogul Empire*, 2nd edn, Delhi: S. Chand & Co., 1968, pp. 98-99; Craig Davis, *Dara Shukuh and Aurangzib: Issues of Religion and Politics and their Impact on Indo-Muslim Society* (PhD dissertation, Indiana University, 2002), pp. 236, 238.
3. Majumdar, *op. cit.*, pp. 299-300.
4. In 1659, shortly after his grand coronation, he sent a considerable sum of money to the Sharif, to be distributed to the needy there. But to his dismay, the authorities in Mecca turned down his gift for the same reason his own jurists had initially rejected his claims to the throne, that he could not legally be sovereign as long as his father was still alive. Undeterred, several years later he sent gifts valued at Rs. 6,60,000 to the Sharif. Finally, in 1666, shortly after Shah Jahan

had died, the Sharif sent 'Alamgir a belated congratulation on his accession, together with a sacred relic, the broom and some dust from the Prophet Mohammad's tomb in Medina, which the emperor received with much solemnity. (William Irvine (tr.), Niccolao Munucci's *Storia Do Mogor,* (1907), vol. II, London, pp. 114-15; Jadunath Sarkar (1947), tr. of Saqi Must'ad Khan's *Maasir-i-Alamgiri*, Calcutta, p. 32.)

5. V.G. Khobrekar (ed.), Jadunath Sarkar (tr.), *Tarikh-i-Dilkasha* (*Memoirs of Bhimsen Relating to Aurangzeb's Deccan Campaigns*), Bombay: Department of Archives, Government of Maharashtra, 1972), p. 215.
6. S. Moinul Haq (tr.), Khafi Khan's *History of Alamgir*, Karachi: Pakistan Historical Society, 1975, p. 257; Jadunath Sarkar, *History of Aurangzib,* 1912; repr. New Delhi: Orient Longman, 1973, vol. 3, pp. 198-99; Manucci, vol. III, *op. cit.*, p. 247.
7. S.A.A. Rizvi (1965). *Muslim Revivalist Movements in North India in the Sixteenth and Seventeenth Centuries,* Agra, Agra University, p. 375; *Tarikh-i-Dilkasha, op. cit.*, p. 127; Taymiya R. Zaman, "Nostalgia, Lahore and the Ghost of Aurangzeb", *Fragments: Interdisciplinary Approaches to the Study of Ancient and Medieval Pasts* 4 (2015), p. 13.
8. Jadunath Sarkar (tr.), *Anecdotes of Aurangzeb and Historical Essays,* Calcutta: M.C. Sarkar & Sons, 1917, p. 99.
9. *Ibid.*, p. 141.
10. M. Athar Ali (1968). *The Mughal Nobility Under Aurangzeb*, Asia Publishing House, Bombay, p. 31.
11. Audrey Truschke (2018). *Aurangzeb: The Man and the Myth*, New Delhi, pp. 55 & 60.
12. *The Hindus*, *op. cit.*, p. 538.
13. Majumdar, *op. cit.*, p. 235.
14. Edwardes & Garrett, *op. cit.*, p. 114.
15. Finding themselves in this difficulty, their large earnings likely to cease, without there being any other mode of seeking a livelihood, the musicians took counsel together and tried to appease the king in the following way: About 1,000 of them assembled on a Friday when Aurangzeb was going to the mosque. They came out with over twenty highly-ornamented biers, as is the custom of the country, crying aloud with great grief and many signs of feeling, as if they were escorting to the grave some distinguished defunct. From afar Aurangzeb saw this multitude and heard their great weeping and lamentation and, wondering, sent to know the cause of so much sorrow. The musicians

redoubled their outcry and their tears, fancying the king would take compassion upon them. Lamenting, they replied with sobs that the king's orders had killed Music, therefore they were bearing her to the grave. Report was made to the king, who quite calmly remarked that they should pray for the soul of Music and see that she was thoroughly well buried. In spite of this, the nobles did not cease to listen to songs in secret. This strictness was enforced in the principal cities. (Munucci, vol. II, *op. cit.*, p. 8.)

16. *The Religious Policy of the Mughal Emperors*, pp. 127-29.
17. Munucci, vol. II, *op. cit.*, p. 5.
18. *Ibid.*, pp. 5-6.
19. *Ibid.*, p. 7.
20. *Ibid.*, pp. 7-8.
21. Sri Ram Sharma, *op. cit.*, pp. 133-35.
22. Edwardes & Garrett, *op. cit.*, p. 102.
23. *Ibid.*
24. Emperor Aurangzeb had withdrawn the tobacco tax owing to a horrible event. It happened that a soldier of strict habits wanted to enter the city, having with him his wife in a covered vehicle, as usual among Muslims. A tax-gatherer ordered him to halt and asked if he had any tobacco. The soldier replied that he, being a man of serious habits, did not smoke tobacco, neither he nor his wife, who was in the vehicle and he might trust his word. The tax-collector would not believe him and wanted to search the cart. To this the soldier would not consent, not wishing his wife to be seen in public and remonstrated, saying if such an affront were done him, he would repent of it later on. But the tax-collector would not listen to a word and uncovered the vehicle to make his search. The soldier laid hand on his sword and cut off the man's head and also wounded several attendants. Not content with this even, he killed his wife too and a daughter she had with her. He was seized and carried off to prison and a complaint was laid before the king. Upon hearing the soldier's defence, the king abolished the tax and released the soldier, having compassion on him for his loss of temper. Among the Muslims it is a great dishonour for a family when a wife is compelled to uncover herself. By this event tobacco was no longer so dear and numerous merchants lost much from this circumstance, whereby the king conferred a benefit on the poor. William Irvine (tr.), Munucci, vol. II, *op. cit.*, p. 175.
25. Edwardes & Garrett, *op. cit.*, p. 103.

26. Munucci, vol. II, *op. cit.*, p. 8.
27. *Ibid.*
28. *Ibid.*, p. 9.
29. *Ibid.*, p. 12.
30. *Ibid.*, pp. 12-14.
31. *Ibid.* pp. 14-15.
32. *Ibid.* p. 16.
33. Satish Chandra, "Jizya and the State in India during the Seventeenth Century", *Journal of the Economic and Social History of the Orient*, 12, Part 3 (Sept. 1969), pp. 322-40. Bhimsen writes of the violence and oppression of the amins appointed to collect the jaziya that has been [newly] imposed, as they are beyond description? They realise crores of rupees and pay only a small portion of it into the treasury. *Tarikh-i-Dilkasha, op. cit.*, p. 231.
34. Majumdar, *op. cit.*, p. 234.
35. *Ibid.*, p. 372.
36. *Ibid.*, p. 373.
37. *Ibid.* Munucci, vol. II, *op. cit.*, p. 320.
38. *Ibid.*, Munucci, vol. II, *op. cit.*, p. 320.
39. Munucci, vol. II, *op. cit.*, p. 374.
40. Munucci, vol. II, *op. cit.*, pp. 167-68.
41. *Ibid.*
42. *Ibid.*
43. *The Hindus, op. cit.*, pp. 537-38.
44. Sri Ram Sharma, *op. cit.*, p. 180.
45. *Ibid.*, Majumdar, *op. cit.*, p. 236.
46. *Ibid.*, p. 181.
47. Majumdar, *op. cit.*, p. 239.
48. Robert C. Hallissey (1977). *The Rajput Rebellion against Aurangzeb: A Study of the Mughal Empire in Seventeenth-Century India*, University of Missouri Press, Columbia MO, pp. 71, 75.
49. Majumdar, *op. cit.*, p. 240.
50. Munucci, vol. II, *op. cit.*, pp. 28-29.
51. *Ibid.*, pp.103-07.
52. *Ibid.*, p. 135.
53. S. Moinul Haq (1975). trans. of *Khafi Khan's History of Alamgir*, Pakistan Historical Society, Karachi, 1975, p. 193; Surendranath Sen (1920), tr. *Extracts and Documents Relating to Maratha History*, vol. I, University of Calcutta, Calcutta, pp. 61-64.

54. Munucci, vol. II, *op. cit.*, pp. 137-139; *Khafi Khan's History of Alamgir, op. cit.*, p. 193; Surendranath Sen, vol. I, *op. cit.*, pp. 61-64.
55. Satish Chandra (1999). *Medieval India, from Sultanat to the Mughals*, Part 2, 6th edn., New Delhi, p. 326; Surendranath Sen, vol. I, *op. cit.* pp. 113-18; *Aurangzeb: The Man and the Myth, op. cit.*, pp. 51-52.
56. Brij Kishore (1963). *Tara Bai and Her Times*, Asia Publishing House, Bombay, pp. 71-93.
57. *The Hindus, op. cit.*, pp. 545; *Aurangzeb: The Man and the Myth, op. cit.*, p. 52.
58. Sri Ram Sharma, *op. cit.*, pp. 155-67. Here are the names of the Hindu *mansabdars* under Aurangzeb 1659-1707. Commanders of (7,000)— 1. Raja Jai Singh of Jaipur, 2. Raja Jaswan Singh of Jodhpur, 3. Sahu, Shivaji's grandson and a ward of the emperor. Commanders of (6,000)— 4. Maharaja Raj Singh of Mewar, 5. Rao Kanhoji Maratha, 6. Satvad Dafalya Maratha, 7. Santaji Jadun. Commanders of (5,000)— 8. Smbhaji, son of Shivaji, only for a short period, 9. Netoji, Shivaji's Commander in Chief, after Shivaji's escape from Agra his mansab was reduced to 3500, 10. Bijaji, 11. Pratap, 12. Raja Bhim Singh of Banera, 13. Raja Jai Singh of Toda, 14. Raja Ram Singh of Jaipur, 15. Achalaji Nimbalkar, 16. Maharana Jai Singh of Udaipur, 17. Maharana Amar Singh II of Uaipur, 8. Priya Nayak of Sakhar, Deccan, 19. Balaji, 20. Janoji, 21. Nakoji Mamja, 22. Sobhanji, 23. Barna Rao. Commanders of (4,000)— 24. Raja Chhatrsal Bundela, 25. Jaswant Rao, 26. Tarsoji, 27. Babaji, son of Dafalya, 28. Siyaji, 29. Jadun Rai, 30. Ramaji, 31. Raja Indra Man of Dhandhera, 32. Raja Bishen Singh of Jaipur, 33. Raja Rai Singh Rathor, 34. Rabhaji. Commanders of (3,500)— 35. Raja Rajrup of Noorpur, Punjab, 36. Raja Inder Singh, 37. Udai Singh Bundela, 38. Raja Anurudh Gaur, 39. Raja Anup Singh. Commanders of (3,000)— 40. Rao Man Singh of Kishangarh, 41. Raja Sujan Singh Bundela, 42. Rao Dalpat Bundela, 43. Raja Raghunath, Diwan, Imperial Finance Minister, 44. Rao Bhao Singh Hada, 45. Viram Dev Sasodia, 46. Durga Das Rathor, for a short period, 47. Raja Kirat Singh Kachhwaha, 48. Girdhari Das Gaur, 49. Rao Karn Bhurtya of Bikaner, 50. Udaji Ram, 51. Jakoji, 52. Parsoji Bhonsla, 53. Vasudev Singh, 54. Raja Dalip Singh of Urchha, 55. Sunderji, 56. Inder Singh, 57. Himmat Rao Koli, 58. Baji Rao, 59. Sarup Singh, 60. Badarji. Commanders of (2,500)— 61. Rao Shubh Karan of Dattya, 62. Raja Devi Singh Bundela of Urchha, 63. Raja Bhagwant Singh Bundela, 64. Rawat Amar Singh Chandravat,

65. Kishan Singh of Jaipur, 66. Mayaji, 67. Raja Ram Singh Hada of Kota, 68. Raja Anup Singh Bhurtya, 69. Rustam Rao, 70. Khindoji, 71. Baitoji. Commanders of (2,000)— 72. Raja Jai Singh II of Jaipur, 73. Rai Todar Mal, Revenue Department, 74. Raja Vikram Singh of Guler, Himachal Pradesh, 75. Pritam Singh Rathor, 76. Udyat Singh Bhadoria, 77. Ram Chand, 78. Ram Singh Hada, 79. Medni Singh of Srinagar, Garhwal, 80. Arjoji, 81. Mankoji, 82. Madho Narain, 83. Vyas Rao, 84. Tanaji, 85. Raja Jagat Singh Hada, 86. Anil Rai, Diwan, 87. Bahadur Singh, 88. Bhupat Singh, 89. Ram Singh son of Rattan Singh Rathor, 90. Ram Chandra, 91. Auji Ahal Rao, 92. Nimaji Sindhiya. Commanders of (1,500)— 93. Amar Singh Sasodia of Rampura, 94. Raja Babal Singh Sisodia, 95. Bhojraj Kachhwaha, 96. Man Singh, Gwaliar, 97. Raja Prithi Chand, 98. Raja Sarandhar of Jummon, 99. Shiv Singh, 100. Chaturbhuj Chauhan, 101. Amar Singh of Narwar, 102. Raghunath Singh Rathor, 103. Udai Singh Mertia, 104. Bir Singh Chamba, 105. Mahesh Das Rathor, 106. Raja Sarup Singh, 107. Manohar Das, 108. Ajit Singh Rathor, 109. Raghunath Singh Bhurtya, 110. Rai Makrand, 111. Raja Inder Man Bundela, 112. Trimbakji Bhonsla, 113. Bagoji, 114. Rambhaji, 115. Raja Sarup Singh of Bikaner, 116. Raja Mohkam Singh Sisodia, 117. Bhagwant Singh. Commanders of (1,000)— 118. Jagram, 119. Raja Maha Singh Bhadoria, 120. Raja Kishan Singh Chandrawat Tomar, 121. Raja Chatar Singh of Chamba, 122. Raja Kalyan Singh of Bandhu, 123. Raghunath Sasodia, 124. Vijay Singh, 125. Mahoji, 126. Prahladji, 127. Parsoji, 128. Tanaji, 129. Sujan Rao, 130. Raja Udai Singh Chamba, 131. Ram Chand son of Dalpat Bundela, 132. Dankat Rao, 133. Rawal Jaswant Singh of Dungarpur, 134. Guman Singh, 135. Sur Singh, 136. Shiv Singh, 137. Satra Sal, 138. Sambhaji, 139. Ratan Rao, 140. Sarup Singh son of Udyat Singh, 141. Mitra Sen Bundela, 142. Bhim Singh of Srinagar Garhwal, 143. Mandhata son of Rajrup of Nurpur, 144. Bhawani Das Bhurtya, 145. Sher Singh son of Ram Singh Rathor, 146. Suraj Mall Gaur, 147. Harsaj Gaur, 148. Gopal Singh Kachhwaha, 149. Arjun Gaur, 150. Suraj Mall son of Raja Bhim Singh, 151. Dal Singh Sasodia, 152. Arjun Singh, 153. Chatroji, 154. Raja Ram Das Kachhwaha of Narwari, 155. Rawal Ram Singh of Dungarpur, 156. Badan Singh Bhodorya, 157. Narsingh Rao, 158. Bahadur Singh, 159. Ratan Rao, 160. Sarsa.

59. Richard M. Eaton, 'Temple Desecration and Indo-Muslim States', in David Gilmartin and Bruce B. Lawrence (2000), *Beyond Turk and Hindu: Rethinking Religious Identities in Islamicate South Asia,*

University Press of Florida, Gainesville, pp. 246-81; Catherine B. Asher, *Architecture of Mughal India, New Cambridge History of India*, vol. I:4, Cambridge University Press, Cambridge, 1992, pp. 254 & 278; Heidi Pauwels, "A Tale of Two Temples: Mathura's Ke-avadeva and Orchha's Caturbhuvadeva", *South Asia History and Culture* 2, No. 2 (2011), pp. 288-90. (It was learnt that in Multan and Thatta in Sind and especially at Varanasi, Brahmans attracted a large number of Muslims to their discourses. Aurangzeb, in utter disgust, ordered the governors of all these provinces "to demolish the schools and temples of the infidels and with utmost urgency put down the teaching and the public practices of these religious misbelievers". A temple at Mathura was demolished in 1670, under Aurangzeb's command. A decade later, Abu Turab, who had been sent to Amber in Rajasthan to demolish temples there, returned to the court and reported that he had pulled down 66 temples. A year earlier, Khan-i-Jahan Bahadur returned from Jodhpur, having demolished temples and carrying with him, in the chronicler's hyperbolic language, "cartloads of idols" and had audience with the emperor, who praised him highly. The Vishwanath Temple at Varanasi was demolished on the order of the Aurangzeb. In most of the cases, the angry reaction of the royal forces led to the destruction of the temples. In this realm of India, although king Aurangzeb destroyed numerous temples, are thronged with worshippers; even those that are destroyed are still venerated by the Hindus and visited for the offering of arms. Harbans Mukhia, op. cit., p. 25.)

60. Munucci, vol. II, *op. cit.*, p. 154.
61. *The Hindus, op. cit.*, p. 544. Majumdar, *op. cit.*, p. 235.
62. Majumdar, *op. cit.*, pp. 234-35.
63. Harbans Mukhia, *op. cit.*, pp. 25-26. (Harbans Mukhia tells some inverse evidence too of the demolition of mosques by the Hindus and conversion of these into temples. Sher Shah, the Afghan ruler who had snatched the Mughal Empire from the hands of Humayun in 1540, is reported to have vowed to punish the Hindu *zamindars*, who, after destroying the mosques and places of worship of the Musalmans converted them into places for idol-worship and have entered into the quarters of Delhi and Malwa. He also quotes the story told by Mohammad Ufi related to the thirteenth century in India. In the port-city of Cambay in Gujarat, the Parsis instigated the infidels to attack the Musalmans and the minaret (atop a mosque) was destroyed, the mosque burnt and eighty Musalmans were killed. Some of the

Muslims reported the incident to the Hindu ruler, who personally went out to investigate the matter and found it true. The ruler had the mosque restored to its old state, saying it was his duty to see that all his subjects were afforded such protection as would enable them to live in peace. Harbans Mukhia, *op. cit.*, p. 26.)

64. *Aurangzeb: The Man and the Myth*, *op. cit.*, p. 33.
65. *Farman* of Aurangzeb preserved in Bharat Kala Bhawan of Benares Hindu University.
66. *Dainik Jagaran*, Varanasi, 17 December 2005.
67. Jnan Chandra, "Alamgir's Tolerance in the Light of Contemporary Jain Literature", *Journal of the Pakistan Historical Society*, October 1958, vol. 6: 4, pp. 271-72.
68. Jnan Chandra, "Freedom of Worship for the Hindus under Alamgir", *Journal of the Pakistan Historical Society*, January 1958, vol. 6:1, p. 125.
69. Ansari, Mohammad Azhar (1984). *Administrative Documents of Mughal India*, Delhi, No. XV and XVI, pp. 31-33.
70. B.N. Goswami & J.S. Grewal (1967). *Mughals and the Jogis of Jakhbar*, Shimla, pp. 32-33.
71. S.K. Bhatt (1975). *Two Persian Documents Relating to the Religions Policy of the Mughals: A Parwanah of Aurangzeb and a Parwanah of Muhammad Shah, Proceedings of the Indian History Congress*, 1975, pp. 358-60.
72. *Aurangzeb: The Man and the Myth*, *op. cit.*, p. 69. (Pattabhi Sitaramayya writes that Aurangzeb had in his entourage a number of Hindu nobles. They all set out one day to see the sacred Kashi Vishvanath Temple of Benares. Amongst them was a Rani of Cutch. When the party returned after visiting the temple, the Rani of Cutch was missing. hey searched for her and find her in a *tah-khana* (basement) in bereft of her jewellery. It turned out that the *mahants* were in the habit of picking out wealthy and be jewelled pilgrims and in guiding them to see the temple, decoying them to the underground cellar and robbing them of their jewellery. On discovering the wickedness of the priests, Aurangzeb declared that such a scene of robbery could not be the House of God and ordered it to be forthwith demolished. And the ruins were left there. But the Rani who was thus saved insisted on a mosque being built on the ruin and to please her, one was subsequently built. That is how a mosque has come to exist by the side of the Kashi Visweswar Temple which is no temple in the real sense of the term but a humble cottage in which the marble Sivalinga is housed.

By quoting Sitaramayya, B.N. Panday also tells the same story that they found the missing Rani dishonoured and crying, deprived of all her ornaments. The basement was just beneath Lord Vishvanatha's seat. The *rajas* expressed their vociferous protests. As the crime was heinous, the *raja*'s demanded exemplary action. Aurangzeb ordered that as the sacred precincts have been despoiled, Lord Vishvanath may be moved to some other place, the temple be razed to the ground and the *mahant* be arrested and punished. (Pattabhi Sitaramayya (1946), *Feathers and Stones*, Bombay, pp. 177-78; and B.N. Pandey (1987). *Islam and Indian Culture*, Khuda Bakhsh Oriental Public Library, Patna, pp. 44-45.)

73. *Aurangzeb: The Man and the Myth*, *op. cit.*, pp. 70-71.
74. *Dauji Temple Inscription*, Mahavan, Mathura.
75. timesofindia.indiatimes.com, 13 September 2015.
76. Jalaluddin, Some Important Farmans and Sanads of Medieval period in the Institutions of U.P., *Studies in Islam* (Quarterly Journal), Indian Institute of Islamic Studies, New Delhi, January 1978, vol. 15:1, pp. 44-46; *The Milli Gazette*, 27 October 2016.
77. *Ibid.*
78. Jnan Chandra, Aurangzeb and Hindu Temples, *Journal of the Pakistan Historical Society*, January 1957, vol. 5:1, p. 251.
79. Jnan Chandra, Alamgir's Grants to Hindu Pujaris, *Journal of the Pakistan Historical Society*, January 1958, vol. 6:1, p. 57.
80. Allama Yusuf Alqarzavi, Abu Masood Azhar Nadvi (2000). *Islam: Muslims and Non-Muslims*, Delhi, p. 63.
81. *Aurangzeb: The Man and the Myth*, *op. cit.*, p. 66.
82. Jnan Chandra, Alamgir's Atitude Towards Non-Muslim Institutions, *Journal of the Pakistan Historical Society*, January 1959, vol. 7:1, pp. 36-39.
83. *Aurangzeb: The Man and the Myth*, *op. cit.*, p. 66.
84. Archibald Constable (1968). Francois Bernier' translation of *Travels in the Mogul Empire*, 2nd edn, S. Chand & Co., Delhi, p. 303; Rajeev Kinra, "Handling Diversity with Absolute Civility: The Global Historical Legacy of Mughal Sulh-i Kull", *Medieval History Journal*, 16, No. 2, 2013, p. 258.
85. Harbans Mukhia, *op. cit.*, p. 27.
86. Munis Faruqui (2014). *Encyclopaedia of Islam*, Leiden, p. 71.
87. Elliot & Dowson, vol. VII, *op. cit.*, p. 158.
88. *Ibid.*, pp. 158-59.
89. *Khafi Khan's History of Alamgir*, *op. cit.*, pp. 251, 255.

Bibliography

Journals, Newspapers, Gazetteers and Websites

Barabanki District Gazetteer, Lucknow, 1902.
Dauji Temple Inscription, Mahavan, Mathura.
District Gazetteer of Fyzabad, Lucknow, 1905.
Encyclopedia Britannica.
Farman of Aurangzeb preserved in Bharat Kala Bhawan of Benares Hindu University.
tajmahal.org.uk.
heriagewalkcalcutta.com.
International Journal of Trend in Scientific Research and Development (*IJTSRD*), vol. 6, Issue 6, October 2022.
The Journal of the Royal Asiatic Society of Great Britain and Ireland, No. 2, October 1949.
Proceedings of the Indian History Congress, 1975.
Journal of the Economic and Social History of the Orient, 12, Part 3, September 1969.
Fragments: Interdisciplinary Approaches to the Study of Ancient and Medieval Pasts, 4, 2015.
Uttar Pradesh District Gazetteers Faizabad, Allahabad, 1960.
www.ijtsrd.com/papers/ijtsrd52079.pdf
Journal of the Pakistan Historical Society, January 1957, vol. 5:1.
Journal of the Pakistan Historical Society, January 1958, vol. 6:1.

Journal of the Pakistan Historical Society, October 1958, vol. 6:4.

Journal of the Pakistan Historical Society, January 1959, vol. 7:1.

Studies in Islam (Quarterly Journal), January 1978, vol. 15:1, Indian Institute of Islamic Studies, New Delhi.

Dainik Jagaran, Varanasi, 17 December 2005.

Modern Asian Studies, 41, No. 5, 2007.

Modern Asian Studies, 43, No. 1, 2009.

Dawn, (English Daily) 25 December 2010.

South Asia History and Culture 2, No. 2, 2011.

Medieval History Journal, 16, No. 2, 2013.

timesofindia.indiatimes.com, 13 September 2015.

The Milli Gazetteer, 27 October 2016.

Hindustan Times, 10 March 2017.

indiatoday.in. 25 July 2017.

Indian Express, 18 October 2017.

Hindustan Times, Lucknow, 26 October 2017.

history.com, 22 November 2019.

timesofindia.com, 6 December 2019.

Books

Ali, M. Athar (1968). *The Mughal Nobility Under Aurangzeb*, Asia Publishing House, Bombay.

Alqarzavi, Allama Yusuf & Abu Masood Azhar Nadvi (2000). *Islam: Muslims and Non-Muslims*, Delhi.

Ansari, Mohammad Azhar (1984). *Administrative Documents of Mughal India*, Delhi, Nos. XV and XVI.

Asher, Catherine B. (1992). *The New Cambridge History of India*, vol. I, Part. 4, Cambridge University Press, Cambridge.

Bernier, Francois & Archibald Constable (1968). *Travels in the Mogul Empire*, 2nd edn., S. Chand & Co., Delhi.

Beveridge, Annette Susannah (1922). *The Memoirs of Babur* (trs. *Baburnama* of Zahiruddin Muhammad Babur Padshah Ghazi), vol. I, London.

Beveridge, Annette Susannah (1922). *The Memoirs of Babur* (trs. *Baburnama* of Zahiruddin Muhammad Babur Padshah Ghazi), vol. II, London.

Beveridge, H. (1939). *The Akbarnama of Abul Fazl*, (trs. of *Akbarnama* of Abul Fazl), vol. III, Calcutta.

Chandra, Satish (1999). *Medieval India, from Sultanat to the Mughals*, Part 2, 6th edn. New Delhi.

Constable, Archibald & Francois Bernier (1968). trs. of *Travels in the Mogul Empire*, 2nd edn., S. Chand & Co., Delhi.

Davis, Craig (2002). *Dara Shukuh and Aurangzib: Issues of Religion and Politics and their Impact on Indo-Muslim Society*, (PhD dissertation, Indiana University).

Doniger, Wendy (2009). *The Hindus: An Alternative History*, New Delhi.

Edwardes, S.M. & H.L.O. Garrett (1930). *Mughal Rule in India*, London.

Elliot & Dowson (1877). *History of India as Told by Its Own Historians, The Mohammadan Period*, vol. VI, London.

Faruqui, Munis (2014). *Encyclopaedia of Islam*, Leiden.

Fuller, R., W.E. Begley and Z.A. Desai (1990), tr. of *The Shah Jahan Nama of Inayat Khan*, Delhi.

Gilmartin, David & Bruce B. Lawrence (2000). *Beyond Turk and Hindu: Rethinking Religious Identities in Islamicate South Asia*, University Press of Florida, Gainesville.

Gopal, Sarvapalli (1992). *Anatomy of a Confrontation: The Babri Masjid-Ram Janmabhumi Issue*, New Delhi.

Goswami, B.N. & J.S. Grewal (1967). *Mughals and the Jogis of Jakhbar*, Shimla.

Gupta, Laxminarayan (1973). *History of Modern Indian Culture*, Agra.

Hallissey, Robert C. (1977). *The Rajput Rebellion against Aurangzeb: A Study of the Mughal Empire in Seventeenth-Century India*, University of Missouri Press, Columbia MO.

Haq, S. Moinul (1975). Trs. of *Khafi Khan's History of Alamgir*, Pakistan Historical Society, Karachi.

Havell, E.B. (1904). *A Handbook to Agra; The Taj, Sikandara, Fatehpur Sikri and the Neighbourhood*, Calcutta.

Holden, Edward S. (1895). *The Mogul Emperors of Hindustan*, New York.

Hoyland, John (1922). trs. *The Commentary of Father Monserrate*, S.J., on his *Journey to the Court of Akbar*, Oxford University Press, London.

Innes, McLeod (1895). *Lucknow & Oude in the Mutiny: A Narrative and a Study*, London.

Innes, McLeod (1897). *The Sepoy Revolt: A Critical Narrative*, London.

Keene, H.G. (1899). *A Handbook for Visitors to Agra and its Neighbourhood*, Calcutta.

Khobrekar, V.G. & Jadunath Sarkar (1972). (tr. of *Tarikh-i-Dilkasha*), *Memoirs of Bhimsen Relating to Aurangzeb's Deccan Campaigns*, Department of Archives, Government of Maharashtra, Bombay.

Kishore, Brij (1963). *Tara Bai and Her Times*, Asia Publishing House, Bombay.

Koch, Ebba (2001). *Mughal Art and Imperial Ideology: Collected Essays*, Oxford University Press, New Delhi.

Lamb, Harold (1961). *Babur, the Tiger; First of the Great Moguls*, New York.

Leyden, John & William Erskine (1826). *Memoirs of Zaheeruddin Mohammad Babur* (trs. of *Tuzuk-i-Babari* of Zaheeruddin Mohammad Babur), London.

Lowe, W.H. (1899 reprint 1973), *Muntakhabut-Tawarikh* (tr. of *Muntakhabut-Tawarikh* of Abdul Qadir Badauni), vol. 2, Delhi.

Mahajan, Vidyadhar (1979). *Muslim-Kalin Bharat*, Part II, Delhi.

Majumdar, R.C. (1974). *The History and Culture of the Indian People: The Mughal Empire*, vol. VII, Bombay.

Mann, Gurinder Singh (2001), *The Making of Sikh Scripture*, Oxford University Press, New York.

Martin, R. Montgomery (1858). *The Indian Empire*, vol. II, London.

Miller, Barbara Stoler (1992). *The Powers of Art: Patronage in Indian Culture*, Oxford University Press, New Delhi.

Moinuddin, Mohd (1906). *The History of Taj and Buildings in its Vicinity*, Agra.

Moreland, W.H. & P. Geyl (1972). tr. of *Jahangir's India: The Remonstrantie of Francisco Pelsaert*, Delhi.

Mukhia, Harbans (2004). *The Mughals of India*, Malden.

Nath, R. (1972). *The Immortal Taj Mahal: The Evolution of Tomb in Mughal Architecture*, Bombay.

Oak, P.N. (1965). *Taj Mahal Was a Rajput Palace*, New Delhi.

Oak, P.N. (1974 reprint in 1974). *The Taj Mahal is a Temple Palace*, New Delhi.

Oak, P.N. (2000). *Who Says Akbar Was Great*, New Delhi.

Pandey, B.N. (1987). *Islam and Indian Culture*, Patna.

Prasad, Beni (1940). *History of Jahangir*, Allahabad.

Prashad, Ishwari (1939). *A Short History of Muslim Rule in India: From the Conquest of Islam to the Death of Aurangzeb*, Allahabad.

Ranking, George S.A. (1924). *Muntakhbu-t-Tawarikh*, (trs. *Muntakhbu-t-Tawarikh of Al-Badauni*, Abdul Qadir Ibn Muluk Shah), vol. II, New Delhi.

Rapson, Edward James, Sir Wolseley Haig, Sir Richard Burn & Henry Dodwell (1962). *The Cambridge History of India: The Mughul Period*, Cambridge.

Rizvi, S.A.A. (1965). *Muslim Revivalist Movements in North India in the Sixteenth and Seventeenth Centuries*, Agra University, Agra.

Rogers Alexander & Henry Beveridge (1909). *Memoire of Jahangir*, (tr. of *Tuzuk-i-Jahangiri* of Nooruddin Jahangir), 2nd edn., vol. I, London.

Sarkar, Jadunath (1912, reprint 1973). *History of Aurangzib*, vol. 3, New Delhi.

Sarkar, Jadunath (1917), *Anecdotes of Aurangzeb and Historical Essays*, Calcutta.

Sarkar, Jadunath (1947). trs. of *Saqi Must'ad Khan's Maasir-i-Alamgiri*, Calcutta.

Sarkar, Jadunath (1988). *Chaitanya's Life and Teachings*, New Delhi.

Sen, Surendranath (1920). tr. *Extracts and Documents Relating to Maratha History*, vol. I, University of Calcutta, Calcutta.

Sharma, Sri Ram (1954). *Maharana Pratap*, Udaipur.

Sharma, Sri Ram (1972). *The Religious Policy of the Mughal Emperors*, Bombay.

Sitaramayya, Pattabhi (1946). *Feathers and Stones*, Bombay.

Smith, Vincent A. (1917). *Akbar The Great Mogul 1542-1605*, Oxford.

Srivastava, Ashirbadi Lal (n.d.). *History of India (1000-1707)*, Agra.

Tavernier, Jean-Baptiste & V. Ball (1889 reprint 1976), *Travels in India*, vol. I, Lahore.

Thapar, Romila, Akbar, *Microsoft Encarta Encyclopaedia* (Microsoft Corporation: 2001).

Truschke, Audrey (2018). *Aurangzeb: The Man and the Myth*, New Delhi.

Williams, Rushbrook (1918). *An Empire Builder of the 16th Century*, London.

Index